CW01082373

Globe Law
and Business

Great Legal Writing

Writing

Lessons from Literature

Max Barrett

Author
Max Barrett

Managing director
Sian O'Neill

Great Legal Writing: Lessons from Literature is published by

Globe Law and Business Ltd
3 Mylor Close
Horsell
Woking
Surrey GU21 4DD
United Kingdom
Tel: +44 20 3745 4770
www.globelawandbusiness.com

Printed and bound by CPI Group (UK) Ltd, Croydon CR0 4YY, United Kingdom

Great Legal Writing: Lessons from Literature

ISBN 9781787429499
EPUB ISBN 9781787429505
Adobe PDF ISBN 9781787429512

MIX
Paper | Supporting responsible forestry
FSC® C013604

Table of contents

They have very few laws ... For, according to the Utopians,
it's quite unjust for anyone to be bound by a legal code
which is too long for an ordinary person to read right
through, or too difficult for him to understand.
More[1]

A lawyer without history or literature is a mechanic, a mere
working mason; if he possesses some knowledge of these he
may venture to call himself an architect.
Scott[2]

You write with ease, to shew your breeding; But easy
writing's vile hard reading.
Sheridan[3]

[T]his society [of lawyers] has a peculiar cant and jargon ...
that no other mortal can understand, and wherein all their
laws are written ... whereby they have wholly confounded
the very essence of truth and falsehood.
Swift[4]

The truth is rarely pure and never simple. Modern life
would be very tedious if it were either, and modern literature
a complete impossibility.
Wilde[5]

1   Thomas More, *Utopia*, P Turner (trans) (Penguin Books, 2003), 87.
2   Walter Scott, *Guy Mannering* (JM Dent & Sons, 1957), 259.
3   Richard Brinsley Sheridan, "Clio's Protest" in R Rhodes, *The Plays and Poems of Richard Brinsley Sheridan*, vol 3, 117 (Russell & Russell Inc, 1962).
4   Jonathan Swift, *Gulliver's Travels* (John Wanamaker, 1800), 308.
5   Oscar Wilde, *The Importance of Being Earnest* (Walter H Baker Company, 1920), 13.

Foreword

Is all seeking vain, then? Is it useless to try for a clear view of the meaning and method of one's art? Surely not. If no art can be quite pent-up in the rules deduced from it, neither can it fully realize itself unless those who practise it attempt to take its measure and reason out its processes.
Wharton[1]

Lord Macmillan, a former 'law lord', has written that to be a good lawyer it does not suffice to have a knowledge of statutes and law reports.[2] Rather, he suggests, a good lawyer will possess "that width of comprehension ... serenity of outlook and ... catholicity of sympathy which can no-wise be so well acquired as from consort with the great masters of literature".[3] In this book, I consider lessons on writing that may be gleaned from various leading authors of the past and which, I submit, can be brought to bear in crafting more polished legal texts.

It is not clear that lawyers have always appreciated the truth that Lord Macmillan has identified. Henry Fielding, the short-lived 18th-century English novelist and judge, famously decried the legal profession as "little acquainted with the commonwealth of literature".[4] However, some later lawyers have been well acquainted with this 'commonwealth'. Take, for example, two of the great common law judges of the 20th century, Oliver Wendell Holmes, Jr and Lord Denning. Holmes, the son of a prominent author, grew up in the heady literary ambience of early 19th-century Boston, his youthful reading tastes running to British authors such as Dickens, Scott, Tennyson and Thackeray, amongst others.[5] As an older man, Holmes enjoyed reading philosophy and was so grand a 'Yankee' that when he took to reading Plato, his approach, apparently, was "You

---

1   Edith Wharton, *The Writing of Fiction* (Charles Scribner's Sons, 1925), 118–119.
2   Lord Macmillan, *Law and Other Things* (Cambridge University Press, 1937), 138.
3   *Ibid.*
4   See Fielding's untitled essay in *The Covent-Garden Journal* (21 March 1972, No 23), reprinted in Henry Fielding, *The Works of Henry Fielding, Esq.* (Smith, Elder & Co, 1882), 73.
5   David Burton, *Oliver Wendell Holmes, Jr* (Twayne Publishers, 1980), 20.

have been pleasing the world for two thousand years; see whether you can please me".[6] Denning hailed from humbler origins than his American counterpart; his father was a draper, though very much a reading-man and, when asked in later life about his father, Denning would recall that "[h]e could quote poetry and prose from authors, known and unknown, much to our delight".[7] As to his own childhood, Denning wrote in his later years that as a boy he read a lot of books,[8] his preferred reading material included British greats such as Carlyle, Macaulay and Milton. "They have been of the greatest value to me," Denning observed in his old age, "I have read ... and referred to them ... a thousand times".[9]

Both Holmes and Denning were men whose legal writing evinces the highest literary craftsmanship. In this, they were not alone. The American and British judicial benches have long been populated by men and women of great writing skills honed to the highest level through long years in professional practice. The United States Supreme Court has been graced by gifted authors such as Mr Justice Jackson (a "distinctively dazzling writer")[10] and Mr Justice Scalia (a man of "distinctive splendid prose").[11] On this side of the Atlantic, one thinks of the beautiful writing styles of judges such as Lord Atkin (who showed a remarkable "clarity of style and language")[12] and, more recently, Lord Donaldson (a judge with a "beguiling fluidity"[13] to his English).[14]

Such writing skill does not come from nowhere. It is born of years in professional practice spent writing advice and opinions and submissions. Words, after all, are a central concern of all legal professionals and students. Every day, they compose all manner of legal texts filled with carefully chosen words. If a lawyer wishes to achieve distinction in the legal profession, he or she must have a facility with the written word. That is not to say that a lawyer should aspire to the gentle feelings of the poet or the novelist's flights of fancy.[15] Legal prose is typically a more pedestrian venture than a novel or a poem; however, the pedestrian can be done well and even (sometimes) beautifully. The views of the

---

6   *Ibid*, 22.
7   Lord Denning, *The Family Story* (Butterworths, 1981), 11.
8   *Ibid*, 33.
9   *Ibid*.
10   John Barrett, "The Nuremberg Roles of Justice Robert H Jackson" (2007) 6(3) *George Washington University Global Studies Law Review* 511–525, 515.
11   John Roberts *et al*, "In Memoriam: Justice Antonin Scalia" (2016) 130(1) *Harvard Law Review* 1, 9.
12   Seamus Henchy, "*Lord Atkin* by Geoffrey Lewis" (1983) 18(1) (NS) *Irish Jurist* 182, 183.
13   Max Barrett, *The Art and Craft of Judgment Writing* (Globe Law and Business, 2022), 244.
14   *Ibid*.
15   G Nicholls, "Of Writing By Lawyers" (1949) 27(10) *Canadian Bar Review* 1209, 1210.

professional writers considered in this book identify in greater detail how lawyers can write legal prose well and even (sometimes) beautifully.

Lord Macmillan suggests that a lawyer who wishes to attain a good English writing style would be well-advised to start with the King James Version of the Bible, not for the spiritual messages it contains – though Macmillan was a practising Christian – but because it is a "well of English undefiled".[16] Second to this, Macmillan urges lawyers to read the classics of English literature if they wish to avoid ugliness of style.[17] The American author, Edith Wharton, touches on a similar point when she suggests that one should read certain of Henry James's works if one is to appreciate the technicalities of good writing.[18] In this book, I consider the words and insights proffered by some of the great authors of the late 18th to early 20th centuries on the craft of writing. These are accomplished individuals who know that writing is difficult and also a fine art.[19] Between them, they offer hundreds of years of insight into how to approach the complexities of writing so as to make one's prose finer.

When it came to choosing the authors whose observations I consider in the pages that follow much the same approach was adopted by me as was taken by Mrs Barbauld in *The British Novelists*,[20] a trailblazing early 19th-century consideration of the modern British novel at a time when the novel was still a burgeoning form of literature.[21] In her prefatory essay to that book, Barbauld writes:

> *Variety in manner has been attended to. As to the rest, no two people probably would make the same choice, nor indeed the same person at any distance of time. A few of superior merit were chosen without difficulty, but the list was not completed without frequent hesitation. Some regard it has been thought proper to pay to the taste and preference of the public.*[22]

In like manner, this book considers some of the most outstanding English-language authors of the past. Care has been taken to ensure a breadth of opinions, a variety of styles and a mix of genders and sexualities. A particular reason for focusing on the 19th and early 20th

---

16 *Ibid*, 145.
17 *Ibid*.
18 Edith Wharton, *The Writing of Fiction* (Charles Scribner's Sons, 1925), 45.
19 Lord Macmillan, *Law and Other Things* (Cambridge University Press, 1937), 148.
20 Anna Barbauld, *The British Novelists* (FC&J Rivington, 1810), vol 1, 61.
21 Barbauld's publication of what was in effect the first novelistic canon has been described as "one of the instituting moments in … [the] history of the British novel", lending prestige to novel writing and recognising writers as a professional class. (See Claudia Johnson, "'Let Me Make the Novels of a Country': Barbauld's The British Novelists" (2001) 34(2) *Novel: A Forum on Fiction* 163–179, 167.)
22 Anna Barbauld, *The British Novelists* (FC&J Rivington, 1810), vol 1, 61.

centuries is that some of the highly valuable insights of that most literate of eras seem at risk of being forgotten in our (arguably) less literary age.

In writing this book, I have elected to treat with a different author in each chapter, rather than dealing with a different theme in each chapter and identifying what the various authors considered have to say about that theme. This has led to a degree of overlap between the various chapters. However, this overlap is helpful in identifying common (and varying) views of the authors considered. The author-by-author approach also has the attraction of capturing the differences in emphasis, personality and style that each of the writers whose observations are considered manifested in their respective approaches to writing. In practical terms, it also offers the benefit that this book can be read from cover-to-cover or, alternatively, a single chapter – and hence a single author – can be considered by the reader who has less time on his or her hands. Each chapter ends with a section of key propositions on writing that have been identified by the writer who is the subject of that chapter. The reader with very little time on his or her hands may find it beneficial to read those propositions and then proceed to the Afterword.

I suspect that any aspiring or practising legal writer who reads this book or any of its chapters or even the closing propositions at the end of each chapter will find observations on the art and craft and skills of legal writing that can usefully be deployed by them in their respective careers. Additionally, in the Afterword (entitled "Towards a code of good legal writing") I identify various general propositions concerning good legal writing contained in the preceding chapters and work them into a rudimentary code of good legal writing. In the Appendix (entitled "Writing for the young and vulnerable"), I consider some pointers on writing for children and the vulnerable that CS Lewis has identified, along with some that I have learned in my own career as a judge, all of which I believe can usefully be brought to bear when it comes to legal writing more generally.

This book is not an instruction manual on legal writing. Nor does it proceed on a basis of presumption as to the quality of my own legal writing. It involves a consideration of what the great and good of the literary world have to say about literary writing and an application of their insights to the specific context of legal writing – cross-referring when, and as appropriate, the now-extensive academic and professional commentary on good legal writing. If I might pick up on the observations of the five great authors quoted at the outset of this book – More, Scott, Sheridan, Swift and Wilde – the central thematic threads in the pages that follow are these:

- legal writing should never be too difficult to understand;
- great writers have much to teach the legal writer;
- good writing requires hard work; professional jargon is generally best avoided; and
- (here, I respectfully disagree with Wilde – or at least with the views that he has Algernon Moncrieff express in *The Importance of Being Earnest*) truth is always pure, oftentimes simple and generally best expressed in plain English.

Throughout this book, I have used the masculine and feminine form when referring to the notional legal writer, save when this would lead to unwieldy text – in which case, I have used the plural form. I do not mean in this approach to cause any offence to non-binary legal writers. Needless to say, there are all kinds of fine legal writers whose collective diversity hugely enriches the worlds of literature and the law. References in this book to a 'judgment' are – unless the context otherwise indicates – to a written reserved legal judgment rendered by a government-appointed judge in a court of law. In the American context, these would be referred to as 'opinions'; however, for the sake of consistency, I have generally elected to use the term 'judgment' even when referring to an opinion. When I refer to 'legal texts' I have primarily had in mind written formal legal advice, as well as articles, decisions, essays, submissions and judgments, all as composed in the civil context. Though much of what follows will likely also be of interest to criminal law practitioners and judges, the book was not written with them primarily in mind.

This book builds on the analysis undertaken in Chapter 8 of my recent book, *The Art and Craft of Judgment Writing*,[23] in which – proceeding on the basis that the composition of good judicial prose is not so very different from composing any good prose – I look at the lessons that might be gleaned by judgment writers (in truth, all legal writers) from the 'writing on writing' published by 19th- and 20th-century literary stalwarts, such as Somerset Maugham, George Orwell, Edgar Allen Poe, Mark Twain and Edith Wharton. The reader who is disappointed by the absence of those writers from this book is respectfully directed to my consideration of their valuable insights in *The Art and Craft of Judgment Writing*.

I am grateful to my brother, Professor Gavin Barrett, BL, of University

---

23   Max Barrett, *The Art and Craft of Judgment Writing* (Globe Law and Business, 2022), 244.

College Dublin's Sutherland Law School for his helpful comments on an earlier version of this text. Mum, Dad and Conor were, as ever, forthcoming with kindness and reassurance. I must also thank each of my judicial assistants, Ms Katie Winder and Ms Hodel Herlihy, for undertaking helpful proofreads of the near-to-final text and suggesting a number of useful amendments. Agapi, Athena, Petros and Mikhalis were a constant source of welcome love, encouragement and kindness, with Agapi suggesting a number of particularly valuable changes to the text.

All the views expressed in this book are personal and any errors are mine alone. Readers must take professional legal advice and assistance in relation to any legal issue or other query which they may have. This book is not represented as containing (or as a substitute for) legal or other advice or assistance. No warranty is given as to the accuracy or correctness of its content. No liability whatsoever (whether in contract, negligence, negligent misstatement or otherwise at all) is accepted to any person arising out of any reliance on the content of this book.

As this book goes to print a terrible war is being waged on the people of Ukraine and a host of human rights abuses are being visited upon them. All after-tax royalties earned by me from sales of this book will be donated to the Ukrainian relief efforts of the International Red Cross and Red Crescent Movement.

This book is dedicated to the much-loved memory of my late brother-in-law, Kostas Kapelonis (1976–2022), a kind-hearted Greek man who died unexpectedly (and far too soon) as this book was in its final stages of preparation.

Max Barrett
January 2023

1. Lawrence

On morality, aesthetics and other matters

DH Lawrence (1885–1930) was a famous, relatively short-lived English writer who managed during his too-brief literary career to produce an array of novels, poems and short stories that have entered the canon of Western literature. His most prominent works include *Sons and Lovers* (1913) and *Lady Chatterley's Lover* (1928). The sexual freedom in Lawrence's writing made him something of an outcast during his lifetime, "dismissed by many as inflammatory and obscene ... because [he] ... subverted the status quo by inviting the marginal (or unspeakable) into [his] ... work".[1] In death, however, Lawrence has joined the pantheon of great authors. In addition to his fiction and poetry, Lawrence was an accomplished literary critic. His essay, "The Novel",[2] makes numerous points that, I submit, are also of interest when it comes to legal writing.

1. Writing engagingly

Lawrence suggests that it is difficult to read the whole of any novel, that the reader reads a bit and knows what will happen or else decides that he or she simply does not want to read any more.[3] What Lawrence can be seen to be touching upon in this regard are the issues of plot and reader engagement. It has long been suggested that the elements of literary plot development (introduction, rising conflict, climax, resolution and dénouement) can be brought usefully to bear when it comes to drafting persuasive legal texts. So, for example, Chestek – writing of how the elements of literary plot development can be brought to bear when crafting a legal brief – suggests the following (though his observations also arguably resonate when it comes to legal writing more generally):[4]

---

1   Helen Wussow, "Caravaggio and DH Lawrence: Vulgarity to Sainthood" (2014) 39(1) *The DH Lawrence Review*, 51–66, 51.
2   DH Lawrence, *Reflections on the Death of a Porcupine* (Indiana University Press, 1963).
3   *Ibid*, 103.
4   Kenneth Chestek, "The Plot Thickens: The Appellate Brief as Story" (2008) 14 *Legal Writing: The Journal of the Legal Writing Institute* 127–170, 148–150.

- **Introduction:** Here the factual background, including details of the protagonists, should be included.
- **Rising conflict:** The issue (conflict) presenting, the applicable law (and any legal conflict) are now presented.
- **Climax:** The moment of climax in a legal text is when the reader knows the facts, the persons involved and the conflict presenting.
- **Resolution:** In this section, the conflicts presenting are resolved.
- **Dénouement:** A plausible conclusion must now be presented.

Notwithstanding that a clear analogy can be drawn between the elements of a legal text and the various elements of the traditional literary plot, it is important not to take the analogy too far. So, for example, Sir Frank Kitto, a former member of the High Court of Australia, has cautioned against judgments (though the point might be made of legal texts more generally) which descend to 'purple prose', "beginning with élan and proceeding with breathless zest, holding the reader entranced to the ... satisfying and dramatic dénouement".[5]

For a legal text to communicate effectively and persuasively, it should speak with authority and dignity, be impressive but not grandiloquent, its reasoning should be convincing, it should evince clarity of expression and come embellished with the attributes of style, elegance and good phrasing but, above all, it should perform its utilitarian function well (whatever its particular function is): all other attributes of the text are subservient to that.[6]

As to what makes a legal text interesting, some of the relevant factors are considered at length in later chapters. It suffices, for now, to observe that an interesting legal text, should:

- be based on scrupulous research;[7]
- offer sound legal analysis;[8]
- distil the necessary from the dense;[9]
- contribute to the solution of practical problems;[10]
- be brief/concise;[11]

---

5   Frank Kitto, "Why Write Judgments?" in *Judicial Commission of New South Wales, A Matter of Judgment: Judicial Decision-Making and Judgment Writing* (Judicial Commission of New South Wales, 2003), 69.
6   Lord Macmillan, "The Writing of Judgments" (1948) 26 *Canadian Bar Review* 491–499, 491.
7   Bryan Garner, "Legal Writing" (2009) 38(3) *Student Law* 12, 13.
8   American Bar Association, *Internal Operating Procedures of Appellate Courts* (American Bar Association, 1961), 34.
9   Charles Maechling, "Legal Research and the Problems of Society" (1968–1969) 21(1) *Journal of Legal Education* 86–88, 87–88.
10 Adina Radulescu, "Preserving Conceptual Concordance in the Multilingual Translations of EU Legislation" (2012) 4(2) *Contemporary Readings in Law and Social Justice* 318–323, 320.

- be clear;[12]
- be simple/direct;[13]
- be elegant;[14]
- avoid vagueness;[15]
- avoid wordiness;[16]
- avoid grand flourishes; and[17]
- be engaging.[18]

2.   Didacticism and the 'art' of writing

Lawrence accepts that there may be didactic elements to the novel; he does not accept that those are the novel.[19] It is important to distinguish, in this regard, between didactic and purpose fiction. "Novels that preach on a multitude of things ... are considered ... 'didactic'. Novels ... written to champion a specific cause are ... 'purpose' novels."[20] Bringing the just-quoted distinction to bear in the context of legal writing, it follows that – depending on the type of legal text that one is treating with, and on the intentions of the relevant author – a legal text may be a 'didactic' or a 'purpose' text. But what Lawrence's observation suggests is that such aspects of the legal text are not the legal text, that is, the text sits apart from what it seeks to do and falls to be appreciated for what it is (presumably from an aesthetic perspective).

Is it possible to appreciate a legal text such as a judgment from an aesthetic perspective? Widespread "impoverished sensitivity" to the aesthetic nature of law does not mean that it lacks an aesthetic.[21] Judgments are a genre of literature within the body of civic literature.[22]

---

11   Tenielle Fordyce-Ruff, "Cutting the Clutter: Three Steps to More Concise Legal Writing" (2011) 54(1) *Advocate (Idaho State Bar)* 41–46, 41.
12   Benjamin Cardozo, *Selected Writings of Benjamin Nathan Cardozo*, M Hall (ed) (Fallon Publications, 1947), 341.
13   Samuel Murumba, "Good Legal Writing: A Guide for the Perplexed" (1991) 17(1) *Monash University Law Review* 93–105, 100.
14   Jaro Mayda, "On Style and Form in Legal Writing" (1962) 31 *Revista Jurídica de la Universidad de Puerto Rico* 9–32, 9.
15   Karen Sneddon and David Hricik, "Be Inelegant" (2011) 16(7) *Georgia Bar Journal* 76–77, 76.
16   Robert McWhirter, "'Writing Maketh an Exact Man': How Good Lawyers Don't Write Like Lawyers" (2013) 49(6) *Arizona Attorney* 14–29, 21.
17   James Raymond, "Legal Writing: An Obstruction to Justice" (1978) 30(1) *Alabama Law Review* 1–19, 15.
18   Adina Radulescu, "Preserving Conceptual Concordance in the Multilingual Translations of EU Legislation" (2012) 4(2) *Contemporary Readings in Law and Social Justice* 318–323, 320.
19   DH Lawrence, *Reflections on the Death of a Porcupine* (Indiana University Press, 1963), 104.
20   Donald Ross, *Didactic and Purpose Novels in America: The Implications and Effects They Have Had on the Trends in the Novel, 1789–1941* (MA Thesis) (Boston University, 1941), 1.
21   Brian Butler, "Aesthetics and American Law" (2003) 27(1) *Legal Studies Forum* 203–220, 216.
22   Frances Ferguson, "Not Kant, but Bentham: On Taste" in Anthony Julius *et al*, *Bentham and the Arts* (UCL Press, 2020), 179.

And the world of any one judgment (like the invented worlds of any novelist) comprises "a more or less realistic backdrop for the action".[23] Viewed in this way, it seems reasonable to ask if a judgment is beautiful (aesthetically pleasing) and to consider how it might be made beautiful. In this regard, the emphasis placed on utility when it comes to reading judgments seems to have obfuscated their aesthetic merits in the public eye. A good judgment, like a good poem, is wisdom and delight combined.[24] Yet, as Karl Llewellyn (the great American legal philosopher) has observed, beauty has long been "slighted ... by law".[25] By this Llewellyn meant that, when it comes to law, beauty has generally been seen to have no place as a yardstick of accomplishment or a source of meaning. It has even been suggested that no two terms would seem "more incongruous" than beauty and law,[26] even though in commentary on judgments and other public legal texts one often encounters aesthetic verbs, such as 'appealing', 'attractive' or 'enticing'.[27]

Why has beauty been slighted by law? There may be a sense that the philosophy of aesthetics is not sufficiently serious a subject for it to be brought to bear in the legal arena. But the truth is that there is space in the legal realm for aesthetics and that a judgment, like poetry, "enlarges the circumference of the imagination".[28] It can be stated of law, as of art, that its history is a history of responding to "encounters with [the] provocative".[29] Judges in their judgments (and practising lawyers in their legal writings) can produce provocative works; encounters with such works can involve an aesthetic experience; and that experience can be appreciated in the manner contemplated by Lawrence.

3.   Moralising

Lawrence is critical of the moral purpose in which many authors enwrap themselves, suggesting, amongst other matters, that in their moralising – condescending commentary on issues of right and wrong with an unfounded air of superiority – there is a want of reality.[30] It is not possible to

---

23   Peter Lamarque, "Aesthetics and Literature: A Problematic Relation?" (2007) 135(1) *Philosophical Studies* 27–40, 27.
24   Percy Shelley, *A Defence of Poetry* (Bobbs-Merrill Co, 1904), 29.
25   Karl Llewellyn, "On the Good, the True, the Beautiful, in Law" (1942) 9 *University of Chicago Law Review* 224–265, 227.
26   Henry Chandler, "Attitude of the Law Toward Beauty" (1922) *ABA Journal* 470–474, 470.
27   Richard Moran, "Kant, Proust, and the Appeal of Beauty" (2012) 38(2) *Critical Inquiry* 298–329, 301.
28   Percy Shelley, *A Defence of Poetry* (Bobbs-Merrill Co, 1904), 34.
29   Paul Ziff, "Art and Sociobiology" (1981) 90 (360) *Mind* 505–520, 505.
30   DH Lawrence, *Reflections on the Death of a Porcupine* (Indiana University Press, 1963), 107.

comment on whether Lawrence's observation holds true in the context of all legal texts. However, moralising condescension is certainly not an unknown trait among lawyers, who have been spoken of as having a "heritage of disdain"[31] and of using language that is "un-clear, boring, [and] haughty".[32] Judge Posner, a distinguished American judge, has urged judges to substitute "humble, fact-bound, policy-soaked, instrumental ... 'reasonableness' for [the] ... legal and moral rightness"[33] with which judgments can come cloaked, and such urgings can surely be applied to lawyers more generally.

Lawrence clearly holds disdain for writers who presume to preach from a self-perceived position of superiority (a disdain which, incidentally, echoes the Old Testament injunction, "Let not the wise man glory in his wisdom").[34] Professional journals repeatedly caution practising lawyers to avoid condescension. So, for example, one finds it stated that:

- condescension destroys lawyer-client relations;[35]
- nobody willingly seeks the company of those who belittle them;[36]
- many lawyers (wrongly) seem to think condescension a hallmark of education;[37]
- the lawyer who aims at clear and persuasive legal writing should seek to explain but avoid condescension;[38] and
- it is a wise practising lawyer who avoids condescension (because avoiding condescension can only benefit his or her client's interests).[39]

4. Detachment

Lawrence expresses a dislike for novels into which the author intrudes as a presence.[40] When it comes to legal writing, the general consensus is that lawyers should evince detachment in their legal writing (with a want of detachment typically being associated with a want of perspective).[41]

---

31 Douglas Abrams, "Legal Writing: Sense and Nonsense" (2018) 74(2) *Journal of the Missouri Bar* 94–97, 94; and Harold Lloyd, "Plain Language Statutes: Plain Good Sense or Plain Nonsense" (1986) 78(4) *Law Library Journal* 683–696, 683.
32 Adam Johnson, "A Mild Case for Latin" (2012) 69(3) *Bench & Bar of Minnesota* 25–27, 26.
33 Richard Posner, *The Problems of Jurisprudence* (Harvard University Press, 1990), 130.
34 Jeremiah 9:23.
35 Bryan Yeazel, "On Giving Advice: Maximising Value for Your Client" (2015) 9(33) *International In-House Counsel* 1–9, 5.
36 *Ibid*.
37 *Ibid*.
38 Benjamin Norris, "Writing to Win: Improving Your Law Practice Through Attention to Detail" (2000–2001) 37(4) *Arizona Attorney* 32–37, 34.
39 Richard Gorman, "The Expert Witness" (1943–1944) 34(6) *Journal of Criminal Law and Criminology* 418–419, 419.
40 DH Lawrence, *Reflections on the Death of a Porcupine* (Indiana University Press, 1963), 109–110.
41 Nancy Rice, "Tips on Legal Writing" (2015) 44(5) *Colorado Lawyer* 61–62, 61.

Students going to law school are often taught that it is unprofessional[42] (perhaps even unseemly) to show feelings. Indeed, the very mention that a legal writer or legal text evinces emotion is often meant as a deprecatory observation[43] (emotion being seen in this context as a "corruptive force",[44] requiring to be excised from the legal reasoning process lest it diminish the logic and reason at play).[45] This traditional notion of detachment as a professional virtue among lawyers may, to some extent, derive from the classist notion once posited by Adam Smith that "the mob ... never bear any envy to their superiors".[46] Yet, in one way, the affection that lawyers as a professional class have long manifested for professional detachment seems a little odd. After all, emotion pervades the legal arena,[47] and lawyers and judges are no different from everyone else in tending to react "sympathetically"[48] (emotionally) to the world around them. In truth, it seems both unnatural and unattainable to excise emotion from legal affairs when modern studies, in fields such as psychology and neurobiology, suggest that – even in ostensibly emotionless moments – emotion and cognition function and fuse, shaping perception and reactions.[49]

A number of reasons present as to why emotion continues so widely to be perceived as a deficiency insofar as it features in legal analysis, namely that:

- the legal field has not kept pace with modern reassessments of the interplay between emotion and cognition;
- the individual emotion of each case presents a challenge for a discipline aimed at systemic regulation; and
- a sense that the legal process is meant to proceed mechanically.[50]

However, in light of modern science, a question surely arises as to whether there is a necessary tension between detachment and empathy. After all, does not detachment create the space necessary for an

---

42   Tamara Piety, "Smoking in Bed" (2003) 57(3) *University of Miami Law Review* 827–852, 843.
43   Laura Little, "Negotiating the Tangle of Law and Emotion" (2001) 86(4) *Cornell Law Review* 974–1002, 977.
44   Jeremy Blumenthal, "Does Mood Influence Moral Judgment? An Empirical Test With Legal and Policy Implications" (2005) 28 *Law and Psychology Review* 1–28, 2.
45   *Ibid.*
46   Adam Smith, *The Theory of Moral Sentiments* (Henry G Bohn, 1853), 65.
47   Susan Bandes, "Introduction" to Susan Bandes (ed), *The Passions of Law* (NYU Press, 1999), 1. Little even suggests that emotion's role in law is so great as to require an "organizing principle" (Laura Little, "Adjudication and Emotion" (2002) 2 *Florida Coastal Law Journal* 205–218, 218).
48   Neal Feigenson, "Sympathy and Legal Judgment: A Psychological Analysis" (1997) 65(1) *Tennessee Law Review* 1–78, 78.
49   Susan Bandes, "Introduction" to Susan Bandes (ed), *The Passions of Law* (NYU Press, 1999), 7.
50   *Ibid.*

"imaginative reconstruction"[51] of the feelings/interests at play in a particular legal matter (and hence in a legal text relating to the same)?

To the extent that detachment continues to be perceived as a virtue among legal writers, it is, of course, possible to be 'excessively detached', one prominent American author cautioning against "cosmic detachment",[52] that is, an approach to writing which ignores the people who are at the centre of legal matters and directs itself to some unhuman "cosmic void".[53] Thus, while Lawrence cautions against the intrusion of the author into a literary text, he may, to some extent, be a creature of his time, with the more modern understanding of cognition and emotion being that emotion is an inescapable facet of the cognitive process. In short, there is an evolving modern sense that it is undesirable to promote a sense of detachment between lawyers and the suffering that they are often asked to resolve.[54]

5. Writing intelligently, coherently and honestly

Lawrence suggests that a novel has to be "quick", "interrelated" and "honourable".[55] By "quick", he appears to mean, in essence, that it is possessed of intelligence.[56] By 'interrelated' he means that a text should be coherent. By 'honour' what Lawrence has in mind is that the author must be a servant to the truth in what he or she depicts.[57] These points have a resonance in the legal writing context also. It seems scarcely controversial to posit that a legal text should:

- exhibit intelligence;
- depict coherently the interrelationship between the applicable law, facts and conclusion reached; and
- that in his or her selection of law and facts and in the analysis of the same a legal writer should be honest.

Turning to consider each of these attributes in some more detail, the following observations might be made:

- **Intelligence:** Aristotle posited that there are three facets to being persuasive as an advocate: *ethos* (character), *logos* (reasoning) and

51 Richard Posner, "Emotion versus Emotionalism in Law" in Susan Bandes (ed), *The Passions of Law* (NYU Press, 1999), 309–329, 324.
52 Richard Wydick, *Plain English for Lawyers*, 2nd edition (Carolina Academic Press, 1985), 63.
53 *Ibid*.
54 Elaine Craig, "Judicial Audiences: A Case Study of Justice David Watt's Literary Judgments" (2018) 64(2) *McGill Law Journal* 309–348, 344.
55 DH Lawrence, *Reflections on the Death of a Porcupine* (Indiana University Press, 1963), 116.
56 *Ibid*, 110.
57 *Ibid*, 115–116.

pathos (emotional appeal). Of the three, Aristotle considered *ethos* to be the most important, observing that moral character possesses "the most sovereign efficacy in making credible".[58] Or, as one modern author has said of *ethos*/character, it offers the greatest basis for belief.[59] In terms of legal writing, it has been suggested that the key elements of *ethos* are character (truthfulness), goodwill (reasonableness) and intelligence.[60] As to intelligence, this is more than a mere matter of intellect: it has been suggested that the intelligent writer is, amongst other matters, well-informed, good at research (and reasoning), articulate/eloquent, empathetic, practically minded, hard-working and creative.[61]

- **Coherency:** Coherency is an ingredient of clarity, with clarity (clearness) being one of the fundamental attributes of good legal writing.[62] In addition, it is a characteristic of a clear legal text that its structure is logically coherent (simple, sincere and direct)[63] and involves an exactness in the deployment of words.[64] In essence, what is meant by coherency is that a legal text is organised logically in such a manner that the reader understands what the writer is thinking (and seeking to state). A want of a coherent structure/theme in a legal text is a particular 'bugbear' for legal readers.[65] And a hallmark of persuasive legal writing, it has been suggested, is that it not only explains the applicable facts and law clearly but ties all the matters at play into a coherent whole.[66]

- **Honesty:** When it comes to honesty in legal writing one is back again to Aristotle's concept (discussed previously above) of *ethos* (character) as a bedrock of credibility and hence persuasiveness. Judge Ripple of the United States Court of Appeals has spoken of the desirability of honesty in writing style.[67] A legal text, he suggests,

58 Aristotle, *Treatise on Rhetoric*, T Buckley (trans) (Henry G Bohn, 1850), 12.
59 Eugene Garver, *For the Sake of Argument: Practical Reasoning, Character, and the Ethics of Belief* (University of Chicago Press, 2004), 7.
60 Michael Smith, *Advanced Legal Writing: Theories and Strategies of Persuasive Writing*, 3rd edition (Aspen Publishing, 2013), 127.
61 Anne Mullins, "Source-Relational Ethos in Judicial Opinions" (2019) 54(4) *Wake Forest Law Review* 1089–1134, 1093.
62 Benjamin Cardozo, *Selected Writings of Benjamin Nathan Cardozo*, M Hall (ed) (Fallon Publications, 1947), 341.
63 George Rossman (ed), *Advocacy and the King's English* (Bobbs-Merrill Co, 1960), 769.
64 *Ibid.*
65 Susan Kosse and David ButleRitchie, "How Judges, Practitioners, and Legal Writing Teachers Assess the Writing Skills of New Law Graduates: Comparative Study" (2003) 53(1) *Journal of Legal Education* 80–102, 86.
66 James McElhaney, "The Art of Persuasive Legal Writing" (1996) 82(1) *ABA Journal* 76–82, 76.
67 Kenneth Ripple, "Legal Writing in the New Millennium" (1999) 74(3) *Notre Dame Law Review* 925–932, 929.

should be well-organised, lucid in presentation and free of "guile"[68] in terms of word choice. After all, one has scant hope of arriving at truth in law if the person helping one to navigate the shoals of law is less than honest. Legal writing involves distilling a mass of law and facts into a coherent, comprehensible and compelling whole. Such a process involves a high risk of inadvertent error. However, writers do an injustice to their readers and diminish themselves if they do not always seek to state/summarise all the material bearing on the matter at hand,[69] or, to put matters otherwise, if they do not constantly seek to be honest and candid.

Key propositions

- There may be didactic elements to a legal text but they are not the legal text; the legal text opines upon/decides whatever issues have been placed before the legal writer.
- Moralising ought to be avoided in a legal text – a legal writer is asked to decide issues of fact and law, not to opine or rule upon matters of personal morality.
- Though emotion may be difficult to eschew, it is undesirable that the persona/predilections/preferences of a legal writer should intrude unduly into a legal text. The writer selects the facts and law and shapes the text but its abiding hallmark should be that the substance of the text predominates, not a sense of the author.
- A legal text should exhibit intelligence and accurately depict the interrelationship between the applicable law, facts and conclusion reached. The writer, in his or her selection of law, facts, analysis and conclusions should be a servant of truth.
- The legal writer who engages in moralising will diminish his or her work by departing from the pursuit of truth.
- By chaining themselves to a particular perception of morality, legal writers are ultimately chaining themselves to a star that is doomed to fade. Honour and truth should be the guiding stars of the legal writer.

---

68 *Ibid.*
69 I Campbell, "Legal Writing" (1999) 30(2) *Victoria University of Wellington Law Review* 427–434, 429.

2. Besant

On the 'laws' of fiction and other matters

Sir Walter Besant (1836–1901) was a prolific English novelist and essayist of the Victorian era. Though widely respected in his own time, he is somewhat overlooked today. This chapter focuses on his work, "The Art of Fiction".[1] Originally delivered as a lecture at the Royal Institution in April 1884, Besant uses this text to canvass three key propositions: that fiction is an art as great as any other; that as an art it is governed and directed by identifiable laws; but that those laws cannot be taught to those who are not endowed with certain natural gifts.

1.   Writing engagingly

Besant contends that in fiction the human dimension is critical, with nothing commanding interest and sympathy more than a simple and faithful love story.[2] Legal texts offer stories of fact and law, and thus can be written in an engaging manner that draws the reader in and makes whatever the legal writer has to say more interesting, memorable and commanding of sympathy. One great example of a well-written judgment, in which a judge renowned as a master writer presents the facts like a novel writer, is the 1928 judgment of Chief Judge Cardozo (as he then was) in *Palsgraf v Long Island Railroad Co.*[3] This decision of the New York Court of Appeals remains a leading authority in the United States on liability to an unforeseeable plaintiff. The opening paragraph of Cardozo's judgment reads like the introductory passage to a novel and its literary effects were considered in an article by Frank Cooper, a law professor at the University of Michigan whose book, *Effective Legal*

---

1   Walter Besant, *The Art of Fiction* (Cupples, Upham & Co, 1885). Besant also considers the craft of writing in his autobiography where he compares the writer's process of roughing out, reviewing and refining to the process of hollowing out a tunnel by initial boring and blasting, followed by a process of refinement (Walter Besant, *Autobiography of Sir Walter Besant* (Hutchinson & Co, 1902), 102–103).
2   Besant (1885), *ibid*, 11.
3   248 NY 339, 162 NE 99 (1928).

Writing (1953), remains an eminent American text on legal writing. Some of Cooper's observations appear in square brackets in the extract from *Palsgraf* that follows:[4]

> *Plaintiff was standing on a platform of defendant's railroad after buying a ticket to go to Rockaway Beach.* [What difference does it make where she was going? ... [D]oes its inclusion add some element of human interest, and pique the curiosity?] *A train stopped at the station, bound for another place. Two men ran forward to catch it.* [Here, a bit of suspense ...] *One of the men reached the platform of the car without mishap, though the train was already moving. The other man, carrying a package, jumped aboard the car, but seemed unsteady, as if about to fall.* [Here is a scene that has been pictured hundreds of times in cartoons and motion pictures ...] *A guard on the car, who had held the door open, reached forward to help him in, and another guard on the platform pushed him from behind. In this act, the package was dislodged and fell upon the rails. It was a package of small size, about 15 inches long, and was covered by a newspaper. In fact, it contained fireworks, but there was nothing in its appearance to give notice of its contents.* [Why didn't he simply say it was a package of fireworks?] *The fireworks when they fell exploded. The shock of the explosion threw down some scales at the other end of the platform, many feet away. The scales struck the plaintiff, causing injuries for which she sues.*

What Cooper does not comment on is the brilliant shift of focus at the end of the just-quoted text from all the pushing and shoving at one end of the platform to the completely unexpected event with the weighing scales at the other end. Joined with this shift of focus is the unexpected discovery that it is not (as readers, perhaps instinctively, expect as they proceed through the paragraph) one of the male passengers or the helpful guards who has sued for damages but the woman whom the reader encounters for the first time at the end of the paragraph. If ever there was a closing to the initial paragraph of a legal text that invites (even excites) the reader to read on, Cardozo's opening paragraph in *Palsgraf* is surely it. A masterful writer, Cardozo has pitched his judgment in such a way as to emphasise the human dimension and thus command interest and sympathy in the manner contemplated by Besant.

---

4   The extract from *Palsgraf* appears in the law reports, ibid, 340–341. Cooper's comments appear (with the text from *Palsgraf*) in Frank Cooper, *Effective Legal Writing* (Bobbs-Merrill Co, 1953), 28–29.

2.   Sympathy and writing

Fiction, Besant contends, requires sympathy in the author and excites it in the reader.[5] By 'sympathy', he means the power to pity, understand and respect the individual.[6] As to appeals to sympathy in legal texts, even though legal reasoning has an ostensible preference for the logical, the objective and the rational, there is a place for emotion in such texts, provided it comes in a semantic form acceptable in legal reasoning,[7] for example, in the description of facts, the deployment of analogy and the denoting of theme and tone.

3.   Selection in writing

A key feature of fiction, Besant maintains, is its emphasis on suppression and reticence.[8] By this, Besant means to refer to the process whereby the author selects characters, incidents and moments to realise a story that does not contain unnecessary detail.[9] The legal writer engages in a similar task of distillation (selection, extraction and condensation)[10] when realising the best legal text that he or she can. The legal writer's task, to draw on Besant, is to aim at completeness without needless complexity/error.[11]

4.   Elevation of mind

Fiction, Besant writes, and the same might be contended of a legal text, is a vehicle for thought.[12] In this observation, Besant means that words express thinking as thoughts are 'pressed out' and made public.[13] However, there is also a school of thought that knowledge derives from what is expressed.[14] Indeed, legal texts might be contended to be something of an example *par excellence* in this last regard, with law and facts being combined into a particular conclusion through the analysis that the legal writer brings to bear. Whatever the precise nature/function of a legal text (be it as a vehicle for thought or as a predicate for knowledge), it seems safe to assert that in the best legal texts, the mind

5   Walter Besant, *The Art of Fiction* (Cupples, Upham & Co, 1885), 14.
6   *Ibid*, 13.
7   Kathryn Stanchi, "Feminist Legal Writing" (2002) 39 San Diego Law Review 387–436, 397.
8   Walter Besant, *The Art of Fiction* (Cupples, Upham & Co, 1885), 14.
9   *Ibid*, 15.
10   I Campbell, "Legal Writing" (1999) 30(2) *Victoria University of Wellington Law Review* 427–434, 429.
11   Walter Besant, *The Art of Fiction* (Cupples, Upham & Co, 1885), 15.
12   *Ibid*.
13   John Fischer, "Reading Literature/Reading Law: Is There a Literary Jurisprudence?" (1993) 72(1) *Texas Law Review* 135–160, 141.
14   Kristen Robbins and Amy Vorenberg, "Podia and Pens: Dismantling the Two-Track System for Legal Research and Writing Faculty" (2015) 31(1) *Columbia Journal of Gender and Law* 47–64, 58.

of the writer and reader are elevated: the writer writes what he or she sees and the reader is enabled to see that vision closely and distinctly.[15]

5.   'Laws' of writing

Besant moves on to consider various 'laws' of fiction, by which he means to refer to certain precepts that (he contends) fiction writers must master before they can hope for success. These 'laws' include the following:

Anything in fiction which does not derive from personal experience/observation is useless.

Today, this is an accepted truism of writing. So, for example, in *Home Before Dark* (2020), an Apple TV series, a journalist father tells his young daughter, an aspiring journalist, that she is a talented writer but "to get a great story, you gotta … actually live".[16] Putting this in the context of legal writing, perhaps the point to be derived is that it is important for a legal text to be honest and sincere, demonstrating the writer's legal knowledge but drawing also on personal experience.[17] That cannot occur if the level of professional detachment brought to bear in a legal text suggests that the legal writer is an unfeeling automaton. To be aimed for is a difficult balance between professional detachment, a certain pithiness in one's prose and the sense that a human being with a heart has crafted the text.[18]

Any author 'worth his salt' must be a master of descriptive power.[19]

By this observation, Besant means to refer to the faculties of observation/ selection (and the avoidance of needless complexity). Besant also suggests that observation plays no part in commercial writing.[20] However, it may be that he is not quite right in this. So, for example, it has been suggested that, for a lawyer, the power of observation is a key aspect of treating with the vagaries of human behaviour.[21] As to selection, what is at play in this regard is the selection of right and relevant facts and law and the excision

---

15   Walter Besant, *The Art of Fiction* (Cupples, Upham & Co, 1885), 16.
16   Season 1, Episode 6.
17   Kathryn Stanchi, "Feminist Legal Writing" (2002) 39 *San Diego Law Review* 387–436, 389.
18   Bryan Garner, "Legal Writing" (2002) 30(8) *Student Law* 9–10, 10. Garner is writing of demand letters but his observations have a wider resonance.
19   Walter Besant, *The Art of Fiction* (Cupples, Upham & Co, 1885), 20.
20   *Ibid*, 23.
21   Arthur Vanderbilt, "A Report on Prelegal Education" (1950) 25(2) *New York University Law Review* 199–290, 272.

of material that does not advance a text.[22] (As a profession, lawyers are generally credited with a tendency to be needlessly accurate,[23] filling their texts with true facts and correct law that do not advance their point or bring focus to their analysis.) As to the nature of the text that falls to be excised, there are perhaps three main candidates for excision: the obvious, the repetitive and the unnecessary.[24]

Closely connected with selection is the skill of presenting matters as forcibly as possible.[25]

Dramatic presentation is a key skill in terms of producing a legal text that is as persuasive as possible. To achieve optimal persuasiveness a variety of goals require to be achieved. So, for example, one might reduce the number of adjectives to verbs, accept what has been described as "the gospel of the active verb",[26] avoid the inactive/intransitive/impersonal,[27] excise that which seems particularly finely written (one can have too much of a good thing), and depart from good grammar where to proceed otherwise would diminish the energy of one's thoughts.[28]

When it comes to dramatic presentation, it was said of Lord Denning (one of the common law world's "great stylists")[29] that he was an aficionado of the "brief dramatic statement".[30] That so great a legal writer had such a penchant for the dramatic points surely to the legitimacy of the dramatic as a device in legal writing. (That said, because one of the golden requirements of legal writing is brevity,[31] the potential for the dramatic must always, I submit, yield to that golden rule.[32]) Suspense, to the extent it is thought desirable, can often be yielded through punctuation.[33] As to being forcible (vigorous and strong) in one's writing, this is not the same as being uncivil – civility counts.[34]

---

22   Walter Besant, *The Art of Fiction* (Cupples, Upham & Co, 1885), 24.
23   Patrick Barry, "Uselessly Accurate" (2018–2019) 18 *Scribes Journal of Legal Writing* 27–36, 27.
24   Joseph Kimble, "The Straight Skinny on Better Judicial Opinions" (2003–2004) 9 *Scribes Journal of Legal Writing* 1–42, 15.
25   Walter Besant, *The Art of Fiction* (Cupples, Upham & Co, 1885), 24.
26   Eugene Gerhart, "Improving Our Legal Writing: Maxims from the Masters" (1954) 40(12) *ABA Journal* 1057–1060, 1059.
27   *Ibid.*
28   *Ibid.*
29   Brady Coleman, "Lord Denning and Justice Cardozo: The Judge as Poet-Philosopher" (2001) 32(2) *Rutgers Law Journal* 485–518, 498.
30   Jim Corkery, *Study of Law* (Adelaide Law Review Association, 1988), 129.
31   Edward Re, "Legal Writing as Good Literature" (1985) 59(2) *St John's Law Review* 211–227, 223.
32   *Ibid.*
33   James Raymond, "Legal Writing: An Obstruction to Justice" (1978) 30(1) *Alabama Law Review* 1–19, 8.
34   Stephen Carter, *Civility: Manners, Morals, and the Etiquette of Democracy* (Basic Books, 1998), 74.

> *Every personality should be sketched clearly and*
> *without hesitation.*[35]

Putting this observation in the context of legal writing, perhaps the point to be made is that in treating with individuals and incidents clarity of prose is a paramount value. Commenting in this regard, Justice Cardozo has ranked clarity as a key virtue of judicial writing (and this is true of almost all legal writing).[36] He continues, however, with the observation that clearness:

> *... though the sovereign quality, is not the only one to be pursued ... The opinion will need persuasive force, or the impressive virtue of sincerity and fire or the mnemonic power of alliteration and antithesis, or the terseness and tang of the proverb and the maxim. Neglect ... these ... and it may never win its way.*[37]

Specifically, when it comes to sketching personalities (parties/ witnesses) in judgments (personality descriptions seem unlikely generally to be required in other legal texts), Besant's observation rings true. And in the want of hesitation to which Besant points, there seems less potential for embroidery of the truth.

In his "Essay on Language",[38] the 18th-/19th-century English philosopher, Jeremy Bentham, identifies various rules as regards clarity in language, among which are the following:

- When language has a word which conveys precisely what one seeks to convey, avoid using another word.[39]
- Use the singular in preference to the plural where possible.[40]
- If a particular object has been given a particular name, use that name.[41] (Conversely, do not wrongly designate an object with a name typically used for another object.[42])
- Prefer verbal nouns (eg, 'arrival') to verbs ('to arrive').[43]
- When a word would yield ambiguity, use one that does not.[44]

---

35   Walter Besant, *The Art of Fiction* (Cupples, Upham & Co, 1885), 25.
36   Benjamin Cardozo, *Selected Writings of Benjamin Nathan Cardozo*, Margaret Hall (ed) (Fallon Publications, 1947), 342.
37   *Ibid.*
38   Jeremy Bentham, "Essay on Language" in Jeremy Bentham, *The Works of Jeremy Bentham*, John Bowring (ed) (William Tait, 1843), vol 8, 290–338.
39   *Ibid*, 313.
40   *Ibid*, 315.
41   *Ibid.*
42   *Ibid.*
43   *Ibid.* The modern tendency is to use whatever form yields the greatest concision without loss of meaning.
44   Jeremy Bentham, "Essay on Language" in Jeremy Bentham, *The Works of Jeremy Bentham*, John Bowring (ed) (William Tait, 1843), vol 8, 316.

The importance of style cannot be overestimated.[45]

This seems but a truism when brought to bear in the context of legal writing. Thus, in a legal text as in a novel, to borrow from Besant:

> *There ought not to be ... a single sentence [that is] carelessly worded, [or] a single phrase which has not been considered ... There should be no unfinished places, no sign anywhere of weariness or haste ... The writer must so love his work as to dwell tenderly on every page and be literally unable to send forth a single page of it without the finishing touches.*[46]

These are not just aesthetic principles. Style in legal writing is also attributable to practical sense on the part of the legal writer, for if something is worth writing about then it is surely worth writing well about. It has even been suggested that it is naïve to focus on substance over form,[47] still less to assume that style is inferior to form.[48] Or, as Justice Cardozo once put it:

> *Most of our so-called noble thoughts have been at bottom pretty prosy and commonplace sentiments. It is the vitalizing power of style that lends them force and loftiness, and imparts a semblance of novelty to notions as old as man.*[49]

Mayda suggests that the essence of style in legal writing is having something to say and saying it clearly.[50] He also espouses ten useful rules on style in legal writing that are too long to recite in full but can be summarised as follows:[51]

- style involves the maximum/minimum of clarity/words;
- clarity in thought and writing is of paramount importance;
- clear thinking is an absolute virtue when it comes to style;
- clear thinking is a predicate for (not a guarantee of) good style;
- flatness of style will not yield clarity;
- clarity does not demand a journalistic or colloquial style;
- clarity often derives from brevity;
- brevity is a product of both thinking and writing;
- clarity and brevity should yield simplicity/readability; and
- readability can be tested by reading aloud.

---

45   Walter Besant, *The Art of Fiction* (Cupples, Upham & Co, 1885), 30.
46   *Ibid*, 30–31.
47   Patrick Hugg and Melanie McKay, "Classics Teach Legal Writing" (1985) 2(2) *Journal of Paralegal Education* 13–52, 51.
48   *Ibid*.
49   Benjamin Cardozo, *Selected Writings of Benjamin Nathan Cardozo*, Margaret Hall (ed) (Fallon Publications, 1947), 70.
50   Jaro Mayda, "On Style and Form in Legal Writing" (1962) 31 *Revista Jurídica de la Universidad de Puerto Rico* 9–32, 13.
51   *Ibid*, 13–15.

The most important part of the novel (and arguably the most important part of any legal text) is the central story.[52]

Fiction would soon lose its fans if it ceased to care for the story. Likewise, legal writing involves a legal writer telling whatever 'story' he or she has resolved upon to tell in terms of fact, law, analysis and conclusion. It is well known that when American juries sit they are looking for the "central 'story'"[53] each side has to tell, and there is no reason to believe that the juries of other nations are any different. The same is true of any legal text: there is a central story of facts and law that is (or ought to be) the focus of the legal writer. Thus, it has been suggested of the story woven by trial lawyers (but the same is true of all legal writers) that the central story should guide every beat.[54] The author of this suggestion moves on to make a number of related observations that also apply to legal writing, including that:[55]

- every story should have a beginning a middle and an end;
- the burden of proof (desire for persuasiveness) can influence the structure of the legal text;
- focused rebuttals work well – 'scattergun' reasoning does not;
- opening with a theme, proceeding with thematic blocks and closing with a return to theme is a powerful approach;
- coherence is key;
- great stories end with a harkening back to the beginning;
- a tale of facts and law is better told in the writer's own voice – affectation rings false, authenticity rings sincere and sincerity appeals; and
- a lawyer who aims for factual and emotional truth will communicate more effectively than one who writes without empathy.

One way of becoming a good story writer is to read past masters of the art.[56]

It surely has to be a beneficial exercise for the legal writer to read, for example, past judgments written by great judges and to consider, say, how they approached reciting facts, describing law, applying law to the

---

52   Walter Besant, *The Art of Fiction* (Cupples, Upham & Co, 1885), 33 *et seq.*
53   Anon., "Solid to the Core" (1995) 7(12) *Trial Excellence* 7–8.
54   Nathalie Kane, "Narrative, the Essential Trial Strategy" (2008) 34(4) *Litigation* 52–58, 57.
55   *Ibid*, 57–58.
56   Walter Besant, *The Art of Fiction* (Cupples, Upham & Co, 1885), 35.

facts and formulating conclusions. Certainly, Blackstone stresses the importance for the student and practitioner of law of reading the finest case law, coupled with the finest textbooks.[57] Besant, of course, suggests, in the context of *literary* writing, that reading the best *literary* works will improve a *literary* writer. But Lord Macmillan, it will be recalled, makes a similar point as regards a lawyer reading good literature.[58] And on the other side of the Atlantic, Judge Posner has suggested that reading literature yields a number of positives, including "[offering] surrogate experience … [and] templates for interpreting one's actual experiences, sharpening one's writing and reading skills; expanding one's emotional horizons; obtaining self-knowledge; [and] gaining pleasure".[59]

As to whether literary texts should feed into legal texts, that is another matter. Posner does not believe that literature offers practical lessons for living.[60] However, as will be seen (eg, in Chapter 3), there are commentators who have taken a different view. Another American commentator has suggested that fiction offers a crutch for the legal writer/reader treating with the ineffable.[61] And, if one looks at some recent English cases in which works of fiction have been quoted, it does seem that fiction/poetry is only ever used as a crutch, to copper-fasten the credibility of what a writer has to say by referring to a popular fictional character/work with which readers are likely to be at least vaguely familiar. So, for example, if one takes the search term 'Sherlock Holmes', and inserts it into the Lexis® database one finds that quotes from Sherlock Holmes stories (as opposed to cases involving an entity/enterprise with the name 'Sherlock Holmes') were used three times by the English courts in 2020 alone, in each case by way of 'crutch'. Thus, in *East-West Logistics LLP v Melars Group Ltd*,[62] a case concerned with whether the English courts had jurisdiction to wind-up a company which had moved its registered office to Malta, Baister J observed:

> *I agree with Mr Comiskey that it is for the petitioner to make out its case, but as Sherlock Holmes noted, sometimes it is the dog that does not bark that gives the clue: silence can sometimes be a powerful indicator of what is most likely to be true. In this case I do draw adverse inferences from the company's failure to provide even the most basic information about what it does where.*[63]

So, Baister J did not decide the case by reference to *The Adventure of*

57 William Blackstone, *Commentaries on the Laws of England* (Rees Walsh & Co, 1898), vi.
58 Lord Macmillan, *Law and Other Things* (Cambridge University Press, 1937), 138.
59 Richard Posner, *Law and Literature*, 3rd edition (Harvard University Press, 2009), 481–482.
60 *Ibid.*
61 JM de Stefano, "On Literature as Legal Authority" (2007) 49(2) *Arizona Law Review* 521–552, 539.
62 [2020] EWHC 2090 (Ch).
63 *Ibid*, para 25.

Silver Blaze, the Sherlock Holmes story in which the fact that a dog did not bark in the night pointed to the solution of the mystery that presented. Instead, he used it as a crutch to support his suggestion that sometimes silence can be telling as to where the truth might lie.

Likewise, in *Kardi Vehicles Ltd*,[64] a decision of the First Tier Tax Tribunal, it was noted that "HMRC officers are not required to exercise the deductive powers of Sherlock Homes",[65] which was a shorthand way of saying that persons in tax investigations need to help themselves by explaining matters to revenue officials, rather than 'dumping' materials on those officials and leaving them to deduce the intended/true significance of those materials. So, again the reference to Sherlock Holmes is a 'crutch', saving the author from spelling out in detail what can briefly and clearly be stated by reference to a fictional character.

Lastly, in *Stark v Walker*,[66] Deputy Judge Halpern QC,[67] referred back to the dictum of Lord Brandon in *Rhesa Shipping Co SA v Edmunds*,[68] when pointing to it being inappropriate for a trial judge when engaged in fact-finding, to apply the renowned (fictional) observation of Sherlock Holmes "that when you have eliminated all which is impossible, then whatever remains, however improbable, must be the truth".[69] (Lord Brandon's reasoning as to the type of logic deployed by Holmes in *The Adventure of the Blanched Soldier* was 'crutch-style' reasoning used to bring a point home in a winning style).[70]

None of these mentions of 'the Great Detective' would have worked had the decision-makers and decision-readers not themselves at some point read or gleaned an understanding of the Sherlock Holmes stories relied upon – a fact which points to the need for lawyers to be good readers if their legal texts are to be engaging and persuasive and also if they are properly to understand literary references. Sherlock Holmes is also so embedded into the public consciousness as a fictional character that relying on him escaped the double sins of pretentiousness and lack of clarity.

---

64   [2020] UKFTT 254 (TC).
65   *Ibid*, [73].
66   [2020] EWHC 562 (Ch).
67   *Ibid*, [77]–[78].
68   [1985] 1 WLR 948, 955–956 (HL).
69   Arthur Conan Doyle, *The Case Book of Sherlock Holmes* (John Murray and Jonathan Cape, 1980), 63.
70   While the line referred to by Deputy Judge Halpern (and indeed Lord Brandon) is the most famous line from Doyle's story, it does not represent the entirety of Holmes's thesis which runs as follows:
      I will give my process of thought [said Holmes] … "That process … starts upon the supposition that when you have eliminated all which is impossible, then whatever remains, however improbable, must be the truth. It may well be that several explanations remain, in which case one tries test after test until one or other of them has a convincing amount of support" (ibid).

A certain lightness of style helps in the telling of a story.[71]

There are two aspects to this proposition. The first aspect is not that a storyteller – for which one might substitute the legal writer – should play the role of comic. Rather, it is that he or she should evince a degree of empathy/sympathy without emoting.[72] The second aspect is to not be (to use a colloquialism) 'too clever by half'.[73] (That said, it also seems necessary to proceed without fake modesty.)

Key propositions

- Legal texts are stories of fact and law that can be written in an engaging manner which draws the reader in (making the texts more interesting and memorable).
- Although legal reasoning prefers the logical/objective/rational, there is a place for emotion in legal texts, provided it is couched appropriately.
- The legal writer's task is to select and compress in a bid at completeness, avoiding undue complexity and unwarranted error.
- In the best legal texts, the minds of the writer/reader are elevated: the writer writes what he or she sees; the reader is enabled to see that vision clearly.
- A legal text should be honest and uncontrived, demonstrating the legal writer's legal knowledge but drawing also on personal experience. That cannot occur if the level of professional detachment brought to bear suggests the legal writer to be an unfeeling automaton.
- The power of observation is a critical skill for legal writers.
- As to the power of selection, a legal text should exclude unnecessary detail.
- Active verbs aid a text; the impersonal, inactive and transitive do not.
- A legal writer should depart from good grammar where to proceed otherwise would diminish the expression of his or her thoughts.
- Lord Denning's judgment style points to the legitimacy of the

---

71   Walter Besant, *The Art of Fiction* (Cupples, Upham & Co, 1885), 37.
72   *Ibid.*
73   *Ibid.*

dramatic in legal writing; however, the potential for the dramatic must yield to the need for brevity.

- Suspense, to the extent it is thought desirable in legal writing, can be yielded through punctuation.
- Being forcible/vigorous/strong in one's writing is not the same as being uncivil, and civility counts.
- Clarity of prose is a paramount value.
- Writing unhesitatingly leaves less time for that storytelling to which lawyers may be prone.
- The importance of style cannot be overestimated. In a legal text, as in a novel:

  There ought not to be ... a single sentence [that is] carelessly worded, [or] a single phrase which has not been considered ... There should be no unfinished places, no sign anywhere of weariness or haste ... The writer must so love his work as to dwell tenderly on every page and be literally unable to send forth a single page of it without the finishing touches.[74]

- Legal writing involves a legal writer telling whatever 'story' he or she has resolved to tell in terms of facts, law, analysis and conclusion.
- It is beneficial for the legal writer to read, for example, past judgments written by great judges and to consider how they approached reciting facts, describing law, applying law to the facts and formulating conclusions.

---

74   *Ibid*, 30–31.

3. Conrad

On bringing light to truth and other matters

Joseph Conrad (1857–1924) was a prominent Polish-British author who did not speak English fluently until he was in his twenties, yet managed to attain such distinction in his use of English that Virginia Woolf later described him as a writer for whom "it seemed impossible … to make an ugly or insignificant movement of the pen".[1] Arguably, Conrad's most famous work is *The Children of the Sea* (1897).[2] In the preface to that novel (considered below), Conrad muses for a time on the interrelationship between art (writing) and truth in terms which, I submit, also have a resonance when brought to bear in the context of the legal writing.

1. Bringing light to truth

'Art' is defined by Conrad as a single-minded effort at "bringing light to the truth".[3] Indeed, in an imperfect world where even the truths arrived at by a court by reference to the applicable standard of proof may not be the full truth it has been suggested that fiction has a role to play.[4] That is not to say that the truth of a legal matter is to be found in fiction, but that in difficult cases insights into human behaviour gleaned from works of fiction may be useful in pointing to where the truth perhaps lies in real life. This is neither a new nor especially radical proposition. Thus, as John Wigmore (the original author of the definitive American work on evidence, *Wigmore on Evidence*) observed when he once volunteered a list of legal novels that merited reading by lawyers:

> [T]he novel – the true work of fiction – is a catalogue of life's characters. And the lawyer must know human nature. He must deal understandingly with

---

1   Virginia Woolf, *The Common Reader* (The Hogarth Press, 1948), 283.
2   Joseph Conrad, *The Children of the Sea* (The Heritage Press, 1965). I have elected to use the original American title of Conrad's novella, rather than the deplorably racist title by which it is also known.
3   Joseph Conrad, *The Children of the Sea* (The Heritage Press, 1965), xv.
4   Marianne Wesson, "Three's a Crowd: Law, Literature, and Truth" (1999) 34 *Tulsa Law Journal* 699–712, 704–705.

its types, its motives. These he cannot find – all of them – close around him; life is not long enough, the variety is not broad enough for him to learn them by personal experience before he needs to use them. For this learning, then, he must go to fiction, which is the gallery of life's portraits.[5]

The artist, Conrad suggests, is engaged in trying to find what is of fundamental value in life.[6] In a similar vein, the legal writer is seeking to identify the truth of whatever matter has been placed before them. "Law", says Auden's priest, "with a priestly look/ ... Law is the words in my priestly book".[7] However, in secular society, lawyers take the role that Auden's priest would otherwise arrogate onto himself of deciding on matters of truth and justice. Indeed, in early societies, when law purported to represent the will of the gods, the priests were lawyers; it is in modern society where law is the fruit of the collective will that "the lawyers are priests".[8] And that observation brings one right back to Conrad, for just as Conrad sees the artist (writer) to be engaged in the search for what is of fundamental value, likewise it does not suffice for lawyers to hide behind the fig leaf of the scientific judgment,[9] failing in the process to consider the value premises[10] that underpin the law at any one time. Such a failure leads to a situation in which (to put matters in 'Conrad-ian' terms) legal issues depart from a search into what is of fundamental value into unnaturally technical questions that avoid the true issue/s presenting.[11]

2.   Different author types

Conrad draws a distinction between (on the one hand) the thinker/scientist and (on the other hand) the artist. The thinker/scientist, he posits, speaks to the reader's common sense and intelligence.[12] The artist looks within to the spiritual.[13] Again, this raises the type of issues touched upon immediately above, for reading Conrad's distinction one might instinctively expect that the spiritual realm would not be one into which legal writers would stray when writing. And yet a question arises

---

5   John Wigmore, "List of Legal Novels" (1907–1908) 2(9) *Illinois Law Review* 574–593, 579.
6   Joseph Conrad, *The Children of the Sea* (The Heritage Press, 1965), xv.
7   WH Auden, "Law Like Love" in *The Collected Poetry of WH Auden*, 3rd edition (Random House, 1945), 74–76, 75.
8   Rennard Strickland, "The Lawyer as Secular Priest – A Call for Attorneys Who Are More than Legal Engineers" (1976) 3(3) *Learning and the Law* 40–44, 42.
9   *Ibid.*
10   *Ibid.*
11   *Ibid.*
12   Joseph Conrad, *The Children of the Sea* (The Heritage Press, 1965), xv.
13   *Ibid*, xvi.

as to whether this is so? Latterly, there has been increasing recognition that law is a derivative discipline that draws on ideas from outside the legal arena.[14] Viewed in this context, the notion that the law would *not* have scavenged in the spiritual field for some of its informing ideas seems almost eccentric. As Justice Silberg, formerly of the Supreme Court of Israel, has observed, "Every law protects something, corporeal or spiritual, deserving protection in the eyes of the creator of the laws".[15] Assuming this to be so, that is, that law often exists in part to protect the spiritual,[16] it seems a small jump from Conrad's observation (that the artist looks within to the spiritual) to the notion that the lawyer too would look within when approaching their interpretation of the law. After all, from where else does one derive a sense of where right lies in a close run legal matter if not in those 'spiritual' (ethical) values that bind societies and which are imbued/instilled in childhood?[17] As Lord Denning once observed of the common law, religion (spirituality) has long been a guide in its formulation,[18] not always (it should be noted) to the benefit of those who came before the courts or the general development of the law,[19] but a guide nonetheless.

3.   Emotion, morality and writing

All art, Conrad posits, shows the meaning of things and creates the emotional and moral atmosphere of the times.[20] In this regard, a parallel with the law arises, as can be seen in the following assertions of Lord Gifford, a one-time Master of the Rolls, in a public address delivered in 1878, when he observed on the relationship between public law and the national sense of right and wrong:

> *The deliverance which the municipal and positive law of any country gives upon a question of morality – upon a question of right or wrong – is generally the most weighty and authoritative that can be given. Surely what the law declares to be right must really be so. Surely what the law compels*

---

14   E Donald Elliott, "The Evolutionary Theory in Jurisprudence" (1985) 85 *Columbia Law Review* 38–94, 38.
15   Moshe Silberg, "Law and Morals in Jewish Jurisprudence" (1961) 75 *Harvard Law Review* 306–331, 328.
16   Mihai Bădescu, "Law, Normativity, Legal Order" (2017) 3(6) *Journal of Law and Public Administration* 70–75.
17   Joseph Conrad, *The Children of the Sea* (The Heritage Press, 1965), xvi.
18   Lord Denning, *The Influence of Religion on Law* (Canadian Institute for Law, Theology, and Public Policy, Inc, 1997), 33.
19   One has only to think of the (sadly continuing) history of unbridled prejudice so often visited on the LGBTQ+ community as a result of the religiously inspired view that homosexuality is morally objectionable to see how awful the effects of the Christian spirituality to which Lord Denning refers has in practice sometimes been.
20   Joseph Conrad, *The Children of the Sea* (The Heritage Press, 1965), xvii.

or enforces must be inherently and in the highest sense lawful ... [T]he civil or municipal law gives tone and colour to the morality of the nation ... And when at last a law is discovered by a few ... enlightened minds to be morally imperfect or morally wrong, how difficult it often is to break its thrall or procure its repeal or amendment! How the masses cling to it as good enough for them! How are the reformers stigmatized as utopian or visionary! The wisdom of our ancestors is declared to be better than the speculations of innovators, and the old landmarks are preferred to the new limits and definitions of an upstart ethics.[21]

There is, however, another sense in which the law acts as something of a moral bellwether (and which chimes with Conrad's perception of art as showing the true meaning of things and creating the emotional and moral atmosphere of the times). For are not legal writers in their legal texts seeking to endow passing events with their true meaning (legal import)? Do not legal texts (such as judgments) create a 'moral atmosphere' (as to the desirability of conformity with law)? And do not legal texts seek to appeal to the senses (in particular, the sense of justice)?

4.   Pursuit of truth

Conrad points to how artists seek always to go as far down the road of truth as their strength will carry them.[22] In his own case, he writes, he saw his task as being to make the reader feel, think and see, and thereby to arrive at a vision of truth.[23] Though legal texts wear the cloak of rationality, legal writers are, to some extent, involved in a similar task of making the recipient/reader feel, think and see a particular perceived truth.

Conrad suggests that art inspires, its effect lingers and that, at its best, it attains a vision of truth.[24] In a similar vein, when law and truth are combined in a legal text it can be a potent combination. One finds this particularly in the field of transitional justice (the area of law which seeks to come to grips with, for example, a history of past abuse or repression in a bid to attain accountability, justice, and reconciliation).[25] And, as it is in transitional justice, so it is more generally. Certainly, Conrad would have one believe that the text which lingers in the mind is that which

---

21   Lord Gifford, "Law a Schoolmaster; or the Educational Function of Jurisprudence" (1879) 23 *Journal of Jurisprudence* 57–112, 63.

22   Joseph Conrad, *The Children of the Sea* (The Heritage Press, 1965), xvii.

23   *Ibid.*

24   Joseph Conrad, *The Children of the Sea* (The Heritage Press, 1965), xviii–xix.

25   Anne Orford, "Commissioning the Truth" (2006) 15 *Columbia Journal of Gender and Law* 851–884, 851.

most closely approaches the truth. One is reminded in this regard of Gandhi's considerations on the relationship between the pursuit of law as a profession and the pursuit of truth, and his recognition that by serving truth lawyers can produce "lasting unity from damaging conflict".[26]

Key propositions

- Although the truth of law is not to be found in fiction, in difficult cases, insights gleaned from fiction may point to where the truth perhaps lies.
- The artist tries to find what is of fundamental value. The legal writer seeks to identify the truth of whatever matter is placed before him or her.
- Law is a derivative discipline that has scavenged in the spiritual field for some of its informing ideas.
- A sense of where right lies in a close-run legal matter may be found in the 'spiritual' values which bind societies and tend to endure, even if our understanding of them changes.
- All art, Conrad posits, shows the true meaning of things and creates the emotional/moral atmosphere of its times. In this regard, a parallel with legal writing arises.
- Though legal texts come veiled in rationality, legal writers are to some extent involved in the task of making the reader feel/think/see a particular truth.
- When law and truth are combined in a legal text it can be a potent combination. (In the field of transitional justice, the notion of truth is especially significant at the individual and collective level, as a means of individual healing.)
- The text which lingers in the mind is likely the text which most closely approaches the truth.
- By serving truth lawyers can create "lasting unity from damaging conflict".[27]

---

26 Paul Lannon, Jr, "A Lawyer in Pursuit of Truth and Unity: Mohandas Gandhi and the Private Practice of Law" (2011) 44(3) *Suffolk University Law Review* 665–682, 672.
27 *Ibid.*

4. Crawford

On moralising, flippancy and other matters

Francis Marion Crawford (1854–1909) was an American author who once rivalled Henry James and Mark Twain in popularity,[1] and was renowned for the Italian settings of many of his notably successful books.[2] (Crawford was born and grew up in Italy and lived at a villa in Sorrento in his later life).[3] Having written numerous novels, in the 1890s Crawford published a non-fiction book, *The Novel: What It Is*.[4] In it, Crawford identifies his understanding of the novel in terms that apply with equal rigour, I submit, to the art and craft of legal writing.

1.   Types of text

Crawford gives a threefold definition of the novel: as a saleable commodity,[5] as an artistic luxury[6] (because it is not judged by any of the material senses) and as an intellectual luxury[7] (a conception of the mind un-judged by the material senses).

Crawford's conception of the novel is also capable of being applied to the legal text. It is a saleable commodity – the number of law reports and online legal databases is surely testament to this, though there can be a danger in seeing judgments as a commodity rather than as a process or as "an exercise in justice".[8] Judgments and other legal texts such as law books can also be viewed as an artistic luxury and an intellectual luxury, in each sense as defined by Crawford.

As texts produced in the ordinary course of professional practice are

---

1   John Pilkington, "Francis Marion Crawford (1854–1909)" (1971) 4(2) *American Literary Realism 1870–1910*, 177–182, 187.
2   *Ibid.*
3   John Russo, "A Hundred Years After: New Light on Francis Marion Crawford" (2012) 30(1) *Italian Americana* 110–113, 110.
4   Francis Crawford, *The Novel: What It Is* (Macmillan & Co, 1893).
5   *Ibid*, 8.
6   *Ibid.*
7   *Ibid.*
8   Frank Macchiarola, "Teaching in Law School: What Are We Doing and What More Has to Be Done" (1994) 71(3) *University of Detroit Mercy Law Review* 531–542, 538.

not luxuries (they are produced to meet a need), they do not quite come within Crawford's threefold categorisation, albeit that their value ultimately is not judged by the material senses.

2.   Purpose of text

Crawford also suggests the novel to have a twofold and possibly a threefold purpose: to amuse, to interest and, perhaps, to also instruct. By contrast, a legal text aims to answer and also, to some extent, to instruct and interest. But, I submit, it ought never to contain humour. Admittedly, opinions vary when it comes to the potential for amusement (humour) in legal writing. In *El Farargy v El Farargy*,[9] a case where attempts at judicial humour by a High Court judge were found to have crossed the line of what is tolerable,[10] Ward LJ, for the English Court of Appeal, acknowledges the general consensus that jokes are not a good idea,[11] though he seems immediately to depart from this standard with his wry observation that "Of course they are [a bad idea] when they are bad jokes".[12] However, in bringing this good joke/bad joke dichotomy to bear, the problem that immediately presents itself is that what is funny to you may not be funny to me, so why take the risk in the serious business of law of trying to be funny at all? Indeed, *El Farargy* is possibly something of a case *par excellence* in this regard. In that case, the trial judge saw what he was saying merely to involve colourful language.[13] However, the affronted litigant considered the judge's words to be disparaging and mocking of him, and the Court of Appeal agreed.[14]

Hori, in an in-depth consideration of judicial humour (though his observations have a wider resonance in the legal writing field), concludes that:

- although various writers object to judicial humour, some cases are naturally funny;
- a rule against judicial humour/wit would be impossible to police; and
- judges should be free to use various writing styles.[15]

---

9   [2007] EWCA Civ 1149 (CA).
10   *Ibid*, [31].
11   *Ibid*, [30].
12   *Ibid*.
13   *Ibid*.
14   *Ibid*, [31]. In a statement issued through the Judicial Communications Office immediately after the issuance by the Court of Appeal of its judgment, the trial judge apologised unreservedly for his words (see https://web.archive.org/web/20080905114445/http://www.judiciary.gov.uk/docs/judgments_guidance/singer_statement.pdf).
15   Lucas Hori, "*Bons Mots*, Buffoonery, and the Bench: The Role of Judicial Humor in Judicial Opinions" (2012) 60 *UCLA Law Review Discourse* 16–37, 35–36.

As against this it might be contended that:
- while the facts of a case may be funny the litigation that arises from those facts typically is not;
- while one cannot prohibit humour/wit, a legal writer who seeks continuously to deploy humour seems likely ultimately to be viewed as a clown;[16] and
- freedom of expression is to some extent constrained by the substance and seriousness of the issue/s being addressed in any one legal text.

For the legal writer minded to include humour in a text, Hori offers some useful guiding principles for judges (but again his observations have a wider resonance), namely:
- that they should keep any instances of humour brief;
- that they should consider any intended deployment of humour from the litigants' perspective; and
- that scorn is never appropriate.[17]

So far as a novel that instructs is concerned, Crawford uses the term "purpose-novel", by which he means a novel that seeks to impart some form of moral lesson.[18]

Crawford suggests that the purpose-novel represents a violation of the unwritten contract between writer and reader as to what the former is providing to the latter.[19] Thus, he writes, a man should not buy a purported work of fiction, bring it home, prepare to enjoy it and only then discover that he is actually being given someone's views on, say, politics or religion.[20] Many lawyers, it has been suggested, view legal texts as involving the construction of morality tales,[21] that is they approach their writing task as a purposeful one in which they have a beneficial didactic lesson to teach.[22] This does not present with the same difficulty

---

16   Justice Cardozo, writing of humour in judgments, recounts the following salutary tale: "The story is told by Bernard Shaw of a man who wished to consult the writings of the great naturalist Buffon, and who startled the clerks in the bookstore by the pompous and solemn query, 'Have you the books of the celebrated Buffoon?' One of the difficulties about the humorous opinion is exposure to the risk of passing from the class of Buffoons where we all like to dwell and entering the class of celebrated Buffoons." (Benjamin Cardozo, *Selected Writings of Benjamin Nathan Cardozo*, M Hall (ed) (Fallon Publications, 1947), 350).

17   Lucas Hori, "*Bons Mots*, Buffoonery, and the Bench: The Role of Judicial Humor in Judicial Opinions" (2012) 60 *UCLA Law Review Discourse* 16–37, 37.

18   Francis Crawford, *The Novel: What It Is* (Macmillan & Co, 1893), 12.

19   *Ibid.*

20   *Ibid*, 13.

21   Helen Leskovac, "Legal Writing and Plain English: Does Voice Matter?" (1988) 38 *Syracuse Law Review* 1193–1222, 1219.

22   *Ibid.*

that Crawford ascribes to authors engaged in writing 'purpose-novels', save in one regard: in legal writing, there is nothing wrong with writers having any views they like, provided such views do not impinge upon the correctness of the law as they state it to be.[23]

3. Effect of writing

Crawford suggests that a novel may educate, cultivate, purify and even fortify the intellect but should never seek to deprave.[24]

It seems uncontroversial to posit that a legal text typically educates the reader about some aspect of the law (albeit that legal writing does not *have* to be didactic to engage the reader).[25]

As to cultivation of the mind, this derives from the Socratic notion that cultivation of the mind is the goal of education;[26] however, in a globalised world there is perhaps now a greater awareness among western thinkers of the Confucian notion of self-betterment whereby education develops the character.[27] So, although Crawford ploughs the same furrow that Socrates once tilled, it is perhaps fair to say that for the legal reader/writer, a legal text can both expand depth of knowledge about the world and (because of the focus of much legal writing on truth and the pursuit of truth – as Gandhi once observed, a lawyer has a permanent and prior retainer for truth[28] there is also that Confucian development of the character).

As to fortification (strengthening) of the intellect, one cannot but recall Washburn's one-time contention (perhaps slightly exaggerated for effect) that there is no discipline which demands "so many and such variety of ... a man's best powers" as law,[29] with the rigours presenting not ending with whatever the student has learned at law school but continuing throughout a lifelong professional existence. Thus, Washburn continues, the more a lawyer brings his (*sic*) law school training to bear in practice, the easier he acquires knowledge, until the acquisition of new knowledge becomes instinctive, automatic and ongoing.

---

23   Stephen Wesler, "Teaching Law, McLuhan Style" (1999) 7 *Law Teacher* 1–12, 4.
24   Francis Crawford, *The Novel: What It Is* (Macmillan & Co, 1893), 16.
25   Deborah Gordon and Kaitlin O'Donnell, "The Committed Legal Writer" (2020) 24 *Legal Writing: The Journal of the Legal Writing Institute* 365–412, 412.
26   Peter Huang, "Adventures in Higher Education, Happiness, and Mindfulness" (2018) 7 *British Journal of American Legal Studies* 425–484, 428.
27   *Ibid.*
28   Mohandas Gandhi, *The Law and Lawyers* (Navajivan Publishing House, 1981), v.
29   Emory Washburn, "Legal Education" (1873) 21(7) *The American Law Register* 409–414, 410. Emory Washburn (1800–1877) was a successful attorney, a sometime member of the Harvard Law School Faculty, succeeded in being elected at various times to the Massachusetts House of Representatives and the Massachusetts Senate, and served for a year as Governor of Massachusetts.

Finally, as to Crawford's mention of depravity, the whole tenor of the legal system in liberal democracies is such that legal texts formulated within that context seem unlikely to consciously seek to deprave – though again it is perhaps worth recalling Gandhi's observation that the law and lawyers and hence legal writers are not invariably the benign influence within society that they may imagine themselves to be. Thus, Gandhi writes:

> *Whatever instances of lawyers having done good can be brought forward, it will be found that the good is due to them as men, rather than as lawyers … [T]he profession teaches immorality; it is exposed to temptations from which few are saved. The Hindus and the Mahomedans have quarrelled. An ordinary man will ask them to forget all about it … The lawyers … will, as a rule, advance quarrels, instead of repressing them … [M]en take up that profession, not … to help others … but to enrich themselves … [T]hey are glad when men have disputes … It is the lawyers who have discovered that theirs is an honorable profession. They frame laws as they frame their own praises.*[30]

One cause of Gandhi's ire against lawyers rests in the fact that, as he saw matters, without lawyers the British colonial legal system in India could not have been established and so the British could not have ruled in India.[31] Whether or not one agrees with all that Gandhi has to say, his observations suggest that even in law a tendency to immorality may be found – and hence that Crawford's observation that a novel should never seek to deprave (incline to immorality) may not always and altogether be irrelevant.

4.   Moralising

Crawford cautions against moralising in the novel, suggesting that it is one thing to depict some moral ideal and to depict it in such a way as to make it appealing; however, he deprecates the notion that a novel might be written as a guidebook on morality.[32] The same might reasonably be contended of a legal text such as a judgment, namely that while it may exhibit an ideal worthy to be imitated, it is not a vehicle through which secular judges should seek to pronounce on matters moral. In this regard, the story is told (in various forms) of an over-lunch encounter between two of America's most famous judges, Learned Hand and Oliver Wendell

---

30   Mohandas Gandhi, *Hind Swaraj or Indian Home Rule* (GA Natesan & Co, 1921), 46–47.
31   *Ibid*, 49.
32   Francis Crawford, *The Novel: What It Is* (Macmillan & Co, 1893), 19.

Holmes, Jr. As recounted by Judge Bork (formerly of the United States Court of Appeals), after lunch had finished and Holmes was leaving, Hand cried to him to 'do justice', to which Holmes reprovingly replied, 'That is not my job. It is my job to apply the law'.[33] The point being made by Holmes was that judges administer justice according to the law; justice by reference to morality is for elected lawmakers to achieve by changing the law. So (like Crawford when writing of literature generally), Holmes did not see a judgment as a 'guide to morality' – though clearly, Hand was minded to take a different view.

5.   Flippant and colloquial writing

Crawford suggests that oftentimes in children's literature one finds that the author includes an element which converts the text from one suitable for younger minds into one wholly unsuitable.[34] In legal texts, the danger lies in a different direction, namely, that content that is too flippant or colloquial for a legal text may be included, thus diminishing its quality as professional prose. It has been suggested that in a legal text one should never be flippant.[35] This is because flippancy seems likely to strike the reader as condescending or inappropriate and perhaps even diminishing the seriousness of the matter at hand. That said, avoidance of the flippant does not mean that a legal writer has to veer immediately into the dreary and dry.

As to colloquialisms, when it comes to judgment writing Judge Posner strikes a middle note, objecting to excessive, self-consciously professional jargon and also to an 'impure' writing style that is excessively colloquial.[36] An overly colloquial tone in legal writing suggests that a want of seriousness and perhaps even undue emotion is being brought to bear by the legal writer.[37] One comparatively recent survey as to which type of writing American judges found more persuasive (and hence the type of legal writing that legal writers ought to aim at producing, at least when writing for judges) showed a general preference for plain English over stilted English, provided the plain English was not excessively colloquial.[38]

---

33   Robert Bork, *The Tempting of America: The Political Seduction of the Law* (The Free Press, 1990), 6.
34   Francis Crawford, *The Novel: What It Is* (Macmillan & Co, 1893), 33.
35   Collyn Peddie, "Improving Legal Writing: The Triumph of Hope Over Experience" (1993) 13(1) *Review of Litigation* 83–104, 102.
36   Richard Posner, "Legal Writing Today" (2001–2002) 8 *Scribes Journal of Legal Writing*, 35–38, 35.
37   Pamela Samuelson, "Good Legal Writing: Of Orwell and Window-Panes" (1984) 46(1) *University of Pittsburgh Law Review* 149–170, 156.
38   Sean Flammer, "Persuading Judges: An Empirical Analysis of Writing Style, Persuasion and the Use of Plain English" (2010) 16(1) *Legal Writing: The Journal of the Legal Writing Institute* 183–222, 211.

So much for judges, but what do non-lawyers find desirable in a legal text? The American humourist, Will Rodgers, probably captured best what the public expects to find in legal writing when he observed (back in the 1930s) that the moment a person reads something they cannot understand, they can be sure that it was drafted by a lawyer, adding that plain and concise wording understandable in one way will invariably be written by a non-lawyer.[39] This possibly understates the level of skill involved in writing any work of prose so that it is comprehensible. However, the problem of 'legalese' is so bad that in the United States it has even acquired an acronym, being described as a 'VIPER', that is, verbose, inert, pompous, euphemistic and redolent.[40] But the antidote to VIPER poison, I submit, is not to have recourse to the excessively colloquial but rather to reach for the triple goal of brevity, clarity and simplicity in one's legal writing. As Justice Robert Jackson, among the most gifted legal writers ever to have graced the United States Supreme Court once observed, a good lawyer "will master the short ... word that pierces the mind like a spear and the simple figure that lights the understanding ... [and] will never drive the [reader to a] dictionary".[41]

6. Self-discipline

Crawford suggests that after writing a few romantic novels, the attractions of romance writing tend to wane for novelists.[42] In its place comes a recognition that the novelist will need to write (in Crawford's opinion) about 20 novels to sustain a career, and in that recognition there often comes a waning of the self-discipline necessary to produce the highest-quality prose.[43]

Notably, one finds, even in the output of the very best legal writers, both good and bad legal texts – testament perhaps to the fact that even the best legal writers occasionally abandon the restraints and constraints that yield the best-quality prose. A good example of this is Lord Denning, who has given some of the strongest and also perhaps some of the weakest opening lines/paragraphs of all of the judgments that have been issued in the courts of England and Wales. Possibly his strongest

39   Will Rodgers, "Weekly Article 657", *Will Rogers Today*, 28 July 1935, www.willrogerstoday.com/quotes/will-rogers-on-lawyers/.
40   David Mellinkoff, *The Language of Law*, 3rd edition (Little, Brown & Co, 1978), 298.
41   Robert Jackson, "Advocacy Before the United States Supreme Court" (1951) 25(2) *Temple Law Quarterly* 115–130, 129. Jackson is writing of the use of language in courtroom advocacy but his observations arguably apply with equal vigour when it comes to legal writing more generally.
42   Francis Crawford, *The Novel: What It Is* (Macmillan & Co, 1893), 35.
43   *Ibid*, 36.

(certainly one of his most famous) openers came in *Miller v Jackson*,[44] a claim concerning the operation of a local cricket ground, in which Denning observes:

> *In summertime village cricket is the delight of everyone. Nearly every village has its own cricket field where the young men play and the old men watch. In the village of Lintz in County Durham they have their own ground, where they have played these last 70 years. They tend it well. The wicket area is well rolled and mown. The outfield is kept short. It has a good club house for the players and seats for the onlookers. The village team play there on Saturdays and Sundays. They belong to a league, competing with the neighbouring villages. On other evenings after work they practise while the light lasts. Yet now after these 70 years a judge of the High Court has ordered that they must not play there any more.*[45]

This paean to traditional English life falls to be compared with Denning's opening paragraph in *George Mitchell (Chesterhall) Ltd v Finney Lock Seeds*,[46] a case arising from the fact that the plaintiffs had requested the supply of one form of cabbage seed and been provided with another. In a notably weak opening to his judgment, Lord Denning observes as follows:

> *Many of you know Lewis Carroll's* Through the Looking Glass. *In it there are these words (Ch. IV):*
> *"The time has come," the Walrus said,*
> *"to talk of many things:*
> *Of shoes – and ships – and sealing-wax –*
> *Of cabbages – and kings – "*
> *Today it is not "of cabbages and kings" – but of cabbages and what-nots.*[47]

The overall decline in the quality of Denning's judgments from the late 1950s through to the 1980s – albeit that many of his opening lines/paragraphs are possessed of an almost startling eloquence – is striking, and has invited speculation as to its cause. Mr Justice Hogan of the Irish Supreme Court, writing extrajudicially, has suggested that it may be that Denning's writing abilities just left him,[48] or, alternatively, that he yielded to a desire for public acclaim in preference to eloquence in his writing.[49] A further, third possibility which presents is that posited by

---

44   [1977] QB 966 (CA).
45   *Ibid*, 976.
46   [1982] 3 WLR 1036 (CA).
47   *Ibid*, 1040.
48   Gerard Hogan, "Holmes and Denning: Two 20th Century Legal Icons Compared" (2007) 42 *Irish Jurist* 119–135, 127.
49   *Ibid*.

Crawford,[50] namely that Denning was 'guilty' over his long incumbency as a judge of a waning of that self-discipline which is necessary to produce the highest-quality prose.

7. Brevity, simplicity, etc

Crawford posits the idea of the perfect novel as a work that is simple, keen, possessed of pathos and even sublime.[51] Taking each of these characteristics in turn, the perfect legal text might likewise be posited as a text that is as simple as possible. Indeed, simplicity, with brevity and clarity, is a 'triple crown' of legal writing. Thus, Lord Bingham, one of the more prominent English judges of the early 21st century, has observed in the context of judgment writing (but his observations have a wider resonance) that the ideal/effective judgment will be possessed of brevity, clarity and simplicity.[52]

What, however, of keenness (enthusiasm), *pathos* (feeling) and sublimity (beauty)? Are these also desirable traits in legal writing? Enthusiasm certainly has its aficionados. So, for example, it has been suggested that there is no quality more essential to good writing than enthusiasm on the part of the writer as that enthusiasm tends to yield "dynamic vitality".[53] Lawyers are typically paid to write but there is no reason why they should be wanting in enthusiasm (indeed a client/litigant might well perceive a want of enthusiasm to be unprofessional). *Pathos* is not an everyday word in the English language but it too has its aficionados when it comes to legal writing. Indeed, it has been suggested that appeals to emotion are a critical element in being persuasive in writing.[54]

As for sublimity, one *can* find transcendent idealism in legal texts such as judgments. As good an example as any is Holmes' soaring (and searing) dissent in *United States v Schwimmer*[55] – a case concerning the refusal of citizenship to a woman who was so committed to pacifism that she was unprepared to swear that she would take up arms for the United States, if necessary. In his dissent, Holmes lauds free thought in the following terms:

50   Francis Crawford, *The Novel: What It Is* (Macmillan & Co, 1893), 36.
51   *Ibid*, 44.
52   Lord Bingham, "What Is the Law?" (2009) 40(3) *Victoria University of Wellington Law Review* 597–612, 609.
53   I Campbell, "Legal Writing" (1999) 30(2) *Victoria University of Wellington Law Review* 427–434, 427.
54   Kathryn Stanchi, "Feminist Legal Writing" (2002) 39 *San Diego Law Review* 387–436, 397.
55   279 US 644 (1929).

[I]f there is any principle of the Constitution that more imperatively calls for attachment than any other it is the principle of free thought – not free thought for those who agree with us but freedom for the thought that we hate. I think that we should adhere to that principle with regard to admission into, as well as to life within this country. And recurring to the opinion that bars this applicant's way, I would suggest that the Quakers have done their share to make the country what it is, that many citizens agree with the applicant's belief and that I had not supposed hitherto that we regretted our inability to expel them because they believe more than some of us do in the teachings of the Sermon on the Mount.[56]

That is beautiful prose and the substance of Holmes' thinking is beautiful too. After reading it, one cannot but feel the same sense as the notional prisoner released from Plato's cave who had previously seen only shadows of what was now placed before him. Indeed, in style and substance, the majority opinion is so thoroughly eclipsed by Holmes' text that it is difficult not to pity Justice Butler (the author of the majority opinion) who comes across as somewhat of an amateur athlete in a race in which a Titan has deigned to compete.

Holmes captures, in a nutshell, the essence of what freedom of thought involves ("not free thought for those who agree with us but freedom for the thought that we hate").[57] He reminds the reader of the glorious part that Quakers – men such as Thomas Paine and General Nathaniel Greene – had in the creation of America's great (if now internally imperilled) democracy, and he even brings in a self-deprecatory reference to the fact that the Quakers have adhered more closely than some to the 'Sermon on the Mount' (a sermon delivered by Jesus shortly after he commenced his public ministry in which he teaches the central tenets of what we now know as 'Christianity'). Even Holmes' disagreement with Ms Schwimmer's view that peace was bound to triumph over war-making in a flawed human world is beautifully expressed:

I do not share that optimism nor do I think that a philosophic view of the world would regard war as absurd. But most people who have known it regard it with horror, as a last resort, and even if not yet ready for cosmopolitan efforts, would welcome any practicable combinations that would increase the power on the side of peace.[58]

---

56   *Ibid*, 654–655.
57   *Ibid*, 655.
58   *Ibid*, 654.

Not everyone can write like Holmes. His achievements are the product of long work and effort but also likely involve an element of natural genius. For lesser writers, a well-constructed text involves "fine cabinetwork",[59] that is, it is something to be pieced together with the minimum of glue. By eliminating excess glue/words from one's sentences one can craft prose that is more eloquent than would otherwise be the case.

8. Illusion, truth and writing

Crawford suggests that a great novel yields the same type of illusion as a good play; however, he emphasises that the 'play' should be the writer's focus, with the illusion being but a tool to success.[60] Transposing this into the context of legal writing it might be posited that a legal text is excellent to the extent that it produces a coherent illusion of real life; even so, real life (not the illusion) is the true focus, albeit that the illusion is necessary to success. One American commentator has treated with this interplay of illusion and truth in the working life of the practising lawyer, noting how a complainant's statement will be less complete than reality, that when matters go to court lawyers will pull from that statement what best suits them (and seek to have the rest excluded), that a jury will therefore not adjudicate on the whole of the truth but on which version of the truth that has been presented to jurors is the more credible, and that the job of an attorney, it follows, is to create something of an "illusion of truth".[61]

9. Realising the author's conception

Crawford posits that the object of the novel writer (and the same is true of the legal writer) is to make the reader realise to the greatest extent possible the author's conception of his or her tale. The English philosopher, John Locke, had something similar in mind when he wrote in his *Essay Concerning Human Understanding* (1689) that: "The chief end of language in communication being to be understood, words serve not well for that end ... when any word does not excite in the hearer the same idea which it stands for in the mind of the speaker."[62] Both the author and legal writer have no means of achieving the end identified by Crawford and Locke, save by way of language.[63]

---

59 Richard Wydick, *Plain English for Lawyers*, 4th edition (Carolina Academic Press, 1998), 10.
60 Francis Crawford, *The Novel: What It Is* (Macmillan & Co, 1893), 50.
61 Christina Bailey, "The Illusion of Truth" (2001) 25(3–4) *Legal Studies Forum* 365–376, 375.
62 John Locke, *An Essay Concerning Human Understanding* (Ward, Lock & Co, 1881), 383.
63 Francis Crawford, *The Novel: What It Is* (Macmillan & Co, 1893), 52.

Language is also the means whereby legal writers create as *persuasive* a legal text as possible, deploying such words as are necessary to do so, and bringing to bear their experiences of life and law in writing the best legal text possible. When it comes to the interrelationship of thought and prose, it has been suggested that lawyers should not write for other lawyers or non-lawyers but with an awareness of law's "conceptual structure",[64] that is, the process whereby relevant facts are extracted and the rule of law is brought to bear upon them.[65]

Writing with an awareness of how one should write is more likely to yield good legal prose/reasoning. And representing a complex concept/ thought accurately does not mean that one has to abandon the object of simplicity. A legal argument is only as good as it is convincing to the reader[66] – and a reader can be convinced only if he or she is presented with text that is clear and simple and thus readily capable of being understood. In short, style is necessary, but substance is critical.

Bringing all of this back to Crawford, what he essentially points to is that the communication of substance can be corrupted through deficiencies of style and that the aim of the writer (the legal writer included) should be to keep such deficiencies/corruption to a minimum. Simply put: "Clarity of expression stems in the main from clarity of thought, but even when a writer's ideas are clear he has to strive to use words that convey his ideas with equal clarity."[67]

10. Using foreign words

When it comes to the use of foreign language, Crawford observes of the writer of fiction that he or she may legitimately deploy certain dialects.[68] For legal writers, a different reality applies. Yes, a legal writer may use legal terms of art and foreign language terms such as Latinisms if he or she wishes but in doing so to any great extent a certain want of clarity seems likely to present for many readers. Specifically, with regard to Latinisms, it has been suggested that although Latin enriches writing it should be used sparingly.[69] However, Crawford suggests another possibility to present. Thus, the question he asks of a novel writer might

---

64   Richard Hyland, "A Defense of Legal Writing" (1986) 134(3) *University of Pennsylvania Law Review* 599–626, 600.
65   *Ibid*, 613.
66   *Ibid*, 620.
67   I Campbell, "Legal Writing" (1999) 30(2) *Victoria University of Wellington Law Review* 427–434, 434.
68   Francis Crawford, *The Novel: What It Is* (Macmillan & Co, 1893), 53.
69   Peter Macleod, "Latin in Legal Writing: An Inquiry into the Use of Latin in the Modern Legal World" (1997) 39 *Boston College Law Review* 235–252, 251.

also be put to the legal writer who is tempted to use foreign words: could greater clarity be achieved through their avoidance? Lebovits, writing of the desirability of using English in English-language judgments, lightly posits a number of sensible points, namely:

- avoid Latin if you wish to be understood as a writer;
- prefer English-language words over foreign words;
- avoid Latin and Norman French; and
- if compelled to use Latin, avoid Latin errors.[70]

11. Digression

Treating with the issue of how to write a novel, Crawford observes that the writer's guiding star must be truth.[71] Perhaps the lesson to be drawn from Crawford's observation when it comes to legal writing is that a legal writer should not become distracted from his or her pursuit of truth, digressing into side issues that serve only to display erudition rather than advance a legal text or enlighten a reader. As one commentator has observed, digression is a fault that merely distracts from the main idea.[72] That said, there is an alternative view, namely, that digression can sometimes lighten the chore of writing/reading, provided it is not done to excess.[73] If digression is to be entertained, it may be that the fact that one is engaging in digression is best identified by placing it in a footnote; that way there is no deviation from the single-minded pursuit of truth in the main substance of the legal text.

12. Life experience and writing

Crawford suggests that life experience forms the true education of a novelist.[74] Interestingly, there is evidence to suggest that in practice law clerks and *in*experienced lawyers tend to be impressed by legalistic reasoning whereas judges (typically older and with more life experience under their belts) tend to look to the human drama at play before them and hence enjoy a narrative.[75]

The desirability of life experience of which Crawford writes points also to the desirability of having a diverse legal profession and a diverse

---

70   Gerald Lebovits, "On *Terra Firma* with English" (2015) 16 *Scribes Journal of Legal Writing* 123–126, 125.
71   Francis Crawford, *The Novel: What It Is* (Macmillan & Co, 1893), 67.
72   Arthur Vanderbilt, *Studying Law* (Washington Square Publishing Corporation, 1945), 26.
73   William Wilson, "How I Write" (1993) 4 *Scribes Journal of Legal Writing* 79–81, 81.
74   Francis Crawford, *The Novel: What It Is* (Macmillan & Co, 1893), 79.
75   Lance Long, "Is There any Science Behind the Art of Legal Writing?" (2016) 16 *Wyoming Law Review* 287–298, 295.

judiciary to make sure that, at all levels of the legal system, the widest experience is brought to bear in reducing offensive words and expressions in legal texts. With all western nations now facing a reckoning over historical racism (particularly but not only as regards the slave trade) there is also a necessary reconsideration of words and phrases in the legal realm that may be controversial. Examples of such words include 'grandfather clause' and 'Chinese wall',[76] with gender pronoun usage also now offering another area ripe for sensitive change in terms of the pronouns deployed in legal texts.[77] When it comes to making such changes the years necessary to attain that life experience to which Crawford points as a virtue may yet prove an incumbrance to the sensitive development of the law. This is because younger people seem more likely to be alert to the evolving meaning of words than older people, if only because younger people tend typically to be more actively involved in that evolutionary process.

13.   Amusement/humour in writing

Ought a legal text to be amusing? When it comes to amusement in the context of novel writing, Crawford observes that the novel amuses at the intellectual level, rather than being downright comical; that it needs to be carefully balanced, not trying to be excessively emotional or humorous (with an excess of either being unnatural).[78] Much the same might be said of a good legal text, that is, that it should amuse, not in the sense of yielding laughter but in the sense of being a finely-balanced creation that is captivating, compelling, and convincing. 'Amusement' in this sense means to be diverting, rather than funny. Attempts at funniness seem best avoided. So, for example, it has been said that misplaced judicial humour threatens to make a joke of a case,[79] that

---

76   The phrase 'grandfather clause' has racist overtones because, to borrow from footnote 11 of the judgment of Milkey J for the Massachusetts Appeals Court in *Comstock v Zoning Board of Appeals of Gloucester* 153 NE3d 395 (Mass A Ct, 2020), "the phrase ... originally referred to provisions adopted by some [formerly Confederate] states after the [US] Civil War in an effort to disenfranchise African-American voters by requiring voters to pass literacy tests or meet other significant qualifications, while exempting from such requirements those who were descendants of men who were eligible to vote prior to 1867" (*ibid*, 400). As to the phrase 'Chinese Wall' (a phrase hitherto used in professional firms to refer to the notional 'screening off' of some employees to avoid internal conflicts of interest) in a concurring opinion in *Peat Marwick, Mitchell & Co v Superior Court* 245 *Cal Rptr* 873, Low J has indicated that the phrase involves a form of linguistic discrimination against people of Chinese ancestry. See generally on this area, John Browning, "Should Legal Writing Be Woke?" (2022) 20 *Scribes Journal of Legal Writing* 25–50.
77   *Ibid*, 48.
78   Francis Crawford, *The Novel: What It Is* (Macmillan & Co, 1893), 82.
79   Thomas Baker, "A Review of Corpus Juris Humorous" (1993) 24 *Texas Tech Law Review* 869–890, 872.

making fun of the less articulate/educated is "outright abuse",[80] and that credibility is imperilled by a joke that is not funny.[81] There is an alternative school of thought which (not without some justification) contends that humour can make a legal text more accessible/persuasive, and that sometimes it simply offers an attractive pace-change.[82] However, in the face of the multiple potential downsides presenting, one has to wonder why any legal writer would run the risk of incorporating humour into a text knowing that if the attempt at humour misfires it will not rebound well on the writer.

14. The ethics of writing

Crawford suggests that the foundation of good fiction writing is ethics, not aesthetics.[83] An ethical work of fiction, he posits, must appeal to the heart, by which he means to refer to all of one's beliefs, impulses, and instincts.[84] In the context of legal writing, this body of instincts, impulses, and beliefs is perhaps best viewed as 'justice'. So, what Crawford arguably points to in the legal writing context is that fundamentally a legal text is an ethical (not an aesthetical) work and that to be ethical it must appeal to the ideals of justice – though this raises the point already touched on in the tale of Learned Hand and Wendell Holmes recounted above, that is, does this mean justice in accordance with law or some separate code of morality? That is, to some extent, an unanswerable question. Certainly, it is a question that cannot properly be addressed in the space available here. The significance of Crawford's observation is that for all the importance of style to writing – and style matters ("bad writing infects thinking")[85] – in essence, legal writing is an ethical exercise, not an aesthetic one.

15. Sympathy

In terms of sustaining reader appreciation, Crawford suggests that sentiment (feeling) heightens the value of a work, but that sentimentality (schmaltz) lowers it.[86] Bringing this to bear in the context of legal writing,

---

80   Paul LeBel, "Legal Education and the Theatre of the Absurd: 'Can't Anybody Play This Here Game?" (1992) 17 *Brigham Young University Law Review* 413–426, 414.
81   Alex Long, "(Insert Song Lyrics Here): The Uses and Misuses of popular Music Lyrics in Legal Writing" (2007) 64(2) *Washington and Lee Law Review* 531–582, 565.
82   *Ibid*, 575.
83   Francis Crawford, *The Novel: What It Is* (Macmillan & Co, 1893), 86.
84   *Ibid*, 85.
85   James Lindgren, "Style Matters: A Review Essay on Legal Writing" (1982) 92(1) *Yale Law Journal* 161–187, 187.
86   Francis Crawford, *The Novel: What It Is* (Macmillan & Co, 1893), 95.

it might be contended that a legal text which evinces a degree of sympathy is likely to be more persuasive than a legal text containing a surfeit of emotion. However, the notion that emotion might have any role to play in legal reasoning has not always been accepted. Sir Edward Coke, the great English jurist, writing in the 17th century, invoked a Latin maxim to the effect that 'Nothing that is contrary to reason is lawful' as a basis for positing the theory that the common law is the "perfection of reason".[87] Coming closer to our own time, however, there is the renowned observation of Oliver Wendell Holmes, Jr in his book, *The Common Law* (1881), that "The life of the law has not been logic: it has been experience",[88] an observation which draws a clear distinction between logic (reason) and experience – with experience again surely being informed by emotion.

As a practising judge, the notion that emotion plays a part in the due administration of justice chimes with my own courtroom experience: a judge wants to achieve fairness in what he or she does and there is always scope within the parameters of the law to achieve what appeals to one's sense of justice on the particular facts presenting. That is why, for example, it has been suggested that one of the great 'dos' of courtroom advocacy is to attract sympathy for one's case and not to shrink from showing how an injustice might happen.[89] In fact, this advice likely holds good across much legal writing. But what happens when one goes too far and treads into the area of sentimentality (schmaltz) to which Crawford refers?

Perhaps surprisingly, there is good reason to believe that some degree of sentimentality (schmaltz) can be a powerful force to bring to bear in advocacy. So, for example, it has been said that in the *Bush v Gore* cases, which contested various aspects of the American presidential election of 2000, the Republican side "exploited sentimentality masterfully", constantly hammering home to the average American voter how his or her vote was "to be effectively recast by petty functionaries".[90] As it is in advocacy so, it might be contended, it is across a range of legal writing.

If emotion (sympathy/sentimentality) suffices to make a case more persuasive to a judge then surely the same emotional tricks that it is

---

87   Edward Coke, *The First Part of the Institutes of the Laws of England* (Robert H Small, 1853), vol 1, §138.
88   Oliver Wendell Holmes, Jr, *The Common Law* (Macmillan & Co, 1882), 1.
89   Roger Miner, "Twenty-Five Dos for Appellate Brief Writers" (1992) 3 *Scribes Journal of Legal Writing* 19–26, 24.
90   Larry Cata Backer, "Using Law Against Itself: *Bush v Gore* Applied in the Courts" (2003) 55(4) *Rutgers Law Review* 1109–1174, 1161.

sought to play on a judge can in turn be deployed by that judge in a bid to make her text more persuasive. However, care is required if appeals to emotion are not to backfire and become perceived instead as part of an exercise in manipulation, rather than part of an exercise aimed at discerning the truth presenting in any one context.

Key propositions

- A legal text is a marketable commodity and an artistic/intellectual luxury.
- A legal text may aim to answer/instruct/interest; it should not seek to amuse.
- A legal text has one purpose: to answer one or more issues presenting; legal writers should not stray into addressing issues that are not before them.
- The tenor of the legal system in liberal democracies is such that legal texts formulated within that context seem unlikely to deprave the mind (they regularly improve and inform it).
- While a judgment may exhibit worthy ideals, it is not a vehicle through which judges should seek to pronounce on matters moral.
- To be guarded against in legal writing is the inclusion of words that are too flippant/colloquial, diminishing the quality of a legal text as professional prose.
- The perfect legal text might be posited as a text that is clear, brief, simple, passionate and possessed of a certain transcendent idealism.
- A legal text is excellent to the extent it produces a coherent illusion of real life; even so, real life, not the illusion, is its true focus (albeit that the illusion is necessary for success).
- The object of the legal writer is to make the reader realise the writer's conception of the 'tale' of fact and law recounted.
- Language is the means whereby a legal writer creates as persuasive a legal text as he or she can, deploying the words necessary and bringing to bear his or her experiences.
- The legal writer may use legal 'terms of art' and Latinisms; however, the legal writer who uses fewer terms of art and Latinisms can hope to produce more compelling texts.
- A legal writer should not digress down logical sidetracks which

display erudition rather than advancing an argument or informing the reader.

- Lawyers are expected to bring a knowledge of people and life to bear in their advice, opinions, etc – their knowledge of the law is assumed.
- A good legal text may legitimately amuse, not by yielding laughter but through being a balanced creation that is captivating/compelling/convincing.
- A legal text is meant to be ethical; as such, it must appeal to the ideals of justice.
- In terms of sustaining reader appreciation, sentiment (feeling) can heighten the value of a legal text, while sentimentality (excessive feeling) lowers it.
- A legal text that evinces a degree of sympathy is likely to be more persuasive/powerful than a legal text possessing a surfeit of emotion.

5. De Maupassant

On honesty, simplicity and other matters

The French writer, Guy de Maupassant (1850–1893), is an acknowledged master of the short-story form, his name "often associated with Tolstoy, Chekhov, Somerset Maugham, and ... Henry".[1] However, de Maupassant was also a distinguished novelist. In what is perhaps his greatest novel, *Pierre and Jean* (1888), he describes the evolution of the relationship between two brothers when and after the suspicion arises that they have different fathers. For present purposes, *Pierre and Jean* is of interest because of de Maupassant's preface concerning the novel as a form of literature,[2] the substance of which is considered below and then applied in the context of legal writing.

1.   Originality

All writers, de Maupassant writes, compose their works in accordance with their own sense of originality.[3] This almost expressivist concept of writing (expressivist writing involves a personal writing style that proceeds heedless of rules) has never really taken hold among teachers of legal writing who have traditionally favoured a cognitivist approach to writing (whereby writing is viewed as a complex, conscious, cognitive task).[4] Indeed, even the concept of originality has a somewhat ambiguous position when it comes to legal writing. Thus, it has been suggested that an excess of the creative in a legal text will likely be both "bad and dangerous".[5]

Reconciling the need for originality with the constraining demands of

---

1   Harold Bloom (ed), *Bloom's Major Short Story Writers: Guy de Maupassant* (Chelsea House Publishers, 2004), 17.
2   Guy de Maupassant, *Pierre and Jean* (PF Collier & Son, 1902), xli–lxiii.
3   *Ibid*, xliii–xliv.
4   See, eg, J Rideout and J Ramsfield, "Legal Writing: A Revised View" (1994) 69(1) *Washington Law Review* 35–100, 51.
5   Mary Ellen Gale, "Legal Writing: The Impossible Takes a Little Longer" (1980) 44(2) *Albany Law Review* 298–343, 315.

precedent is a demanding process, likely not helped by the fact that an oftentimes conservative legal profession is hesitant to embrace innovation. But law is not the only field of endeavour that wrestles with drawing on a repository of accepted knowledge and yet also proceeding in such a way that one is interpreting or even innovating. One recent review article has drawn an analogy in this regard between legal writing and hip-hop writing – hip-hop musicians also being confronted with how to borrow from earlier works and yet also managing to innovate without succumbing to 'biting' (the hip-hop term for plagiarism).[6] What is fascinating about such analysis is that hip-hop styles have radically transformed since the emergence of hip-hop as a musical genre in the 1970s. By contrast if, for example, a Tudor lawyer time travelled to the 2020s he (only men practised law in Tudor times) would not find a great deal of difference between the judgments of his time and ours.

There seems something counter-evolutionary about a writing form that has barely evolved in hundreds of years. Unless one accepts that the common law world settled early on a form of judgment writing which is incapable of improvement (which seems unlikely) the very different experiences of the legal and hip-hop worlds when it comes to innovations in style suggest that the legal profession has not yet fully resolved how to reconcile tradition with originality.

2. Expectations as to form

De Maupassant notes the tendency for critics to hold certain expectations as to the form of a novel and to reject works which do not conform to their pre-conceived notions of the aesthetically pleasing.[7] He also suggests that critics should instead seek out that which least resembles existing words and encourage young authors to go down new paths.[8]

Only a few decades into the Internet Age, these observations can be applied to modern legal writing. Thus, previous means of communication in the legal world are rapidly being overtaken by new means of communicating information. For example, whereas previously a piece of legal analysis would have been committed to a formal letter/ memorandum, nowadays one is just as likely to find one or more emails taking the place of such a letter/memorandum. Yet it would be a mistake to conclude that communication by email is simply a new way of writing

---

6   Kim Chanbonpin, "Legal Writing, the Remix: Plagiarism and Hip Hop Ethics" (2012) 63 *Mercer Law Review* 597–638.
7   Guy de Maupassant, *Pierre and Jean* (PF Collier & Son, 1902), xliii.
8   *Ibid.*

a letter/memorandum. For example, it also replaces conversation, and it takes place in a medium that has its own rules of intercourse, proceeding like a conversation, but a conversation that is being entirely recorded in lasting form – a fact which doubtless shapes what parties are prepared to state, and how.

Determining which traditional form of communication a particular email replaces can be a useful pointer as to what form an individual email ought to take.[9] Other more immediate and casual messaging systems may also be used in place of email, for example, SMS texts, Facebook Messenger®, WhatsApp® and (for business users) Microsoft Teams® and Slack®, all of which have their own rules of social etiquette and their own advantages/drawbacks. In this brave new world, de Maupassant's observations point to the need for open-mindedness as to the expected nature and form of communications, with younger legal writers to be encouraged to try the new, though without altogether eschewing the old.

As one commentator has observed in this last regard, many of today's legal students (as well as more recently qualified lawyers) are "digital natives"[10] accustomed to online exchanges but perhaps, as a consequence, less used to face-to-face conversations. As a result, as much as contemporary students need to be able to converse (and converse appropriately) online, they also need to know how to speak out loud (and speak appropriately) in real-life situations.[11]

3. The pursuit of truth

De Maupassant notes the school of thought which holds that a novel comprises truth.[12] This is a conception that holds true of good legal texts also. That does not mean that the law comprises (or can be reduced through legal texts) to a finite number of universal propositions that apply unfailingly in all instances like scientific truths: "law is contextual".[13] What it does mean is that each legal text is, or ought to be, engaged in the identification of the legal truth of whatever situation it is concerned with.

De Maupassant then proceeds to consider the novelist who alters truth[14] and the novelist who seeks to depict life accurately.[15] The former

---

9   Jennifer Will, "Call It an E-Convo: When an E-Memo Isn't Really a Memo at All" (2020) 24 *Legal Writing: The Journal of the Legal Writing Institute* 269–314, 298–299.

10   *Ibid*, 312.

11   *Ibid*.

12   Guy de Maupassant, *Pierre and Jean* (PF Collier & Son, 1902), xliii.

13   David Romantz, "The Truth About Cats and Dogs: Legal Writing Courses and the Law School Curriculum" (2003) 52(1) *University of Kansas Law Review* 105–146, 105.

14   Guy de Maupassant, *Pierre and Jean* (PF Collier & Son, 1902), xlvii.

15   *Ibid*.

type of novelist: "manipulate[s] events ... [yielding] a series of ingenious combinations."[16] In short, he or she engages in selection and manipulation that is aimed at a particular end and is disrespectful of truth and the reader. If such an approach were deployed in the legal writing context it might yield a persuasive text but (I submit) it would be a flawed text. Persuasive legal writing demands accuracy and truth.[17]

Notably, when it comes to the writer who seeks to depict life accurately, de Maupassant suggests that this writer too may be guilty of falsity. Why so? Because he or she cannot tell the reader everything that makes up the truth: that would be too long and cumbersome a thing to do.[18] So there must be some selection of relevant incidents. But if such a choice must be made (and it must) this deals a blow to the theory that a novel could ever represent the whole truth of a subject.[19] The novel that purports to depict the whole truth (and likewise the legal text that purports to depict the whole truth) cannot be the whole truth. This is why it is so important to seek to be as honest as possible in the process of selection and statement, for if the legal writer proceeds dishonestly, he or she (and his or her text) can no longer be believed.[20]

4.   Detachment

As to the potential for objectivity in a text, de Maupassant considers that writers necessarily bring something of themselves and their worldview to their writing.[21] Lawyers, by contrast, have long been taught to believe that in legal writing objectivity reigns supreme,[22] that it should be the law which shines through a legal text and not the author. This is a very ancient concept. Cicero, a lawyer, philosopher, and politician of the late Roman republic, wrote in the 1st century BCE that "[I]t can truly be said that the magistrate is a speaking law, and the law a silent magistrate".[23] (In other words, the magistrate's voice is simply the law made vocal.) Two millennia later, we know that voice in many guises *can* creep into a legal text. In a consideration of voice, self and persona in legal writing,[24]

---

16   *Ibid.*
17   Mark de Forrest, "Introducing Persuasive Legal Argument via 'The Letter from a Birmingham City Hall'" (2009) 15(1) *Legal Writing: The Journal of the Legal Writing Institute* 109–164, 136–137.
18   Guy de Maupassant, *Pierre and Jean* (PF Collier & Son, 1902), 1.
19   *Ibid.*
20   James McElhaney, "The Art of Persuasive Legal Writing" (1996) 82(1) *ABA Journal* 76–82, 78.
21   Guy de Maupassant, *Pierre and Jean* (PF Collier & Son, 1902), lvi.
22   James Elkins, "What Kind of Story is Legal Writing?" (1996) 20(1) *Legal Studies Forum* 95–136, 113.
23   Cicero, *De Re Publica, De Legibus*, T Page (ed) (William Heinemann, 1928), 461.
24   J Christopher Rideout, "Voice, Self, and Persona in Legal Writing" (2009) 15(1) *Legal Writing: The Journal of the Legal Writing Institute* 67–108.

Rideout points, for example, to the professional (objective) voice, the personal (individual) voice, the social voice (which reflects the context in which the writer is embedded), the discoursal voice (deployed within the context of a discourse), and (in the context of judgment writing, the typified (standard), monologic (composite), and self-dramatising (writer as judge, advising lawyer, etc) voice). When matters are viewed so, the potential for complete objectivity seems less than convincing – and in truth presents with a number of problems, for example, it ignores that language has its own life,[25] and in idealising the objective it may struggle to recognise subjective concepts such as hope, candour and love.[26]

In learning to write 'legal writing' a lawyer acquires a legal writer's voice,[27] which is not a personal voice in the way that a literary author such as de Maupassant might understand it, but neither is it wholly impersonal. Confronted with the reality that writers necessarily bring something of themselves and their worldview to their writing, de Maupassant maintains that the skill of the author in this context consists in not revealing him or herself to the reader.[28] In the legal context, this is typically achieved through the manifestation throughout a legal text of the so-called 'professional voice'. (Whether this professional voice is the desirable quantity that some of the academic literature in this area considers it to be is a separate question. Thus, it has been suggested, eg, that the pursuit of a professional voice excludes the voices of 'outsiders', ie, those who have traditionally been or felt excluded from the practice of the law.)[29]

5.   Exactness and carefulness

Turning next to the use of language, how, in practical terms, can a legal writer deploy language in such a way as to define and distinguish matters exactly? And exactness is important in the legal context, not just because in any legal text the law should be stated exactly as it is but also because clarity is usually a product of exactness.[30] That said, there can be a tendency to what has been described as a 'cult of precision'[31] on the part

---

25   James Elkins, "What Kind of Story is Legal Writing?" (1996) 20(1) *Legal Studies Forum* 95–136, 119.
26   *Ibid.*
27   J Christopher Rideout, "Voice, Self, and Persona in Legal Writing" (2009) 15(1) *Legal Writing: The Journal of the Legal Writing Institute* 67–108, 105.
28   Guy de Maupassant, *Pierre and Jean* (PF Collier & Son, 1902), lvi.
29   Kathryn Stanchi, "Resistance is Futile: How Legal Writing Pedagogy Contributes to the Law's Marginalization of Outsider Voices" (1998) 103(1) *Dickinson Law Review* 7–58.
30   Eugene Gerhart, "Improving Our Legal Writing: Maxims from the Masters" (1954) 40(12) *ABA Journal* 1057–1060, 1058.
31   Matt Keating, "On the Cult of Precision Underpinning Legalese: A Reflection on the Goals of Legal Drafting" (2018–2019) 18 *Scribes Journal of Legal Writing* 91–122.

of legal writers, that is, a tendency to write to such a rarefied degree of exactness that what results is impenetrable to all but the initiated.

Two fundamental problems with the 'cult of precision' have been identified. First, that it fails to understand that precision and clarity can co-exist (indeed precision can be a predicate for clarity). Second, that it proceeds on the notion that exactness should necessarily trump clarity, whereas the modern view is that clarity is something of a paramount virtue.[32]

De Maupassant offers some practical tips on exactness, suggesting, for example, that there is only ever one noun/verb/adjective that expresses precisely what a writer wishes to say and that he or she should take the time to find the right word, rather than settling for a word that is good but not quite right.[33] The type of writing tips of which de Maupassant makes mention have previously been considered by me in *The Art and Craft of Judgment Writing*[34] and are not replicated here. (As the title suggests, that book is focused on judgment writing. However, its observations have a resonance as regards legal writing more generally.)

Closely related to exactness is the attribute of carefulness. Curiously, while brevity, clarity, and simplicity are the 'triple crown' of legal writing,[35] carefulness seems almost like the 'Fourth Musketeer' of the legal writing world, that is, a somewhat underrated presence (perhaps because it will be assumed that a legal writer will be careful in *what* he or she states of the law, though that, of course, is separate from *how* he or she states it). In the introduction to his book, *The Careful Writer*,[36] Theodore Bernstein identifies a number of merits to carefulness. These might be stated as follows: it enhances the chances that one will produce a high-quality written work; it fosters clarity, logic, originality and good phrasing; and it enables the writer to communicate effectively with his or her reader yielding a product that is a pleasure to read (and in which the writer can take pride in his or her writing).

Bernstein sees there to be three principal writing styles which he conceives of as overlapping glass doors (as shown in the boxes below),

---

32   *Ibid*, 91.
33   Guy de Maupassant, *Pierre and Jean* (PF Collier & Son, 1902), lxi.
34   Max Barrett, *The Art and Craft of Judgment Writing* (Globe Law and Business, 2022).
35   The importance of brevity seems sometimes almost forgotten in a legal world where, eg, some writers revise a text by increasing its length, rather than aiming for conciseness (see Ross Buckley, "Legal Scholarship for New Law Teachers" (1997) 8(2) *Legal Education Review* 181–212, 200).
36   Theodore Bernstein, *The Careful Writer: A Modern Guide to English Usage* (Atheneum, 1982).

specifically a narrow door (marked 'Formal'), a wider door marked 'Reputable', and a third, much-the-widest door (marked 'Casual'):[37]

Casual	Reputable	Formal

Bernstein's view is that over the course of the 20th century, formal language retreated behind the 'Reputable' doorway (with legal writing being at the most formal end of reputable).[38] Bernstein also sees 'Reputable' writing to have expanded into much of the 'Casual' space, such that once purely casual English had come to be seen as reputable.[39] From the perspective of legal writing, this suggests two things. First, that excessive formality in legal English runs the risk of placing it at the esoteric end of reputable. Second, that to an increasing extent, the use of casual English in formal contexts is reputable.

It seems to follow from the foregoing that even for the most careful/exact of legal writers, there can be a legitimate move from the extreme end of formal into reputable and even on into the casual without running any risk to one's reputation as a careful writer – and of course with the advantage that what one is writing is likely to be more accessible and comprehensible to all. The problem for legal writing, if it insists on remaining at the esoteric end of formal, is that lawyers will become like the Cabots and the Lowells of old Massachusetts, "Where the Lowells talk[ed] only to Cabots,/And the Cabots talk[ed] only to God",[40] that is, they will produce legal texts that are less accessible/comprehensible to non-lawyers despite the fact that law (unlike many technical disciplines) requires frequent communication with a non-professional audience who neither wish for nor will necessarily understand the "dense jargon"[41] characteristic of professional-to-professional dealings in other technical disciplines.

6. Using simple vocabulary

When it comes to vocabulary, de Maupassant is an apostle of simplicity, writing that there is no need for an unusual vocabulary comprising

---

37   *Ibid*, xiv.
38   *Ibid*.
39   *Ibid*.
40   For the full verse, see William Perry, "The Lowells of Massachusetts ... They talk to the Cabots, but also to the World", *The Berkshire Edge*, 6 December 2020, https://theberkshireedge.com/anyone-for-tennyson-the-lowells-of-massachusetts-they-talk-to-the-cabots-but-also-to-the-world/.

complex or strange words.[42] De Maupassant's 'prayer' when it comes to vocabulary is: "Give us fewer nouns, verbs, and adjectives ... and let us have a greater variety of phrases ... full of sonority and ... rhythm. Let us strive to be admirable in style, rather than curious in collecting rare words."[43] It is difficult enough, de Maupassant maintains, to get a sentence to state what one wants it to state without using all manner of antiquated or novel expressions.[44] That said, law is a discipline that places a particular focus on words and meaning and so a certain richness of vocabulary is a necessary attribute in a competent lawyer so that he or she can express thoughts precisely and with subtlety.[45] Law is also a technical discipline, so there will always be a disjunction between legal language and ordinary English because legal writers will sometimes need to use technical terms that just cannot be avoided.[46]

Bringing de Maupassant's observations to bear in the legal context what he might be contended to point to is the need for a legal text to deploy a vocabulary that is as simple as possible in all the circumstances but no simpler. This is hardly controversial. Nor does it mean that writing must be dull in order to be simple: a writer as talented as de Maupassant would be unlikely to suggest dullness to be somehow desirable. In truth, in legal writing (as in literary writing) the text that uses the fewest and simplest words possible 'sticks in the mind' more than any amount of complex writing.[47]

Key propositions

- All writers compose works in accordance with their sense of originality; however, the potential for originality in legal writing is under-appreciated.
- When it comes to judgments there seems something counter-evolutionary about a writing form that has barely evolved in hundreds of years.
- De Maupassant notes the tendency for critics to hold certain

---

41   Matt Keating, "On the Cult of Precision Underpinning Legalese: A Reflection on the Goals of Legal Drafting" (2018–2019) 18 *Scribes Journal of Legal Writing* 91–122, 117.
42   Guy de Maupassant, *Pierre and Jean* (PF Collier & Son, 1902), lxii.
43   *Ibid.*
44   *Ibid.*
45   Edward Re, "Legal Writing as Good Literature" (1985) 59(2) *St John's Law Review* 211–227, 214.
46   Douglas Litowitz, "Legal Writing: Its Nature, Limits, and Dangers" (1998) 49(3) *Mercer Law Review* 709–740, 711.
47   Thomas Spahn, "The Art of Legal Writing" (1989) 9(2) *Journal of the National Association of Administrative Law Judges* 137–152, 137.

expectations as to form and to reject works which do not conform to those expectations.[48] He suggests that critics should encourage young authors to go down new paths.[49] In a similar vein, in the Internet Age, historical expectations as to writing form may need to change.

- Each legal text is or ought to be engaged in the identification of the legal truth of whatever situation it engages with.
- Honest persuasive argument requires dedication to accuracy/truth.
- When it comes to writers who seek to depict life accurately, they may be guilty of falsity because they cannot tell the reader everything that makes up the truth: there must be some selection of relevant incidents. The same is to some extent true of legal writing; however, if the legal writer proceeds dishonestly, he or she (and his or her text) can no longer be believed.
- 'Voice' in many guises (eg, professional, personal, social and discoursal) can creep into a legal text.
- In learning to write 'legal writing' a lawyer typically acquires a professional voice (albeit one that belongs to the individual writer). This may not be an altogether good thing.
- Legal writers may seek to be detached in their assessment of the law, but they cannot detach themselves from the text that they write.
- The skill of the author consists in not revealing him or herself to the reader. In the legal context, this is often achieved through the acquisition/maintenance of a professional voice.
- In a legal text the law should be stated exactly as it is, thereby yielding clarity. That said, there can be an unhealthy temptation to indulge in the 'cult of precision', that is, to write so exactly as to be incomprehensible.
- Law is a words-focused discipline, so a certain richness of vocabulary is necessary.
- Law is a technical discipline, so legal writers will sometimes need to use technical terms.
- A legal writer needs to deploy a vocabulary that is as simple as possible in all the circumstances – but no simpler.

---

48   See Guy de Maupassant, *Pierre and Jean* (PF Collier & Son, 1902), xliii.
49   *Ibid.*

6. De Quincey

On style and other matters

Thomas de Quincey (1785–1859) is best known for his essay, "Confessions of an English Opium-Eater" (1821). However, de Quincey was, in fact, a prolific essayist whose works often reflect "a kind of nostalgia-laden anxiety disorder".[1] He was also a noted critic, whose output included several essays on style that were originally published in 1840–1841, many of the observations in which can, I submit, be applied by analogy to legal writing.[2]

1. Style and writing

'Style' is defined by de Quincey as a means of constructing individual sentences and weaving those sentences into a coherent whole.[3] (This is not so very different from the definition given in our time to the concept of style by Judge Posner when he described it as the medium through which an author "encodes an idea".)[4] De Quincey also suggests that the British prefer (or at least the British of his era preferred) the substance of prose to its style.[5] As a consequence, he suggests, the British underrate style as an accomplishment.[6]

If this last observation has ever held true in the wider literary context it is difficult to see that it has held good in the context of legal writing, at least in the last three centuries or so. So, for example, the renown of Lord Mansfield – the lord chief justice when de Quincey was born and a man whom Chief Justice Marshall of the United States once described as among the greatest judges ever[7] – rested, in part, on the style of his

1   Elizabeth Fay, "Hallucinogenesis: Thomas de Quincey's Mind Trips" (2010) 49(2) *Studies in Romanticism* 293–312, 293.
2   Thomas de Quincey, *Essays on Style, Rhetoric, and Language*, F Scott (ed) (Allyn & Bacon, 1893).
3   *Ibid*, 104–105.
4   Richard Posner, "Judges' Writing Styles (And Do They Matter)" (1995) 62(4) *University of Chicago Law Review* 1421–1450, 1422.
5   Thomas de Quincey, *Essays on Style, Rhetoric, and Language*, F Scott (ed) (Allyn & Bacon, 1893), 5.
6   *Ibid*.
7   *Livingston v Jefferson* 15 F Cas 660, 664 (1811).

judgments. In the early 20th century, Justice Cardozo described Mansfield's style as "magisterial",[8] by which he meant that it had dignity and power, avoided ornamentation and proceeded confidently and calmly.[9] Those are stylistic accomplishments that seem unlikely to be attained by a man uninterested in style.[10]

In the 19th century, the English bench comprised a remarkable body,[11] peppered with judges whose judgments form an enduring legacy of consummate literary excellence. Likewise, the English bench of the 20th century saw various judges of stylistic brilliance. To the fore among them were Lords Atkin, Denning and Macmillan. Of Lord Atkin, it has been said that his judgments possessed "a flair for … vivid example and … a gift for aphorism and metaphor".[12] And Lord Macmillan's writing style evinced the literary form of a greatly well-read man. But when it comes to writing ability and memorability, they and all other English judges of all centuries past are eclipsed by Lord Denning, perhaps the most significant of England's 20th-century judges.[13] Denning's prose, praised for its felicity and grace[14] and its literary quality[15] is so simple in its presentation that its very simplicity can blind one to the intellectual vigour which it undoubtedly took to arrive at so plain but so perfect an end. In terms of readability, his remarkable corpus of judgments place Denning in a very select group of judges (Justice Holmes of the US Supreme Court is another) whose judgments can still be taken down and read for pleasure today.[16]

Judgment writing is of course just one form of legal writing. However, the fact that in a three-century span so many British judges have wielded

---

8   Benjamin Cardozo, *Selected Writings of Benjamin Nathan Cardozo*, M Hall (ed) (Fallon Publications, 1947), 342.
9   *Ibid.*
10   Despite the praise of men such as Cardozo, there was a dark side to Mansfield's career which no amount of stylistic brilliance can eclipse. Thus, like many prominent people of his era, Mansfield does not escape untainted by the slave trade. Even in *Somerset's Case (R v Knowles, ex parte Somerset* (1772) 98 ER 499 (KB)), in which he famously held that a slave-owner could not forcefully compel a slave to leave England, Mansfield expressly acknowledges (at 510) the validity of positive laws, eg, the statutes of the American Deep South, that sanctioned slavery. And in the later *Zong Case (Gregson v Gilbert* (1783) 99 ER 629 (KB)) – an insurance law case in which slaves had deliberately been drowned by being thrown overboard a slave-ship – Mansfield not only denied justice to the dead slaves but even came close to iterating a doctrine of lawful murder. (In this last regard, see Jeremy Krikler, "The *Zong* and the Lord Chief Justice" (2007) 64 *History Workshop Journal* 29–47, 36.)
11   R Heuston, "James Shaw Willes" (1965) 16 *Northern Ireland Law Quarterly* 193–214, 201.
12   Seamus Henchy, "*Lord Atkin* by Geoffrey Lewis" (1983) 18(1) *Irish Jurist* 182–184, 183.
13   Robert Stevens, *Judicial Legislation and the Law Lords – II* (1975) 10(2) *Irish Jurist* 216–254, 237.
14   Robert Martin, "Criticising the Judges" (1982) 28(1) *McGill Law Journal* 1–30, 7.
15   *Ibid.*
16   For a consideration of Denning's judgments and writing-style, see Max Barrett, *The Art and Craft of Judgment Writing* (Globe Law and Business, 2022), chapter 11, especially 231–243.

their pens to craft persuasive and potent prose – and been assessed and esteemed as judges for their substantive and stylistic skills – suggests that, at least when it comes to judgment writing, de Quincey is just wrong in his suggestion that the British laud substance above style. Of course, substance is critical, but substance without style seems likely always to yield a deficient form of writing. And no less a man than Justice Cardozo has observed that: "For quotable good things, for pregnant aphorisms, for touchstones of ready application, the opinions of the English judges are a mine of instruction and a treasury of joy."[17]

2.   Why is style important?

Why is style so important? For de Quincey the answer lies in the fact that language is the incarnation of thought and style is a part of that thought and essential to the expression of the thought.[18] This is all but a truism of legal writing which, it has been observed, should clearly present whatever thought a writer wishes to communicate.[19] It follows, from de Quincey's reasoning, that bad thinking will yield deficient writing. Almost a century after de Quincey wrote his observations, George Orwell was to take this thinking full circle, positing that bad writing impedes clear thinking.[20] If both men are correct, the end result is to trap the lesser writer into an ever-worsening cycle of bad thinking/bad writing/bad thinking, etc leaving the reader with a 'chicken and egg' style situation where it is not clear which came first but with both unhappily presenting in whatever text is being read.

3.   Writing versus speech

The particular advantage of a book, de Quincey posits – or a legal text, I submit – is that one can return to it repeatedly if needed. This is not true of speech. In speech, because what is said evaporates into the air once spoken, a looseness of style is tolerated.[21] Because some legal texts (such as judgments) continue to be written as though they may be spoken, a judgment can also possess a certain looseness of language that befits an oral pronouncement. Whether such looseness of language is appropriate is questionable. It has been suggested, for example, that the principles for

---

17   Benjamin Cardozo, *Selected Writings of Benjamin Nathan Cardozo*, M Hall (ed) (Fallon Publications, 1947), 347.
18   Thomas de Quincey, *Essays on Style, Rhetoric, and Language*, F Scott (ed) (Allyn & Bacon, 1893), 119.
19   Elliott Biskind, "Effective Legal Writing" (1973) 21(9) *Chitty's Law Journal* 317–321, 317.
20   George Orwell, "Politics and the English Language" (1946) 76(13) *Horizon* 252–265, 253.
21   Thomas de Quincey, *Essays on Style, Rhetoric, and Language*, F Scott (ed) (Allyn & Bacon, 1893), 8.

effective writing apply equally to persuasive speaking, both tasks being aimed at effective communication between two minds.[22] It would seem to follow that any legal text, whatever its form (whether drafted as though for speaking or not), should possess that stylistic polish which is and ought to be the hallmark of a document written for publication.

On a related but different note, one finds it repeatedly suggested in the literature on legal writing that when a writer has completed a particular legal text it is a good idea for him or her to read it aloud (or at the least to read any problematic passages aloud).[23] Smoothness in sound and style, it has been observed, are more frequent 'bed-mates' than might generally be imagined.[24] Reading aloud is a process that offers a different perspective to quiet reading[25] and aids in determining whether, for example, word choices are apposite, punctuation is working and the overall tone is correct. Reading aloud also engages different senses, keeps a tired mind engaged and has been canvassed as an effective means of discerning errors in style and flow.[26]

4. Carelessness in writing

De Quincey suggests that professional authors manifest a carelessness of style.[27] Lawyers are professional writers of a sort and, unfortunately, one does not have to look far to find examples of careless legal writing: complex and convoluted prose abounds in all forms of legal texts. It has been suggested that many practising lawyers write badly because it is in their financial interest to do so,[28] that impenetrable professional language shows them to belong to a specialised caste producing specialised prose for which they can and do charge handsomely.[29] Cynicism born of experience may also play a part. Thus, it has been suggested that because lawyers spend so much time producing words in a bid oftentimes to make something out of nothing, for example, selling a weak case as strong, they "lose faith in the honesty of words"[30] and this engenders a heedlessness in their prose. Both points have the ring of truth about

---

22   George Gibson, "Effective Legal Writing and Speaking" (1980) 36(1) *Business Lawyer* 1–10, 8.
23   See, eg, Jonathan van Patten, "On Editing" (2015) 60 *South Dakota Law Review* 1–40, 35.
24   George Miller, "On Legal Style" (1995) 43(2) *Kentucky Law Journal* 235–273, 268.
25   *Ibid*.
26   Sarah Gerwig-Moore, "Fresh Ears, Fresh Eyes: Final Editing Through Reading Aloud" (2012) 63(3) *Mercer Law Review* 971–974, 974.
27   Thomas de Quincey, *Essays on Style, Rhetoric, and Language*, F Scott (ed) (Allyn & Bacon, 1893), 10.
28   Steven Stark, "Why Lawyers Can't Write" (1985) 10(6) *Bar Leader* 15–17, 15.
29   *Ibid*.
30   *Ibid*, 17.

them. However, de Quincey is also surely right, namely, that carelessness is (at least to some extent) a root cause of stylistic deficiencies in writing, including legal writing. A bad education may also play a part. Bok, in a learned consideration of such underachievement as exists in America's university system, has observed that law school undergraduates have never entered their first year of studies with especially effective writing skills:

> Even in the 1890s, when only a … privileged minority went to college, a … visiting committee concluded that "about 25 percent of … students … admitted to Harvard are unable to write … with … ease …". Since then the problem has … become worse.[31]

As for carelessness, Aristotle saw the power of persuasion to rest in *ethos* (character), *pathos* (emotion) and *logos* (reasoning). Carelessness is the antipathy of professionalism and thus to be deprecated in any lawyer – a lawyer who descends to carelessness can be said to show a want of *ethos*. And carelessness, for example, in the form of bad grammar, bad punctuation, bad sentence structure, etc will diminish the careless writer's *logos*. What then of *pathos*? It has been said of careless legal writers that if they fail in terms of *ethos* and *logos* they may nonetheless excite *pathos*, but in the form of a negative audience response,[32] and a commensurate failure in their attempts at persuasion. In terms of legal writing, the lesson to be taken from this is perhaps that awkwardness, inelegance and unsatisfactory cadence should prompt the remoulding of a clause, the interpolation of a phrase or the striking out of a superfluous word.

De Quincey draws a distinction between, on the one hand, rough and unconsidered prose and, on the other hand, over-refined or overworked text,[33] neither of which he esteems. He also draws a distinction between those whose desire for reputation prompts them to write,[34] those who aim for proper sympathy,[35] and those who seek distinction through unwarranted innovation.[36] Putting all of this in the context of legal writing, perhaps the following might be stated. First, to be avoided in legal writing are the two extremes of carelessness and spurious

---

31 Derek Bok, *Our Underachieving Colleges* (Princeton: Princeton University Press, 2006), 82.
32 Lillian Hardwick, "Classical Persuasion through Grammar and Punctuation" (2006) 3 *Journal of the Association of Legal Writing Directors* 75–107, 99.
33 Thomas de Quincey, *Essays on Style, Rhetoric, and Language*, F Scott (ed) (Allyn & Bacon, 1893), 13.
34 *Ibid.*
35 *Ibid.*
36 *Ibid.*

refinement. Secondly, to be preferred in a legal writer is the prioritisation of sympathy over reputation. Thirdly, to be avoided are tricks of innovation over seriousness of approach. Each of these propositions merits closer consideration:

Avoid carelessness and spurious refinement

The issue of carelessness has been considered immediately above. As for spurious refinement (ornamentation), the problem with producing an overworked piece of prose, that is, text that (to borrow from Justice Cardozo) is "artificial, smelling a little of the lamp",[37] is that the richer the encrust of ornament, the more the author's true human voice is concealed. The reference to the 'human voice' in this context is to plain writing that avoids "professional ornamentation",[38] that is, a writing voice that makes the law more accessible and comprehensible to lawyers and non-lawyers alike.

Prioritise sympathy over reputation

Translating this into the legal context, what de Quincey points to is that a legal text should seek to persuade the reader, rather than be a monument to the writer's vanity. The task of persuading others is a big part of being a lawyer, be it a client, colleague, counterparty, court or someone else.[39] So the de Quincey-derived notion that a legal text should seek to persuade is scarcely controversial; it is with a view to persuasion that many legal texts are drafted. As to using a piece of prose as a vehicle for one's ego, ego is good in the sense of motivating a writer to write a well-crafted piece of prose;[40] where things begin to go wrong is when a practising lawyer seeks to compliment his or her ego by adopting a convoluted writing-style that yields "an aura of mystery".[41] The other problem with ego is that it can blind one to the need for self-

---

37   Benjamin Cardozo, *Selected Writings of Benjamin Nathan Cardozo*, M Hall (ed) (Fallon Publications, 1947), 348. Cardozo's imagery comes from a pre-electrical age. If one worked overnight on a piece of prose one would so with the benefit of a paraffin lamp, so by the phrase *"smelling of the lamp"* Cardozo means to refer to doing long hours of writing late into the night.

38   Julius Getman, "Colloquy: Human Voice in Legal Discourse" (1988) 66(3) *Texas Law Review* 577–588, 582.

39   Joseph Singer, "Persuasion" (1989) 87(8) *Michigan Law Review* 2442–2458, 2442.

40   Allen Hartman, "Legal Writing: A Judge's Perspective" (1991) 79(4) *Illinois Bar Journal* 194–196, 194.

41   Louise Everett *et al*, "Legal, Writing, Is, to, Writing, as, Legal, Fiction, is, to, Fiction" (1975) 4(1) *Student Lawyer* 48–51, 51.

improvement, erecting what one author has described as "ego-defenses"[42] whereby writers persuade themselves that their legal writing is 'good enough' when in truth one can always do better.

Avoid tricks of innovation; adopt a seriousness of approach

Innovation in legal writing takes courage. There are many willing to sneer but in an evolving world, a willingness to innovate is imperative. Some of the general trends likely to impact on legal writing are, I submit:

- Changes in the English language (and the general trend whereby so much casual/conversational language has now also become respectable).[43]
- Changes in English grammar (eg, with the appearance of the 'they/them' pronoun as the pronoun of choice for an increasing number of people it may yet be that 'they' or some variant will become the standard singular pronoun of the future).
- Technology-driven changes (though no one is canvassing for a Twitter-style cap on the number of characters in a legal text, in an age of mass online communication the tolerance threshold for lengthy texts seems to have diminished and the length of legal texts may need to shrink if not quite commensurately then at least to some extent).[44]

What de Quincey points to is the need to avoid stylistic frippery that serves no practical purpose except to irritate the reader. It is hard not to recall in this last regard the reprimand that Don Quixote gives to the hapless Sancho when the latter instead of answering a question directly and to the point comes out with a jumbled string of proverbs that seem to make sense but in truth do not advance the conversation between the two men:

> *"Bless me!" cried Don Quixote, "what a catalogue of musty proverbs hast thou run through what a heap of frippery-ware hast thou threaded together, and how wide from the purpose! Pray thee have done".*[45]

---

42   James Elkins, "The Things They Carry into Legal Writing (and Legal Education)" (1998) 22(4) *Legal Studies Forum* 749–788, 757.

43   *Ibid.*

44   One recent article that touches on the merits of doing law-business online (one being that it tends to give young lawyers an advantage over older, less tech-savvy colleagues) also touches on its implications for legal writing, including that the character limit imposed by service providers such as Twitter® essentially requires a high level of competence in writing. Jordan Couch, "Twitter for Lawyers" (2018) 35(1) *GP Solo* 66–69, 68.

45   Miguel de Cervantes, *The History of Don Quixote* (Cassell & Co, 1892), 170.

As to seriousness of approach, what de Quincey is concerned with in this regard is not the excision of humour but rather treating the very task of writing as something that is serious and requires dedication. It has been suggested (I submit rightly) that legal writers should:

- see themselves to be professional writers[46] (after all much of their time is spent writing for a living);
- learn the professional process of writing;[47]
- thereafter devote the time necessary to keeping their writing technique 'up to speed'; and[48]
- seek to emulate the qualities and skills that literary authors bring to their work.[49]

5.   Media influence on language

De Quincey suggests that newspapers had an influence on the style of written language in his day.[50] In an Internet Age when much of our lives are spent online and traditional news media are increasingly being replaced by online sources,[51] even greater changes would appear to be at play within modern society from those which de Quincey saw to be confronting English society in his day. For example, in our on-screen/online society:

- Multi-modal experiences that use still images, video, audio and music mean that 'writing' has evolved into something quite different from what it was even half a century ago[52] – it can only be a matter of time before multimedia judgments begin to issue as a matter of course.
- It is not just the texts that people can read which have changed but those which they produce; as a consequence, whole new forms of legal writing have become possible.
- When it comes to multi-modal communication the writer has to focus not just on content but on presentation and on the audience

---

46   Patrick Hugg, "Professional Legal Writing Declaring Your Independence" (1991) 11(2) *Journal of the National Association of Administration Law Judges* 114–143, 117.
47   *Ibid*, 121.
48   *Ibid*.
49   *Ibid*, 117.
50   Thomas de Quincey, *Essays on Style, Rhetoric, and Language*, F Scott (ed) (Allyn & Bacon, 1893), 19–20.
51   Dan Milmo, "TikTok is fastest growing news source for UK adults, Ofcom finds", *The Guardian*, 21 July 2022, www.theguardian.com/technology/2022/jul/21/tiktok-is-fastest-growing-news-source-for-uk-adults-ofcom-finds.
52   Sheelah Sweeny, "Writing for the Instant Messaging and Text Messaging Generation: Using New Literacies to Support Writing Instruction" (2010) 54(2) *Journal of Adolescent & Adult Literacy* 121–130, 124.

to an extent that is not required of him or her when it comes to traditional writing.[53]

There is a traditional formality to legal texts. Possible reasons for this include the fact that a lawyer may prefer the safety of a 'tried and tested' form/language rather than the untested. Additionally, a lawyer may enjoy the perceived majesty of traditional language, and may even find that clients expect a degree of formality in legal documents.[54] However, a question arises whether any of these perceived reasons for the traditional level of formality holds good under scrutiny. For example, when it comes to using 'tried and tested' English, there will likely always be a level of technical terminology which requires to be used in a legal text but that does not mean that all possibility of using plain English necessarily falls away. As to a lawyer's love of the traditional language of the law, there seems no reason why a client should be required to join in that love. As to client expectations regarding formality in legal documentation, clients typically want a particular goal to be realised, for example, they want to buy a property, get divorced, or make a will. Once that goal is achieved, a question arises whether they ever bring much focus to the required documentation. In that situation, it might be asked whether it is not better to send them home with documentation that they can later read and understand.

A question must also arise whether 'digital natives' brought up in a world where so much is done online have or will ever have an appetite for lengthy legal documentation in situations where such documentation was traditionally used. There is suggestion in the academic literature that law schools are struggling to get law students who are 'digital natives' to do their paper-based reading.[55] So can it truly be that those same 'digital natives' (and their peers throughout society more generally) are looking for a document-laden experience when they have need of a lawyer? Just as de Quincey saw the language of newspapers (the media of his day) to have an influence on the style of written language, it seems likely that the online media of the present day and the experiences/expectations of online media users will have as great an effect on the legal texts of our day as journalistic language had on the literary texts of de Quincey's day,

---

53   *Ibid.*
54   Debra Cohen, "Competent Legal Writing – A Lawyer's Professional Responsibility" (1999) 67(2) *University of Cincinnati Law Review* 491–526, 511.
55   Liesel Spencer and Elen Seymour, "Reading Law: Motivating Digital Natives to 'Do the Reading'" (2013) 23(1) *Legal Education Review* 177–200.

with an ever greater tendency to ever greater brevity being a likely hallmark of future legal writing.

6.   Unduly long or conditional sentences

De Quincey turns next to a more humdrum deficiency of writing that can also manifest in legal texts: the unduly lengthy or cumbersome sentence. He writes of how the author who writes hurriedly and aims at comprehensiveness tends to produce long sentences full of complex sub-clauses.[56] He champions the ideal of gracefully succeeding sentences,[57] varying between long and short, each one modifying the other, and all of them well connected.[58] Just how sensible de Quincey was being in this regard comes fully home when one has regard to the unintended but still striking overlap between the ideal that he contends for and the following suggestions from a modern text on legal writing, namely:

- write sentences that try to do only one thing, rather than several things;
- keep most sentences short, but vary sentence length to add interest; and
- use transitions to signal the relationships between sentences.[59]

A particular weakness at which de Quincey takes umbrage (and which is related to the problem of length) is the excessively conditional sentence, of which he writes that the particular problem it presents is "the holding-on of the mind"[60] to the point that "the faculty of attention"[61] is simply worn out. The long sentence has also traditionally excited comment in the legal arena, with one commentator succinctly observing that there are two cures for legalese: say less and stick a full stop in the middle, but that unfortunately neither approach has proven popular when it comes to legal writing.[62] One finds basically the same criticism dotted throughout the academic literature in this area. So, for example, another commentator observes that good legal writing is short,

---

56   Thomas de Quincey, *Essays on Style, Rhetoric, and Language*, F Scott (ed) (Allyn & Bacon, 1893), 20.
57   *Ibid.*
58   *Ibid.*
59   Meghan Boyd, *"Legal Writing Style (3d ed). By Antonio Gidi and Henry Wihofen … 2018"* (2020) 19 *Scribes Journal of Legal Writing* 198–202, 200.
60   Thomas de Quincey, *Essays on Style, Rhetoric, and Language*, F Scott (ed) (Allyn & Bacon, 1893), 31.
61   *Ibid.*
62   Terri LeClercq, "First Aid for Sentences, Part I: The Long Sentence" (1988) 51(8) *Texas Bar Journal* 814–817, 814.

clear, and complete, keeps to the point, and is lacking in verbosity.[63] And still another has written that rather than fit all one's thoughts into a single sentence it is preferable to use shorter sentences comprising a single sentence and devoid of qualifying phrases.[64] (This last author also encourages the use of parallelism as a means of bringing clarity to the long sentence, ie, the repetition of the same grammatical form in two or more parts of a sentence, so, eg, not mixing tenses.)[65]

On a related note, one of the banes of modern legal writing is what Justice Cardozo once deprecated as the "agglutinative"[66] tendency (in modern parlance, the tendency to 'cut and paste' long quotations from previous authorities in legal texts). Justice Scalia, a former member of the United States Supreme Court, in a co-authored text with Bryan Garner, the doyen of American legal writing experts,[67] once suggested that when it comes to cutting and pasting (what Cardozo quaintly refers to as "the shears and the pastepot")[68] block quotes ought to be avoided and that because they are likely never read it is better to make one's point in the main text and paraphrase what one was tempted to quote.[69] Separately it has been suggested that one should indicate that a quote is coming and explain to the reader why it is relevant, paraphrasing when the exact language is uncritical and quoting when it is.[70]

7. Using foreign words

De Quincey deprecates Latinisms and the artificiality of prose.[71] Such tendencies in legal writing fall likewise to be deprecated. The use of Latinisms has already been considered. When it comes to the use of any non-English terms in legal writing (save when working in a jurisdiction where a foreign language is among its official languages) one cannot better the frank observation that the main advantages of writing in

---

63   Robert Smith, "Making Sense: Some Reflections on Legal Writing" (1985) 56(41) *Oklahoma Bar Journal* 2563–2577, 2564.
64   Jessica Ronay, "A Mother Goose Guide to Legal Writing" (2014) 36(1) *University of La Verne Law Review* 119–144, 127.
65   *Ibid*, 141.
66   Benjamin Cardozo, *Selected Writings of Benjamin Nathan Cardozo*, M Hall (ed) (Fallon Publications, 1947), 342.
67   Antonin Scalia and Bryan Garner, *Making Your Case: The Art of Persuading Judges* (Thomson/West, 2008).
68   Benjamin Cardozo, *Selected Writings of Benjamin Nathan Cardozo*, M Hall (ed) (Fallon Publications, 1947), 342.
69   Antonin Scalia and Bryan Garner, *Making Your Case: The Art of Persuading Judges* (Thomson/West, 2008), 128–129.
70   Andrey Spektor and Michael Zuckerman, "Legal Writing as Good Writing: Tips from the Trenches" (2013) *Journal of Appellate Practice and Process* 303–316, 305–306.
71   Thomas de Quincey, *Essays on Style, Rhetoric, and Language*, F Scott (ed) (Allyn & Bacon, 1893), 24.

English are "(1) being understood and (2) avoiding ... [coming across as] a pretentious jackass".[72]

There are some Latinisms that are so common in legal terminology (eg, the word *ibid*) that they may be used but on the whole Latin and other foreign language terms seem best avoided when writing in English, again unless one is working in a jurisdiction which has another official language. In my own country, Ireland, there are two official languages – Irish (*Gaeilge*) and English – and although legal texts are typically written in English they may (legitimately) feature words drawn from Irish.

As for the artificiality of prose, it is a truism of legal writing that pretentiousness is off-putting to the reader and detracts from clarity of meaning.[73] One commentator, focusing on the substance of legal letters has commented on the extent to which they often exude formality and artificiality and are just plain hard to read. She suggests applying the simple test 'would I say this if we were face to face?' as a sense-check when drafting a letter (but the approach probably has a wider usefulness).[74]

De Quincey's scorn for artificiality of prose also raises the issue of choice of vocabulary. Among the rules that one finds touted when it comes to choosing the words to use in legal prose are to:

- be precise/unambiguous;
- aim for specificity;
- deploy words that are concrete/familiar;
- use base verbs;
- ignore the 'elegant variation' rule (whereby the same word should not be used again in close proximity to its previous usage);
- avoid unnecessary qualifications; and
- review what one has written to see whether the best words have been used.[75]

8. Different aspects of style

De Quincey draws a distinction between the mechanical/organic dimensions of style. Style, he posits, is mechanical in so far as some words have a determinative or modifying relationship with each other. It is organic insofar as what one writes is connected with and modified by thought. But it is important, de Quincey maintains, not to confuse "that

---

72   Chad Baruch, "Legal Writing: Lessons from the Bestseller List" (2009) 43(3) *Texas Journal of Business Law* 593–632, 617.

73   See, eg, Jim Corkery, *Study of Law* (The Adelaide Law Review Association, 1988), 131.

74   M Floren, "Better Legal Writing" (1967) 13(6) *Practical Lawyer* 77–108, 87.

75   Flora Skelly, "Verbatim" (1985) 13 *Student Law* 54–55.

function by which style maintains ... commerce with thought, and that by which it ... communicates with grammar and ... words".[76] What does this mean in practical terms when it comes to legal writing? Perhaps this: that when it comes to style legal writers should take care that their prose is consistent with their thoughts and that it is also correct in terms of the grammar and words deployed.

In truth, the hard work of writing carefully requires clear thinking;[77] and the clearer one's thoughts the better they can usually be conveyed; indeed one commentator has convincingly suggested that clarity of thought is a necessary precondition to clarity of expression.[78] Good grammar and a commanding vocabulary also have an obvious role to play when it comes to clarity of expression, and have (uncontroversially) been described as "indispensable foundations"[79] of good writing.

9. Punctuation

De Quincey turns next to punctuation, suggesting that it was invented as a by-product of the invention of printing and has had its own influence on style. Whereas people in a pre-printing age relied on purity of syntax as security against misunderstanding, punctuation was invented to maintain the integrity of sense (and the avoidance of error).[80] De Quincey points also to the practice of lawyers, which one still occasionally encounters, especially in property-related documents, of having no punctuation, the logic being that it is better to have no guide to meaning than to mislead.[81] Although de Quincey does not expressly draw these thoughts together, his underlying point seems to be that caution is required when it comes to punctuation as it can bring clarity and confusion. However, when it comes to legal writing, a knowledge of grammar and punctuation is an essential skill.[82] This is because grammar and punctuation errors interfere with the task of communication/persuasion which is the lifeblood of many legal texts.[83] (A consideration

---

76 Thomas de Quincey, *Essays on Style, Rhetoric, and Language,* F Scott (ed) (Allyn & Bacon, 1893), 37.
77 Randall Shepard, "On Lawyers and Writing: Pass the Constitutional Mustard, Please" (1995) 28(4) *Indiana Law Review* 811–818, 817.
78 Edward Re, *Brief Writing and Oral Argument,* 2nd edition (Oceana Publications, 1957), 26.
79 *Ibid,* 19.
80 Thomas de Quincey, *Essays on Style, Rhetoric, and Language,* F Scott (ed) (Allyn & Bacon, 1893), 38.
81 *Ibid.* An alternative solution is to use short sentences so as to avoid the complexities of grammar (see David Ross, "Legal Writing" (2005) 1(4) *Original Law Review* 85–102, 86).
82 Lillian Hardwick, "Classical Persuasion through Grammar and Punctuation" (2006) 3 *Journal of the Association of Legal Writing Directors* 75–107, 75.
83 *Ibid,* 76.

of the rules of grammar and punctuation is beyond the scope of this book).

10. Footnotes

De Quincey also considers the use of footnotes, writing:

> *[A question arises] how far the practice of footnotes … is reconcilable with the laws of just composition … how far … such an excrescence as a note argues that the sentence to which it is attached has not received the benefit of a full development for the conception involved; whether if thrown into the furnace again and re-melted, it might not be so recast as to absorb the redundancy which had previously flowed over into a note.*[84]

In other words, better-composed prose may avoid the need for a footnote, usage of a footnote may point to a want of completed development in the sentence to which it is attached, and re-formulation of a sentence may obviate the need for the "excrescence"[85] of a footnote.

In passing, it seems notable that de Quincey should have used the word 'excrescence' in describing the essential nature of a footnote. No doubt inadvertently, Professor Rodell in the last of his articles entitled 'Goodbye to Law Reviews' – he published a first goodbye in 1937 and a second in 1962[86] – likewise described footnotes as "phony excrescences".[87] For his part, Judge Mikva, formerly of the United States Court of Appeals, believed footnotes (at least in judgments) to be an "abomination".[88] He identified the following problems with footnote usage, namely:

- they distract the eyes into moving up and down the page;
- they present typesetting problems;[89]
- they may start out as a process whereby, for example, citations are moved from the main text to the footnoted text, so as to facilitate the reader – however, the tendency to comment in the footnote on the case there cited leads to an evolutionary process in which 'meat falls from the text into the footnote';[90]
- in a judgment they invite the expression of *obiter* comments; and[91]

---

84   Thomas de Quincey, *Essays on Style, Rhetoric, and Language*, F Scott (ed) (Allyn & Bacon, 1893), 39.
85   *Ibid.*
86   Fred Rodell, "Goodbye to Law Reviews!" (1936–1937) 23(1) *Virginia Law Review* 38–45 and "Goodbye to Law Reviews – Revisited" (1962) 48 *Virginia Law Review* 279–290.
87   *Ibid*, 289.
88   Abner Mikva, "Goodbye to Footnotes" (1985) 56(4) *University of Colorado Law Review* 647–654, 647.
89   *Ibid*, 648.
90   *Ibid.*
91   *Ibid*, 649

- they can become wastebins for excess text from the main body of a work,[92] a resting place for reinforcing points that belong in the main text,[93] and a place where frivolous points are addressed in a surfeit of caution.[94]

In general, it is difficult to flaw the advice that in legal writing one should avoid footnotes so far as possible, and that if something is important enough to be in a particular text, it should be in the main body of the text.[95] However, it may be that footnotes are in any event something of an endangered species, destined to "go the way of the mastodon"[96] and be replaced by e-texts with hyperlinks and URLs – though the explanatory footnote seems likely to remain, subject (hopefully) to an understanding that footnoted text is a place for attribution and main-body text is where the writer engages in elucidation.[97]

11. Repetition and brevity

Turning next to the issue of repetition, de Quincey notes how the French prefer the "*style coupé*"[98] ('cut style') over the "*style soutenu*" ('supported style'),[99] that is, brevity over expansiveness. Yet when it comes to repetition, at least one American style guide observes that deliberate repetition can work in legal writing,[100] and that it need only be avoided where it does not assist in accuracy, emphasis, readability or is not being used to "logically dovetail"[101] a couple of paragraphs or sentences.[102] Save, however, in the foregoing instances it is submitted that:

- Repetition of points is indicative of poor organisation.[103]
- Although good legal writers tend not to adhere to the 'elegant variation' rule,[104] it seems preferable that one does not commence a sentence by repeating half the previous sentence.[105]

---

92   *Ibid*, 651.
93   *Ibid*.
94   *Ibid*.
95   Nancy Rice, "Tips on Legal Writing" (2015) 44(5) *Colorado Lawyer* 61–62, 61.
96   Joan Magat, "Bottomheavy: Legal Footnotes" (2010) 60(1) *Journal of Legal Education* 65–105, 96.
97   *Ibid*, 69.
98   Thomas de Quincey, *Essays on Style, Rhetoric, and Language*, F Scott (ed) (Allyn & Bacon, 1893), 39.
99   *Ibid*.
100   Mary Barnard Ray and Jill Ramsfield, *Legal Writing: Getting It Right and Getting It Written* (West Publishing Co, 1987), 177.
101   *Ibid*, 178.
102   *Ibid*, 177–178.
103   Gerald Lebovits, "Legal-Writing Myths" (2017) 96(2) *Michigan Bar Journal* 50–53, 51.
104   Flora Skelly, "Verbatim" (1985) 13 *Student Law* 54–55.
105   Robert Fugate, "Redundancy and Wordiness in Legal Writing" (2009–2010) 22(3) *Appellate Advocate* 242–246, 242.

- Repetition of unnecessary words ('pleonasm') is easily done and can be quite annoying for the reader. (Examples of pleonasms include '4 a.m. in the morning', 'ATM machine' and 'PIN number'.)[106]

As to de Quincey's notion that brevity may be a virtue but undue brevity can be a hindrance to profundity, there is something of an invisible line that presents in this regard when brevity descends to unwarranted curtailment. Writing of brevity in written submissions, Re observes that while everything of relevance must be included a legal text must nonetheless be concise.[107] That offers a useful sense of what brevity means across the full gamut of legal writing. Brevity can aid in animating and enlivening prose. However, there can be a tendency towards the epigrammatic and oftentimes (though not always) epigrams tend to involve half-truths or untruths,[108] yielding that potential for loss of profundity to which de Quincey refers.

Key propositions

- Style in legal writing is important: language is the incarnation of thought and style is a part of that thought.
- The advantage of a written text is that one can return to it time and again.
- Some legal texts continue to be written as though they will be spoken. As a consequence, they can possess a looseness of language that befits an oral pronouncement while also possessing the stylistic polish of good writing.
- Poor cadence is a predicate for remoulding a clause, interpolating a phrase or striking out a superfluous word.
- To be avoided in legal writing are carelessness, affected refinement and attention-seeking innovations.
- There is a necessary formality to legal texts: legal writers are engaged in serious business. However, there is a greater place for everyday language in legal prose than one typically encounters.
- To be avoided in a legal text is the unduly long/cumbersome

---

106   For these and other examples, see David Ross, "Legal Writing" (2005) 1(4) *Original Law Review* 85–102, 96.

107   Edward Re, *Brief Writing and Oral Argument*, 2nd edition (Oceana Publications, 1957), 25.

108   William Hastings, "Montesquieu and Anglo-American Institutions" (1918–1919) 13 *Illinois Law Review* 419–591, 439.

sentence. De Quincey canvasses for gracefully succeeding sentences, of varying length, one modifying the other, all of them well-connected.

- The excessively conditional sentence is best avoided.
- Artificiality and Latinisms in prose writing are best avoided.
- A legal writer should take care that his or her prose is consistent with their thoughts and correct in terms of the grammar/words deployed.
- Caution is required with punctuation: it can bring both clarity and confusion.
- Better composed prose may eliminate the need for a footnote.
- Usage of a footnote may point to a want of completed development in the sentence to which it is attached.
- Re-formulation of a sentence may obviate the need for the "excrescence"[109] of a footnote.
- Brevity of text may be a virtue, whereas undue brevity may be a barrier to profundity.

---

109   Thomas de Quincey, *Essays on Style, Rhetoric, and Language*, F Scott (ed) (Allyn & Bacon, 1893), 39.

7. Forster

On the text as a story and other matters

Edward Morgan Forster (1879–1970) was one of the greatest English novelists of the 19th/20th centuries. His non-fiction work, *Aspects of the Novel*, is the fruit of a series of lectures concerning various aspects of the novel that were delivered at Cambridge University in the Spring of 1927. Though he is "no systematic critic",[1] Forster's renown as an author gives "depth and strength"[2] to his various observations on novel writing, some of which, I submit, can also be brought to bear as regards legal writing.

1.   Legal texts as stories

In *Aspects of the Novel*, Forster states a truism when he observes that the basic feature of the novel is that it tells a story.[3] Similarly, a legal text tells a story; in fact, the 'story' is critical to any legal matter because humans use stories as a means of understanding facts and resolving issues.[4] Strikingly, the value that a legal reader places on a story appears to be affected in part by the role he or she plays as a lawyer and the point that he or she has reached in their career.

Some of the stories that legal texts concern themselves with are human interest stories that are every bit as engaging as those that any novel tells. To succeed in a legal matter, I submit that one must:

- tell a story that is persuasive;[5]
- tell a short story rather than write a novel;[6]
- remember that a claim needs a story to find support in the law;[7]

---

1   Frederick McDowell, "EM Forster's Theory of Literature" (1966) 8(1) *Criticism* 19–43, 19.
2   EM Forster, *Aspects of the Novel* (Penguin Books, 2005), 43.
3   *Ibid*, 40.
4   James McElhaney, "Legal Writing that Works" (2007) 93 *ABA Journal* 30–31, 30.
5   Elliott Biskind, "Effective Legal Writing" (1973) 21(9) *Chitty's Law Journal* 317–321, 317.
6   Nancy Rice, "Tips on Legal Writing" (2015) 44(5) *Colorado Lawyer* 61–62, 61.
7   Jessica Ronay, "A Mother Goose Guide to Legal Writing" (2014) 36(1) *University of La Verne Law Review* 119–144, 131.

- ensure that the story being told enjoys sound evidential/analytical support;[8]
- ensure that the story being told addresses all relevant issues/points; and[9]
- adhere to the process whereby the law tells its stories, extracting legally relevant facts and then subjecting them to the rule of law.[10]

One of the questions, it is suggested, that a reader should ask herself when reading a sentence (in order to understand the perspective being offered) is 'Whose story is this?'[11] (It also assists if the writer knows this before and when writing the sentence.)

Garner suggests that when presenting a story one should always, so far as possible, unfold the tale in a chronological fashion.[12] That, he suggests, makes it easier to follow and allows the central tale of a case to become memorable as a story.[13] Sometimes, however, an alternative approach may make for a more compelling rendition of the facts; for example, in a judgment, it may work to present the contrasting fact patterns in each side's story.[14]

Although the story can be seen as the backbone of the novel, Forster sees a story as being more like a tapeworm, because where it starts and where it ends are arbitrary.[15] This is perhaps even more true of a legal text than it is of a novel, because a legal text so often takes up from a particular point in the experiences of the relevant parties and leaves off when it has said enough to justify whatever objective it seeks to attain.

2. Writing engagingly

Forster suggests that the novel as a story has one great merit (instilling a desire in the reader to know what happens next) and one great drawback (failing to instil that desire).[16] Lord Denning had much the same point in mind when he wrote in his autobiographical work, *The Family Story*, that

---

8   Kevin Bennardo, "Legal Writing's Harmful Psyche" (2020) 105(1) *Minnesota Law Review Headnotes* 111–127, 126.
9   Arthur Miller, "Some Remarks on Legal Writing" (1955–1956) 18(3) *Georgia Bar Journal (Macon)* 253–269, 267.
10   Richard Hyland, "A Defense of Legal Writing" (1986) 134(3) *University of Pennsylvania Law Review* 599–626, 613.
11   George Gopen, "A New Approach to Legal Writing" (2011) 37 *Litigation* 21–22, 22.
12   Bryan Garner, "Sense and Sensibility: A Primer on Preparing Research Memos" (2010) 38(9) *Student Law* 12–15, 14.
13   *Ibid.*
14   For an example in which this approach was tried, see Chad Baruch, "Legal Writing: Lessons from the Bestseller List" (2009) 43(3) *Texas Journal of Business Law* 593–632, 614–615.
15   EM Forster, *Aspects of the Novel* (Penguin Books, 2005), 41.
16   *Ibid*, 42.

"if you are to persuade your ... readers ... you must cultivate a style which commands attention".[17] In his judgments (perhaps not so much in his extrajudicial books), Denning proved himself a master storyteller. Some of his introductory lines to his judgments read almost like the opening lines to a delightful English novel, for example, "It appears that in 1965 M. Couvreur was interested in acquiring the products of a vineyard in France"[18] and "The centre-piece of this story is a pair of candelabra, made of well-cut glass, each supporting two candles with sparkling pear-drops all about".[19] In *Ex parte Johnson Trust Ltd*, one might be forgiven for thinking that one had stumbled into the opening text of an Agatha Christie mystery:

> *In Sussex, south of Petworth, there are two old villages nestling in the Downs. One is Graffham. The other is East Lavington. They are about a mile apart. In between them is a fine parkland attached to a mansion house called Lavington House. There is a carriage drive through the parkland from Graffham to East Lavington. It passes near to the mansion house. This drive was made over a hundred years ago by the owners of Lavington House so as to give access by carriage to and from their home. It was called the old coach road.*[20]

Somewhere along that road, one half-expects to be told, the body of the late baronet was found. (In fact, it turns out to be a case about whether there was a public right of way along the carriageway.)

In the United States, Judge Learned Hand was also capable of writing riveting text. As good an example as any is Hand's judgment in *Sheldon v MGM Corp* (1936).[21] That was a case in which MGM lost in a copyright infringement action. In his judgment, Hand begins by telling the historical tale that informed the infringing movie. In fairness, the story had been the subject of a play and a movie so it was clearly an engrossing tale, but Hand still tells it well. There is only space enough to include an extract from his second paragraph:

> *An understanding of the issue involves some description of what was in the public demesne, as well as of the play and the picture. In 1857 a Scotch girl, named Madeleine Smith, living in Glasgow, was brought to trial upon an indictment in three counts; two for attempts to poison her lover, a third for poisoning him. The jury acquitted her on the first count, and brought in a*

---

17   Lord Denning, *The Family Story* (Butterworths, 1981), 216.
18   *Ionian Bank Ltd v Couvreur* [1969] 1 WLR 781, 783 (CA).
19   *Reid v Metropolitan Police Commissioner* [1973] QB 551, 557 (CA).
20   [1974] QB 24, 31 (CA).
21   81 F2d 49 (2d Cir 1936).

verdict of "Not Proven" on the second and third. The circumstances of the prosecution aroused much interest at the time not only in Scotland but In England; so much indeed that it became a cause célèbre, and that as late as 1927 the whole proceedings were published in book form. An outline of the story so published, which became the original of the play here in suit, is as follows ...[22]

Even if not quite 'Denning-esque' prose, there are likely few people who would read the quote above and fail to read on further to find out more about the issues that confronted Learned Hand and what he had decided.

In terms of making a piece of prose engaging, the importance of 'pacing' – the speed at which text flows and hence at which a reader reads a piece of legal text[23] – finds some emphasis in the academic literature and also from Chief Justice Roberts of the United States. In a fascinating interview on legal writing, he emphasised the issue of pacing, observing that a judge needs to be taken by the hand and led, with engaging text, through the principal points of a case, adding that if judges are required to struggle through each sentence they will quickly lose interest in whatever arguments are being made.[24]

In *Spunk & Bite*, destined to become (if it is not already) a modern classic on writing style, Plotnik, writing of the literary world generally, though he could just as well be writing of the legal writing community specifically, observes that language/style which is less engaging than that produced by one's rival is "dead on arrival".[25] At least with legal text, the other side or (in court) the judge has to read what one has written. However, it is clear from Chief Justice Roberts' observations that Plotnik is 'on to something' in terms of identifying a need for text to be distinctive if it is to engage.

What about a legal text that does not (to echo Forster) instil a desire in the reader to know what happens next? The possibilities are that that text will not be read or will fail to persuade the reader. Floren, in a relatively dated piece that has aged well, offers a number of precepts that can usefully be observed if one wishes to be read, to be understood, to convince, and to prompt some action (which he sees as the four goals of

---

22 *Ibid.*

23 Julie Oseid, "'Liven Their Life Up Just a Little Bit': Good Pacing Persuades Judges" (2020) 24 *Legal Writing: The Journal of the Legal Writing Institute* 239–268, 240.

24 Anon., "Interview with Chief Justice John G Roberts, Jr" (2010) 13 *Scribes Journal of Legal Writing* 5–40, 11. Elements of the interview are considered in Oseid, *ibid.*

25 Arthur Plotnik, *Spunk & Bite: A Writer's Guide to Punchier, More Engaging Language and Style* (Random House, 2005), viii.

legal writing). It is striking how many of the precepts touch in some way on engagement. Thus, among the issues that Floren touches upon are:

- Is the text readable?
- Have excess words been avoided?
- Is the language pitched properly?
- Have short/simple words been deployed?
- Has needless repetition been avoided?
- Have active verbs been deployed?
- Has care been taken to make the reading experience as easy as it can be and certainly no harder than necessary?[26]

At some level, "good legal writing is simply good writing".[27] What Forster reminds the legal writer is that good writing (and hence good legal writing) engages the reader, whereas bad writing (and hence bad legal writing) does not. A text with which a reader fails to engage will be of limited persuasiveness and lawyers very often need to persuade.[28]

3. Writing and voice

Forster observes that a story is the repository of voice.[29] This is particularly true of judgments which continue to be drafted as though they will be read out in their entirety in court. Edgerton identifies the key elements of voice as tone, vocabulary, imagery and rhythm.[30] It is worth pausing briefly to consider each of these from a legal writing perspective.

Tone

When it comes to tone, part of the task of a lawyer is to keep an eye on the end objective of what he or she is doing, which is often to persuade someone to accept a particular point of view. It has been suggested in the context of advocacy (though the observations would seem to have a wider resonance) that on the way to that end-goal one will have to show patience and restraint, being zealous without being a zealot,[31] evincing a tone of reasonableness in order to arrive at one's desired end.

---

26 M Floren, "Better Legal Writing" (1967) 13(6) *Practical Lawyer* 77–108.
27 Scott Longman, "The Architecture of Legal Writing" (2001) 15(3) *CBA Record* 40–66, 40.
28 Frank Cooper, *Effective Legal Writing* (Bobbs-Merrill Co, 1953), 11.
29 EM Forster, *Aspects of the Novel* (Penguin Books, 2005), 51.
30 Les Edgerton, *Finding Your Voice: How to Put Personality in Your Writing* (Writer's Digest Books, 2003), chapter 6.
31 Kathryn Stanchi, "What Cognitive Dissonance Tells Us About Tone in Persuasion" (2013) 22(1) *Journal of Law and Policy* 93–134, 134.

In writing, restraint often takes the form of understatement. Author after author has emphasised the importance of understatement as part of a lawyer's armoury. One author, describing the ingredients of compelling legal submissions, observes that understatement is preferable to exaggeration.[32] Another, describing how best to fight an appeals case, observes that if one is to err it should be to err towards understatement.[33] Still another observes that when writing for a judge one should prefer understatement to hyperbole.[34]

Tone is also important when it comes to the so-called 'professional legal voice'. It has been suggested that this professional voice is formal, learned, objective, old-fashioned, removed, comfortable with legal jargon and Latin phrases and tends to express itself at a general level.[35] A perceived problem with this conception of the professional legal voice is that it involves the erasure of one's actual voice.[36] That is a process which can lead to a continuing absence of voices which have historically been under-represented in the legal profession, as would-be lawyers abandon finding their own legal voice,[37] adding to the perception of a 'Borg-like' legal profession that only ever speaks with a single, privileged voice.[38]

Vocabulary

As to vocabulary and voice, it has been suggested that the richer the vocabulary and the greater the ability to pick the right word, the more a legal writer will be able to express his or her thoughts precisely and subtly.[39] If that is correct (and it is), it follows that without the right vocabulary both legal text and a lawyer's persuasiveness will suffer. One commentator has observed (I submit, rightly) that as long as human affairs are complicated there will be complex matters that cannot be expressed in plain text.[40] But they can, I contend, helpfully be expressed in the simplest and least technical words that can possibly be deployed, the ultimate aim being balance in approach (avoiding the peculiar, the prolix and the needlessly complex).

---

32   David Cohen, "Writing Winning Briefs" (2000) 26(4) *Litigation* 46–48, 59, 46.
33   William Pannill, "The Classic Guide" (1999) 25(2) *Litigation* 6–11 and 61, 8.
34   James Hinton, "Writing for the Judge" (1983) 9(3) *Litigation* 26 and 63, 63.
35   J Christopher Rideout, "Voice, Self, and Persona in Legal Writing" (2009) 15(1) *Legal Writing: The Journal of the Legal Writing Institute* 67–108, 81.
36   *Ibid.*
37   Teresa Phelps, "The New Legal Rhetoric" (1986) 40(4) *Southwestern Law Journal* 1089–1102, 1102.
38   Kathryn Stanchi, "Resistance is Futile: How Legal Writing Pedagogy Contributes to the Law's Marginalization of Outsider Voices" (1998) 103(1) *Dickinson Law Review* 7–58, 9.
39   Edward Re, "Legal Writing as Good Literature" (1985) 59(2) *St John's Law Review* 211–227, 214.
40   Clinton Markley, "In Defense of Legal English" (1939) 2(8) *Legal Chatter* 28–31, 30.

Imagery/metaphor

It has been suggested that imagery is an important element of persuasive legal writing, with one author asserting that when writing to persuade a judge one should seek to leave the judge with memorable imagery.[41] Still another author commends the legal writer to fix concrete images in the mind of the reader.[42] The language of imagery, it has been suggested, can help to invigorate a case.[43]

All the foregoing being so, it is perhaps somewhat surprising to find that metaphors – a key weapon in the armoury of imagery – have something of a blemished reputation in the legal world. Such antipathy as exists to metaphor seems to arise in part because of the renowned observations of Chief Judge Cardozo (as he then was) in *Berkey v Third Avenue Railway Co*,[44] a decision of the New York Court of Appeals, in which he observed that "Metaphors in law are to be narrowly watched, for starting as devices to liberate thought, they end often by enslaving it".[45]

Five years later, in a published address entitled "What Medicine Can Do for Law", Cardozo returned to this theme, observing that the notion of a mind being 'swept from its moorings' as a determinant of criminal liability was unsatisfactory. "A metaphor", Cardozo wrote, "is, to say the least, a shifting test whereby to measure degrees of guilt that mean the difference between life and death."[46] Yet, for all of Cardozo's eloquent deprecation of metaphor, the truth is that metaphors abound in legal reasoning. So much so that a distinction has been drawn in contemporary academic literature between:

- "doctrinal metaphors"[47] (the expression of legal doctrine by way of metaphor, perhaps the best example being the notion of 'the corporate veil');
- "legal method metaphors"[48] (eg, bringing a 'broad/narrow' interpretation to bear);

41   Scott Longman, "The Architecture of Legal Writing" (2001) 15(3) *CBA Record* 40–66, 43.
42   Collyn Peddie, "Improving Legal Writing: The Triumph of Hope Over Experience" (1993) 13(1) *Review of Litigation* 83–104, 98.
43   Jordan Adalberto, "Imagery, Humor, and the Judicial Opinion" (1987) 41(3) *University of Miami Law Review* 693–728, 700.
44   244 NY 84 (1926).
45   *Ibid*, 94.
46   Benjamin Cardozo, *Selected Writings of Benjamin Nathan Cardozo*, M Hall (ed) (Fallon Publications, 1947), 384.
47   Michael Smith, "Levels of Metaphor in Persuasive Legal Writing" (2007) 58(3) *Mercer Law Review* 919–948, 921.
48   *Ibid*.

- "stylistic metaphors"[49] (ie, the deployment of metaphor in its traditional sense); and
- "inherent metaphors"[50] (ie, metaphors within everyday language such as 'going forward with an appeal').

Thus, the modern (and arguably the better) view seems to be that metaphors can help to simplify explanations of the law.[51] However, one does need to be careful as a legal writer not to slide down the slippery slope into that 'enslavement of thought' to which Cardozo refers.

As to similes, in the 20th century, perhaps the non-legal author most closely associated with the coining of new similes was Raymond Chandler.[52] His creations in this regard include "as phony as the pedigree of a used car"[53] and "as inconspicuous as a tarantula on a slice of angel food".[54] Though 'Chandler-isms' are an art form, in everyday speech, similes are used all the time. They form a sort of conversational shorthand and, at their best, reveal some aspect/characteristic of a subject that had previously gone unnoticed.[55] In addition, they can also add eloquence to legal writing, though the general consensus is that they must be fresh, not clichéd, to be effective.[56] "Shopworn similes"[57] will deaden a text when the aim of a good legal writer should be to craft as attractive/persuasive a piece of legal writing as possible.

Rhythm/cadence

It has been suggested that it does not suffice for legal texts to be as brief as possible, and that good cadence and rhythm are also required.[58] When it comes to rhythm/cadence, Forster distinguishes between the famous opening 'da-da-da-dah' of Beethoven's Fifth Symphony as a rhythm that

---

49   *Ibid.*
50   *Ibid.*
51   J Christopher Rideout, "Penumbral Thinking Re-Visited: Metaphor in Legal Imagination" (2010) 7(1) *Journal of the Association of Legal Writing Directors* 155–192, 190.
52   Stephen Tanner, "The Function of Simile in Raymond Chandler's Novels" (1984–1985) 3(4) *Studies in American Humor* 337–346, 337.
53   Raymond Chandler, "Farewell, My Lovely" in Raymond Chandler, *Four Complete Philip Marlowe Novels* (Avenel Books, 1967), 189.
54   *Ibid*, 160.
55   Patrick Hugg, "Professional Legal Writing Declaring Your Independence" (1991) 11(2) *Journal of the National Association of Administration Law Judges* 114–143, 136.
56   Tenielle Fordyce-Ruff, "Adding Eloquence to Your Legal Writing With Figures of Speech" (2013) 56(5) *Advocate* 48–49, 48.
57   George Gibson, "Effective Legal Writing and Speaking" (1980) 36(1) *Business Lawyer* 1–10, 7.
58   James Madigan and Laura Tartakoff, "Doing Justice to the Potential Contribution of Lyric Poems" (2000) 6 *Legal Writing: The Journal of the Legal Writing Institute* 27–56, 52.

we can all hear, and a separate rhythm that permeates the symphony as a whole. An author, Forster suggests, seeks the first kind of rhythm but it is also possible for a separate rhythm to permeate a legal text as a whole. The first is obvious, the second is less discernible, yet it may be there.[59] With the second category of rhythm what is at play is a feeling that everything within a work fuses into a greater whole than its separate elements, yielding a cadence that appeals to the reader's aesthetic sense.[60]

At its root, rhythm/cadence seems to catch a reader's attention through rigorous conformity to a pattern.[61] The challenge for the writer is, first, to identify a winning pattern, but then to remain consistent with it.[62] Chief Justice Roberts of the United States is noted for his talent at cadence and rhythm,[63] one writer pointing to Roberts' well-known line about the 'hapless toad' as evidence of Roberts' flair for language. That reference came in *Rancho Viejo LLC v Norton*,[64] a US Court of Appeals case concerned with the US Interior Department's blocking of a proposed housing development that, it was believed, would disrupt the habitat of the Arroyo Southwestern toad, a protected species. In a somewhat stinging dissent by Roberts (then an Appeals Court judge) against a denial of an *en banc* rehearing, he observed that:

> *The panel's approach in this case leads to the result that regulating the taking of a hapless toad that, for reasons of its own, lives its entire life in California, constitutes regulating "Commerce ... among the several States".*[65]

Whether or not one agrees with Roberts' reasoning, this is powerful prose which is all the more powerful for being beautiful and all the more beautiful for being rhythmical.

Individual rhythm has been likened to an individual's fingerprints as a hallmark of individuality.[66] In its individuality, it has been contrasted with brevity, clarity and simplicity as common goals of all good legal writers.[67] That said, even as great a communicator as Abraham Lincoln

---

59   EM Forster, *Aspects of the Novel* (Penguin Books, 2005), 146.
60   Mark Osbeck, "What is 'Good Legal Writing' and Why Does It Matter?" (2012) 4(2) *Drexel Law Review* 417–466, 461.
61   See Terri LeClercq, "Examining Other Professional Prose" (2003–2004) 9 *Scribes Journal of Legal Writing* 187–194, 190.
62   *Ibid*.
63   Ross Guberman, "What A Breeze: The Case for the Impure Opinion" (2015) 16 *Scribes Journal of Legal Writing* 57–68, 63.
64   334 F3d 1158 (DC Cir 2003).
65   *Ibid*, 1160.
66   Thomas Spahn, "The Art of Legal Writing" (1989) 9(2) *Journal of the National Association of Administrative Law Judges* 137–152, 137.
67   *Ibid*.

was occasionally prepared to use a long sentence when he thought the cadence to work,[68] as, for example, with his closing line to his First Inaugural Address:

> The mystic chords of memory, stretching from every battlefield and patriot grave to every living heart and hearthstone all over this broad land, will yet swell the chorus of the Union, when again touched, as surely they will be, by the better angels of our nature.[69]

Perhaps the lesson to be derived from Lincoln in this regard is that rhythm/cadence can rescue a long sentence that would otherwise be too long – though one has to wonder just how many people were able to follow the sinewy logic of Lincoln when they heard him speak the long, last-quoted sentence. (It is quite challenging even to follow it in print.)

4. Detachment

Forster touches on the two-fold point of view from which a story may be told: impartially from the outside or omnisciently from within. This observation brings to mind the objective/subjective dichotomy of legal writing/reading. Legal writing (and a legal text) has both objective and subjective dimensions. One sees this clearly in Professor Parker's insightful review of Pirsig's *Zen and the Art of Motorcycle Maintenance* (1974), where Parker seeks to divine what Pirsig's text has to say about the art of teaching. If one substitutes the legal writer into Parker's observations on the objective/subjective nature of the law professor's role, one arrives at a quite brilliant insight into the objective/subjective dichotomy that presents in legal writing and what it is that the legal writer is about. Thus, writes Parker:

> It is true of anyone who teaches [writes] well that he "has something to teach." But what is that something? ... Each teacher [legal writer] has a uniquely different way in which he relates to the law. Some relate to it as craftsmen, working with ... points of authority ... and the inferences allowed by the canons of legal reasoning ... Some like to cut below the legal forms and lay bare the bones of the basic conceptual relations ... Some like to study the law as a social phenomenon. Some study law as a potential instrument of justice ... A teacher's [legal writer's] relation to law is often much deeper than simply a style of analysis ... Teachers [legal writers] also exemplify what the law can be ... the chance for personal redemption ... or

---

68   Megan Boyd, "Legal Writing Lessons from American Presidents" (2018) 15 *Legal Communications and Rhetoric* 287–292, 290.

69   Abraham Lincoln, "First Inaugural Address of Abraham Lincoln", *The Avalon Project*, 4 March 1861, https://avalon.law.yale.edu/19th_century/lincoln1.asp.

intellectual play ... or ... one fascinating set of facts after another. The point is that each teacher [legal writer] relates naturally to the law in his own way and it is that relation and the skills necessary to it which is what he has to teach.[70]

Traditionally, the view taken of law has been that it is not an "objective reality"[71] and that a legal principle only becomes constituted once it is stated in text (written or spoken), with lawyers thereby participating in an "imaginative community of ideas".[72] Since the 20th century, the law and literature movement has challenged the traditionally perceived objectivity of legal texts and the notion that a given legal text is capable of only one meaning, positing instead that in legal texts which historically were viewed as formal, impersonal, technical and objective texts, legal writers are often recounting stories.[73] This alternative view suggests that it is probably best to view a legal text as having both objective and subjective dimensions.

Fundamentally, it is submitted, legal writing is about taking a subjective experience and identifying how it aligns with (or deviates from) objective legal concepts.[74] As a legal reader appraising a text, one has regard to the subjective characteristics of the text such as style and excellence, and to external criteria such as whether the author has had a successful legal career, what the extent of his or her experience in practice is, etc.[75] What Forster highlights is the objective/subjective potential inherent in writing, with the legal writer functioning as an objective narrator or an 'omniscient' insider (or, at least, an insider possessed of specialist knowledge).

5. Plot and writing

Mystery, Forster suggests, is essential to a good plot: something is half-explained now, and its true meaning is explained some pages later.[76] Mystery has a number of points of relevance when it comes to legal writing. So, for example, it has been suggested that poor professional

---

70 Richard Parker, "A Review of *Zen and the Art of Motorcycle Maintenance* with Some Remarks on the Teaching of Law" (1976) 29(2) *Rutgers Law Review* 318–331, 328–329.

71 Sean Mulcahy, "Can a Literary Approach to Matters of Legal Concern Offer a Fairer Hearing than that Typically Offered by the Law?" (2014) 8(1) *Law and Humanities* 111–135, 112.

72 *Ibid.*

73 Robert Hayman and Nancy Levit (eds), *Jurisprudence: Contemporary Readings, Problems, and Narratives* (West Publishing Co, 1994), 267.

74 George Gopen, "The State of Legal Writing: *Res Ipsa Loquitur*" (1987) 86(2) *Michigan Law Review* 333–380, 339.

75 Kim Chanbonpin, "Legal Writing, the Remix: Plagiarism and Hip Hop Ethics" (2012) 63 *Mercer Law Review* 597–638, 623.

76 EM Forster, *Aspects of the Novel* (Penguin Books, 2005), 87.

legal writing is attributable in part to a belief on the part of lawyers that by maintaining a veil of mystery[77] about the texts they craft they will increase public dependence on their services. Viewed in this way legal text can be seen as a communication between legal initiates,[78] offering a sign to both insiders and outsiders that one is an insider.

As to maintaining mystery throughout the course of a legal text, providing a Poirot-like dénouement at the end of a legal text, and occasional cryptic clues as to the solution in the preceding pages, the general consensus is that such an approach to legal writing is best avoided.[79] The thing with mystery novels is that once everything is explained they almost require one to re-read the text to test the accuracy of the explanation.[80] The busy legal reader has neither the time (nor, one suspects, the inclination) to engage in such an exercise: he or she needs to be told everything upfront.[81]

There is a third way in which mystery afflicts legal writing, namely the notion that knowing how to deliver good legal writing is one of the 'mysteries of the universe'.[82] Any such notion is, I submit, nonsense: legal writing is but the use of vocabulary and punctuation, and the application of an adaptive and flexible style, so as to advise/persuade a particular audience as to a particular legal view in as clear and concise a manner as one can.[83]

As to suspense, legal writing proceeds in directly the opposite way to literary writing. Whereas the literary author often redoubles the suspense to entice the reader into reading further,[84] legal writing requires that the fullest context be provided upfront.[85] Good prose, George Orwell once wrote, resembles a windowpane,[86] that is, it lets the fullest light in on a subject; it does not let the light fall selectively.

---

77 Richard Hyland, "A Defense of Legal Writing" (1986) 134(3) *University of Pennsylvania Law Review* 599–626, 604.
78 *Ibid.*
79 Bryan Garner, "10 Tips for Better Legal Writing" (2014) 100(1) *ABA Journal* 24–25, 24.
80 Greg Johnson, "Assessing the Legal Writing Style of Amy Coney Barrett" (2021) 47(2) *Vermont Bar Journal* 24–28, 26.
81 *Ibid.*
82 James Elkins, "What Kind of Story is Legal Writing?" (1996) 20(1) *Legal Studies Forum* 95–136, 107.
83 Julie Clement, "A Community of Writers: Building a Virtual Legal Writing-Center" (2013) 16 *Thomas M Cooley Journal of Practical and Clinical Law* 1–54, 30.
84 James Raymond, "Legal Writing: An Obstruction to Justice" (1978) 30(1) *Alabama Law Review* 1–19, 12.
85 David Hricik and Karen Sneddon, "Ten Tips for Clearer Writing" (2021–2022) 27(5) *Georgia Bar Journal* 62–64, 62.
86 George Orwell, "Why I Write" in George Orwell, *A Collection of Essays* (Harcourt Brace Jovanovich, 1953) 309–316, 316.

6. Writing a conclusion

Though it is possible to overstate the importance of a good conclusion to a legal text,[87] nonetheless it is an important element of such a text, which should not be allowed simply to trail off or suddenly end.[88] Forster suggests that the concluding portion of a novel is often its weakest point because, for example, the plot requires to be closed out[89] or the author has run out of pep.[90] A similar challenge presents itself for the legal writer who, in closing, wants to retain and sustain the reader's interest, encapsulate the essence of what it is that he or she is saying, and excite the reader into doing as one asks (or simply agreeing with one's point of view). Garner suggests that it is useful to say things a little differently from how one has already said them elsewhere in the text and also to find a common thread that joins the beginning to the end.[91]

There is a school of thought which holds that it is a mistake to end on a coldly logical note, at least when seeking to persuade the reader of something – though a judgment can seem unfeeling if it is too coldly legalistic.[92] At heart there are two reasons why a coldly logical ending may not be desirable. First, as Justice Cardozo has noted, logic is not a consistent force of nature:

> *The directive force of logic does not always exert itself … along a single and unobstructed path. One principle or precedent, pushed to the limit of its logic, may point to one conclusion; another principle or precedent, followed with like logic, may point with equal certainty to another. In this conflict, we must choose between the two paths, selecting one or other, or perhaps striking out upon a third, which will be the resultant of the two forces in combination.*[93]

Therefore, cold logic may not be the friend that a legal writer thinks it to be.

A second issue that a coldly logical ending presents is that identified by Lord Halsbury in *Quinn v Leathem*,[94] an early 20th-century trade disputes case, when he cautioned against the assumption that the law is

---

87 Ann Morales Olazábal, "Law as Haiku" (2005) 22(2) *Journal of Legal Studies Education* 123–147, 139. Olazábal is writing of student answer papers but her points hold true as regards legal writing generally.
88 *Ibid.*
89 EM Forster, *Aspects of the Novel* (Penguin Books, 2005), 94.
90 *Ibid.*
91 Bryan Garner, "In Conclusion" (2017) 103(5) *ABA Journal* 24–25.
92 Frank Cooper, *Effective Legal Writing* (Bobbs-Merrill Co, 1953), 140.
93 Benjamin Cardozo, *Selected Writings of Benjamin Nathan Cardozo*, M Hall (ed) (Fallon Publications, 1947), 121.
94 [1901] AC 495 (HL).

a "logical code"[95] when lawyers are aware that the law sometimes just is not logical. In short, while logic has its place, common sense may point in a different direction.

7.   Different types of writer

Forster distinguishes between novelists who are preachers and those who are prophets.[96] A preacher talks about God but never raises one's mind beyond the mortal; a prophet imbues everything with a sense of the divine.[97] Leaving God out of matters, what Forster's observations point to is the distinction between legal writing which is good writing and legal writing which soars. What is it that makes some legal writing inspiring? In my book, *The Art and Craft of Judgment Writing*,[98] I consider the judgment writing styles of common law judges from around the world. All of the judges considered there managed sometimes (though not always) in their careers to write judgments that combined a commanding knowledge of the law and an uplifting use of English. If I were to use that analysis as a basis for identifying what raises judicial prose in any one case from (to borrow from Forster) the 'preacher-like' to the 'prophetic', that is, the good to the inspirational, I would contend that:[99]

- the judges/judgments we most admire are those whose originality makes a connection;[100]
- the best judgments:
  - fuse reason/passion, learning/experience, and erudition/ inspiration;[101]
  - see the larger intellectual/legal significance of a case;[102]
  - state applicable principle clearly, extensively, and methodically;[103]
  - do not involve unmediated expression of self;[104]
  - are not unduly combative;[105]
  - do not surrender substance to style;[106]
  - have a clear style/language;[107]

---

95   *Ibid*, 506.
96   EM Forster, *Aspects of the Novel* (Penguin Books, 2005), 122.
97   *Ibid*.
98   *Ibid*.
99   For the full array of points made, see Max Barrett, *The Art and Craft of Judgment Writing* (Globe Law and Business, 2022), chapters 9–12.
100   *Ibid*, 183.
101   *Ibid*, 184.
102   *Ibid*, 215.
103   *Ibid*, 282.
104   *Ibid*, 216.
105   *Ibid*.
106   *Ibid*, 251.
107   *Ibid*.

- employ vivid examples/imagery;[108] and
- deploy aphorism/metaphor, as appropriate;[109]

- over time, empathy/sympathy for those faring badly in life resonates well;[110]
- distinctive style, snappy 'one-liners' and even occasionally flowery language are all fine, but the best judgments are crisp and persuasive;[111]
- brevity, clarity, and simplicity are the gold standards of judgment writing;[112]
- 'black-letter' legal writing may rise to eloquence but seems never to attain the *éclat* which is a hallmark of the greatest judgments;[113]
- stating the law simply exudes a certain raw power;[114]
- great judgments do not shy from revealing a struggle in the judge's soul;[115] and
- there is no one methodology for writing a great judgment.[116]

If one had to reduce these observations to a series of propositions for legal writing more generally, perhaps the following propositions might be stated:

- Do not fear being original.
- Seek to make an emotional connection.
- Bring reason/passion, learning/experience and erudition/inspiration to bear.
- See the larger intellectual/legal significance of a case.
- State applicable principles clearly, comprehensively and methodically.
- Do not succumb to unmediated expression of self.
- Do not be unduly combative.
- Do not surrender substance to style.
- Have a clear style/language.
- Employ vivid examples/imagery.
- Deploy aphorisms/metaphors, as appropriate.
- Evince a sense of empathy/sympathy for those faring badly in life.
- Be aware that the best legal writing is crisp and persuasive.

---

108   *Ibid.*
109   *Ibid.*
110   *Ibid.*
111   *Ibid.*
112   *Ibid*, 252.
113   *Ibid*, 282.
114   *Ibid.*
115   Pnina Lahav, "Foundations of Rights Jurisprudence in Israel" (1990) 24 *Israel Law Review* 211–269, 216.
116   Max Barrett, *The Art and Craft of Judgment Writing* (Globe Law and Business, 2022), 282.

- Seek always to express yourself briefly, clearly and simply.
- Be aware that stating the law simply can exude a certain raw power.
- Do not shy from revealing weakness.
- Remember that there is no one methodology for good legal writing.

Legal texts that are 'prophetic' may not be as smooth a read as those of lesser legal writers, they may even be provocative, but when they have been read their roughness is forgotten and the memory of their smooth brilliance remains.[117]

8. Patterns in writing and writing models

There are patterns discernible in plots. Forster points to Anatole France's *Thaïs* as a classic example of an hourglass plot. The two main characters start at different points. Their respective paths in life then converge towards a point of confluence and after the moment of confluence, they continue once again on separate paths. The extent to which pattern formation is an element in legal writing is actually quite remarkable. One article contends that there is a kinship between all manner of good writing because all good writing manifests a desire for accuracy, clearness, correctness, elegance and preciseness.[118] Additionally, the practice of law is a social one[119] with its own patterns/styles of argument.[120] Consequently, there are standard patterns discernible in legal texts (and in the writing styles of individual legal writers). And there are patterns that one finds recommended over and again in the academic literature as a skeleton structure on which to build the 'meat' of a legal text, such as the 'FLAC' (Facts–Law–Analysis–Conclusion) and 'IRAC' (Issue–Rule–Analysis–Conclusion) approaches that are commonly used tools for writing all manner of legal texts.[121] Patterns can also be found in judgment writing styles. In *The Art and Craft of Judgment Writing*, I identify various approaches to judgment writing that have been posited over the years. The table set out below (extracted from a more complex table in Chapter 5 of that book) shows some of the principal judgment writing models:[122]

---

117 EM Forster, *Aspects of the Novel* (Penguin Books, 2005), 125.
118 David Kirp, "The Writer as Lawyer as Writer" (1969) 22(2) *Journal of Legal Education* 115–118, 116.
119 J Christopher Rideout and J Ramsfield, "Legal Writing: A Revised View" (1994) 69(1) *Washington Law Review* 35–100, 66.
120 *Ibid.*
121 For a consideration of these and other analytical 'patterns', see Max Barrett, *The Art and Craft of Judgment Writing* (Globe Law and Business, 2022), chapter 5.
122 *Ibid*, 85.

	Model 1	Model 2	Model 3
1	Facts	Introduction	Introduction
2	Law	Facts	Issues
3	Application	Issues	Facts
4	Consideration	Law	Legal Principles
5		Application	Conclusion
6		Remedy	
7		Order	

Along with the above models, one sees in judgments – and in legal texts more generally – how lawyers seek to extract from a given scenario the particular facts that have a legal significance and then bring applicable law to bear on those facts. Thus, it has been noted that lawyers from litigators right up to the highest levels of the judiciary need to be able quickly to recognise fact patterns that are of legal significance.[123]

One thing that Forster expressly cautions against is a too-rigid approach to the shape of a novel, preferring an evolutionary approach whereby a pattern emerges and the distractive is pruned back.[124] In the world of legal writing, there is an extent to which one's freedom as a writer is constrained, individual legal writers being rather wanting in power when it comes to departing from standard/accepted patterns of speaking and writing.[125] That said, while the above-mentioned analytical models undoubtedly assist the task of legal writing one has to be careful not to become trapped in their formulaic simplicity.[126]

---

123 Laurence Trautman, "The Value of Legal Writing, Law Review, and Publications" (2018) 51(3) *Indiana Law Review* 693–772, 696.
124 EM Forster, *Aspects of the Novel* (Penguin Books, 2005), 145.
125 Douglas Litowitz, "Legal Writing: Its Nature, Limits, and Dangers" (1998) 49(3) *Mercer Law Review* 709–740, 738.
126 Philip Meyer, "Confessions of a Legal Writing Instructor" (1996) 46(1) *Journal of Legal Education* 27–42, 40.

Key propositions

- A legal text is like a tapeworm because where it starts/ends is arbitrary – it takes up from a particular point in the experiences of the parties and leaves when it has said enough.
- The legal text as story has one merit (instilling the reader's desire to know what happens next) and one drawback (failing to instil that desire).
- Just as a story is the repository of voice, so too are legal texts.
- Just as novels make the world seem more comprehensible, a legal text can make the world seem more comprehensible.
- A story may be told impartially from outside or omnisciently from within – in legal texts, the external impartial tale predominates.
- A story involves a sequence of events arranged chronologically; a plot involves a sequence of events but its emphasis is on causality; a legal text is akin to a plot.
- Just as mystery is essential to a good plot (something is half-explained now and its true meaning explained later), in legal texts, something is often half-explained now and its significance becomes apparent at the end.
- The concluding portion of a novel is often the weakest because the plot requires to be wound up; by contrast, the concluding portion of a legal text is often its strongest point because it is then that findings become manifest.
- There are legal writers who never raise one's mind from what is written on the pages of a legal text, and there are legal writers (fewer in number) whose words conjure a sense of the majesty of the world and a sense of law's proper place.
- One should avoid taking too formulaic an approach to legal text writing.
- As to rhythm, one can distinguish between the famous opening 'da-da-da-dah' of Beethoven's Fifth Symphony as a rhythm that we all hear, and a second, separate rhythm that permeates the symphony as a whole. A legal writer may seek the first kind of rhythm but it is also possible for a separate rhythm to permeate a great legal text, yielding a feeling that everything within it fuses into a greater whole.

8. Hardy

On sincerity, originality and other matters

Thomas Hardy (1840–1928) was the creator of still popular 'fin de 19e siècle' novels such as *Far From the Madding Crowd* (1874), *The Mayor of Casterbridge* (1886), *Tess of the d'Urbervilles* (1891) and *Jude the Obscure* (1895), all of which cast a critical eye on the mores of 19th-century England. These days, Hardy is also recognised as a significant poet and he was even an accomplished artist, "working in, of all things, coal and ground coffee beans".[1] Three of Hardy's essays on writing form the basis of this chapter: "Candour in English Fiction" (1890),[2] "The Science of Fiction" (1891)[3] and "A Plea for Pure English" (1912),[4] each of which, I submit, makes points of relevance to the art and craft of legal writing.

1. Sincerity

Hardy points to the attraction of sincerity in writing.[5] This is a characteristic of good legal writing also, with one commentator observing that a clear style – unquestionably a desirable style – is, amongst other matters, sincere.[6] And Justice Cardozo, writing of judgments (though his observations have a wider resonance) has suggested that although clearness may be a prime quality of judgments, it is not enough, and that other necessary attributes include sincerity.[7] What does Cardozo mean by 'sincerity'? Most likely, that – consistent with the unobjectionable proposition that one should not seek to deceive other people, still less should one state things that are positively false.[8]

---

1   Nicola Rowan-Brooks, "Thomas Hardy, Victor Hugo, and 'The Sincerest of Flattery'" (2020) 36 *The Thomas Hardy Journal* 65–77, at 66.
2   Thomas Hardy, *Thomas Hardy's Personal Writings*, H Hardy (ed) (University of Kansas Press, 1966), 125–133.
3   *Ibid*, 134–138.
4   *Ibid*, 146–148.
5   *Ibid*, 126.
6   Gibson Witherspoon, "The Importance of Legal Writing to Young Writers" (1960) 6 *Student Lawyer Journal* 20–24, 22.
7   *Ibid*.
8   Micha Schwartzman, "Judicial Sincerity" (2008) 94(4) *Virginia Law Review* 987–1028, 988.

There is a school of thought that sincerity is not always required in writing, that sometimes it is needed to make a text effective (eg, in a letter of apology) but that it is not the *sine qua non* of effective writing.[9] However, while this is an interesting notion, in *legal* writing insincerity, being so closely related to falsehood, is anathema, and the "impressive value of sincerity"[10] is necessary.

"[C]onscientious fiction", Hardy posits – by this, he means writing that aims at sincerity – can prompt real, abiding and reflective interest among thinking readers.[11] What makes a legal text engaging? The secret of good legal writing, one sometimes finds it said, is to know exactly what one wishes to say and how.[12] Brevity, clarity and simplicity are key attainments (the 'triple crown' of legal writing),[13] but what makes a text engaging? Language, sentence length, style (voice), vocabulary, humour (*possibly*)[14] and an ability to elicit pathos and weave a powerful tale have all been offered as elements of engaging legal writing.[15] It is in preparing an engaging script that conscientiousness plays a role.

2. Originality

When it comes to originality in form, Hardy observes that it is the product of much trial and error.[16] When it comes to legal writing one view is that originality is not esteemed.[17] (Academic legal writing may be a little different.)[18] Thus, when it comes to legal submissions it has been suggested that originality can make comprehension of them (and applicable law) more difficult,[19] whereas what judges seek is prose that aids in understanding and applying the law, drawing on applicable authority as appropriate.[20] Judicial originality is frowned upon by some as

---

9   On attitudes to sincerity see Peter Elbow, "Reconsiderations: Voice in Writing Again: Embracing Countries" (2007) 70(2) *College English* 168–188.

10 *Ibid.*

11 Thomas Hardy, *Thomas Hardy's Personal Writings*, H Hardy (ed) (University of Kansas Press, 1966), 127.

12 Samuel Murumba, "Good Legal Writing: A Guide for the Perplexed" (1991) 17(1) *Monash University Law Review* 93–105, 93.

13 Lord Bingham, "What Is the Law?" (2009) 40(3) *Victoria University of Wellington Law Review* 597–612, 609.

14 As will be clear from earlier chapters my own sense is that humour has no place in legal writing.

15 See generally Mark Osbeck, "What is 'Good Legal Writing' and Why Does It Matter?" (2012) 4(2) *Drexel Law Review* 417–466.

16 Thomas Hardy, *Thomas Hardy's Personal Writings*, H Hardy (ed) (University of Kansas Press, 1966), 127.

17 Nancy Wanderer, "Legal Writing: Original Thinking or Patchwork Plagiarism" (2018) 33(2) *Maine Bar Journal* 31–35, 33.

18 Richard Posner, *The Little Book of Plagiarism* (Pantheon Books, 2007), 22–23.

19 Nancy Wanderer, "Legal Writing: Original Thinking or Patchwork Plagiarism" (2018) 33(2) *Maine Bar Journal* 31–35, 33.

20 *Ibid.*

having a destabilising effect on the law.[21] However, there may be a certain sleight of hand at play on the part of judges in this regard, arising from a desire on their part to be perceived as appliers/interpreters (not makers) of law.[22] That there is scope for originality in legal writing, that it does occur, and that legal writing is often the better when it does occur is well-captured in the below, now long ago, observation on originality in the writing efforts of law school students:

> It is not easy to give the student a sense of the degree of originality and creativeness that law work permits. Law is not poetry, and work that is too creative is likely to be bad and dangerous law work. On the other hand, the degree to which legal analysis, research, and exposition can be legitimately individualized is too often ignored. Perhaps the chief impression one has after reading hundreds of student papers is that, to a marked degree, the good paper is good precisely because it adds something to the routine and accurate reporting of authoritative materials. The paper can be made the student's own in many and subtle ways – the style, the proportioning of various aspects of the discussion, the over-all organization, the clarity of transition, the intelligent use of footnote, the wit, the sensitivity to inconsistency. There is ... an extraordinary variety among good papers even though they are on precisely the same topic. Finally, it is, I think, the failure of the intellect thus to shine through ... that makes so much professional textbook and encyclopaedia writing on law so deadly to read. And, I might add, so much the less useful.[23]

It may, in part, be a fear of perceived originality that has seen successive generations of legal writers adhere to the legal writing style of the generation/s that went before. But any such fear of error may also run the risk of hindering advancement in terms of evolving an ever-better system of legal writing that is better suited for each new generation of court users. If Rodell was right when he wrote in the mid-1930s that the two things wrong with nearly all legal writing are style and content,[24] a question surely arises whether writing has changed sufficiently since the 1930s to overcome this then-perceived deficiency.

Hardy suggests that the magazines and circulating libraries of his time, all aimed at middlebrow reading, tended to monopolise literary space.[25]

---

21   Richard Posner, *The Little Book of Plagiarism* (Pantheon Books, 2007), 22.
22   *Ibid*.
23   Harry Kalven, "Law School Training in Research and Exposition: The University of Chicago Program" (1948) 1(1) *Journal of Legal Education* 107–123, 118–119.
24   Fred Rodell, "Goodbye to Law Reviews" (1936–1937) 23(1) *Virginia Law Review* 38–45, 38.
25   Thomas Hardy, *Thomas Hardy's Personal Writings*, H Hardy (ed) (University of Kansas Press, 1966), 128.

In a similar vein, it might be contended that the great mass of legal texts, all drafted in a similar style – a style that evolved over centuries – have monopolised the legal writing space, leaving no ground for innovative legal writing styles. Hardy writes in this regard of an "interference with spontaneity"[26] in English fiction. A question arises as to whether a similar 'interference with spontaneity' presents in legal writing. Former US Supreme Court Justice Felix Frankfurter certainly seemed to think so, writing once of "inevitable lawyer's writing ... [with] dull qualifications and circumlocutions ... that preclude grace and stifle spontaneity".[27] (One might reasonably dispute his notion as to such writing being an inevitability.)

3. Detachment

Hardy writes that the price that one must pay for the privilege of writing in the English language is the extinguishment of sympathy in his or her prose.[28] A similar deficiency presents (I submit) in the context of legal writing, with legal writers consistently expected to write emotionally detached legal texts. One commentator has observed that while many people come to law school with a view on the world and its woes, they are soon encouraged to abjure their feelings, avoid personal pronouns, and adopt the declarative form in their statements of the law, all of the foregoing proceeding on the (questionable) basis that "Detachment is lawyerly. Passion is not".[29]

The principal dictionary definition of 'detachment' is 'the state of being objective or aloof' and that is the meaning that seems most often brought to bear in the legal writing context. There is division in the academic literature as to whether such detachment is in fact a virtue. One prominent American guide on plain English for lawyers urges its readers to "Avoid Cosmic Detachment",[30] noting that while every legal problem involves real people legal writing often ignores these people and is addressed instead "to some ... cosmic void".[31] Yet the extent to which the concept of detachment pervades the world of legal writing suggests that it is perceived by many people to present with advantages. What could

26   *Ibid*, 129.
27   Felix Frankfurter, *Law and Politics: Occasional Papers of Felix Frankfurter*, A MacLeish and E Prichard (eds) (Harcourt, Brace & Co, 1939), 104.
28   Thomas Hardy, *Thomas Hardy's Personal Writings*, H Hardy (ed) (University of Kansas Press, 1966), 130.
29   Tamara Piety, "Smoking in Bed" (2003) 57(3) *University of Miami Law Review* 827–852, 843.
30   Richard Wydick, *Plain English for Lawyers*, 2nd edition (Carolina Academic Press, 1985), 63.
31   *Ibid*.

those be? As an approach to legal writing it seems to have sprung from the same well that yielded the ideal of the 'disinterested judge', namely that the law is "neutral, objective, and devoid of [subjective] values"[32] and a judge should be too. As it was for judges, so for practising lawyers. But a question arises whether this traditional concept of the law and of judges was ever correct. Justice Cardozo clearly did not believe in the dispassionate judge, famously observing:

> We [judges] like to figure ... the processes of justice as coldly objective and impersonal. The law, conceived of as a real existence, dwelling apart and alone, speaks, through the voices of priests and ministers, the words which they have no choice except to utter. That is an ideal of objective truth ... It has a lofty sound; it is well and finely said; but it can never be more than partly true.[33]

It has been suggested too that attempts at avoidance of emotion in legal writing have tended to yield a form of writing that is neurotically flat, with a psychological barrier between the text as written and life as lived.[34] And there is a certain oddity to the fact that so much legal writing is so emotionally restricted:[35] after all, emotion is a central feature of human existence; and so emotion has a part to play in advocacy and in the task of persuasion more generally.[36] That this is so has been recognised since at least the time of Aristotle's treatise on *Rhetoric*. Yet many modern lawyers, it has been observed, tend to focus on the logical and organisational dimensions of their tasks, ignoring (at their peril) the emotional dimension.[37]

Good lawyers, it has been suggested, do not (and should not) shrink from the emotional. Rather they should emphasise the positive emotions that support their clients (just as they pray in aid legal argument and case law).[38] Admittedly, appeals to emotion may not always benefit one's case:

32   Jeffrey Shaman, "The Impartial Judge: Detachment or Passion?" (1996) 45(3) *De Paul Law Review* 605–632, 614.
33   Benjamin Cardozo, *Selected Writings of Benjamin Nathan Cardozo*, M Hall (ed) (Fallon Publications, 1947), 178–179. Cardozo also suggests that it does not help the cause of truth for judges to perpetuate the untruth that they proceed unmoved by the world around them (*ibid*, 178).
34   James Elkins, "What Kind of Story is Legal Writing?" (1996) 20(1) *Legal Studies Forum* 95–136, 119.
35   Douglas Litowitz, "Legal Writing: Its Nature, Limits, and Dangers" (1998) 49(3) *Mercer Law Review* 709–740, 726.
36   See generally Michael Frost, "Ethos, Pathos and Legal Audience" (1994) 99(1) *Dickinson Law Review* 85–116.
37   *Ibid*, 85. Frost is writing of oral advocacy but his observations arguably have a resonance as regards legal writing.
38   John Shepherd and Jordan Cherrick, "Advocacy and Emotion" (2006) 3 *Journal of the Association of Legal Writing Directors* 154–165, 159.

they may be viewed as overly sentimental, they may suggest that one's legal case is weak, they may distract from the intellectual task at hand,[39] and they may even suggest a want of (detached) perspective.[40] Even so, Hardy's notion that the price that one pays for the privilege of writing in English is the extinguishment of sympathy in one's prose seems not to sit well in the legal writing context: one *can* write legal English in a detached manner and it has long been the general practice to do so. However, it seems likely to yield prose that is less rich and less persuasive than if it were vested with some emotion.

4.   'Laws' of writing

Hardy maintains that when it comes to writing it is futile to hope to state comprehensively the science of what is an art form. Even so, he nonetheless identifies some precepts of interest:

A novel should keep as close to reality as it can[41]

It has been suggested (in the context of advocacy) that, in fact, it does not suffice for a lawyer to recount a true story, that his or her story must possess verisimilitude (the appearance of being true or real) if it is to be optimally persuasive.[42] To the extent that verisimilitude is an objective to be striven for by the legal writer, the following skills (amongst others) seem desirable: intellectual agility,[43] trustworthiness,[44] believability,[45] savviness[46] and a certain lack of empathy (or a certain presence of detachment).[47] The key skill, in terms of conveying verisimilitude, seems to be to provide enough detail to form an image in the mind of one's audience which must then be woven into a coherent and convincing narrative.[48]

---

39   *Ibid*, 157.
40   Nancy Rice, "Tips on Legal Writing" (2015) 44(5) *Colorado Lawyer* 61–62, 61.
41   Thomas Hardy, *Thomas Hardy's Personal Writings*, H Hardy (ed) (University of Kansas Press, 1966), 135.
42   Cathren Page, "Stranger than Fiction: How Lawyers Can Accurately and Realistically Tell a True Story by Using Fiction Writers' Techniques That Make Fiction Seem More Realistic than Reality" (2018) 78(3) *Louisiana Law Review* 907–944, 909.
43   Jayne Barnard, "Securities Fraud, Recidivism, and Deterrence" (2008) 113 *Penn State Law Review* 189–228, 206.
44   *Ibid*, 207.
45   *Ibid*.
46   *Ibid*.
47   *Ibid*, 210.
48   Cathren Page, "Stranger than Fiction: How Lawyers Can Accurately and Realistically Tell a True Story by Using Fiction Writers' Techniques That Make Fiction Seem More Realistic than Reality" (2018) 78(3) *Louisiana Law Review* 907–944, 944.

There is discriminative choice (selection) at play in fiction[49]

There is also discriminative choice at play when it comes to legal writing. The writer has to determine which law and facts are sufficiently relevant and significant to include in a piece of prose. Of course, different writers will differ when undertaking this process (a process of selection is invariably subjective)[50] and error will naturally arise in a system of human appraisal. However, a writer will not enhance his or her reputation if he or she does not seek always to state/summarise all relevant material impartially and objectively.[51] Additionally, when disagreeing with a point of view he or she needs to be careful not to exclude material that would support that point of view.[52]

It is impossible to replicate the entirety of experience in prose[53]

Nor would anybody wish for such a piece of prose: it would be too long. Yet one sometimes senses, at least when reading contemporary legal judgments, that sight of this truth has been lost by many. Former Lord Justice Jacob, writing in an extrajudicial capacity has observed that "modern judgments have become far too long … [being] nearly twice as long as they were 50 years ago".[54] There are various suggested reasons for this increased length of modern judgments, for example, judicial behaviours (a tendency to engage in minute analysis with copious citation of precedent, a tendency to address unnecessary points and multiple audiences, an expectation of long judgments, a possible lack of time to reduce judgments in length, and personal ambition), attorney/litigant behaviour (with counsel citing lots of cases and judges feeling that they must include cited cases in their judgments), technology-related factors (eg, the easiness with which text can be cut and pasted).[55] However, what is truly odd about this trend in judgment

---

49   Thomas Hardy, *Thomas Hardy's Personal Writings*, H Hardy (ed) (University of Kansas Press, 1966), 135.
50   Patrick Hugg and Melanie McKay, "Classics Teach Legal Writing" (1985) 2(2) *Journal of Paralegal Education* 13–52, 52. The authors are considering a different form of selection process but the observation seems to hold good in the above context also.
51   I Campbell, "Legal Writing" (1953) 1(3) *Faculty of Law – Victoria University of College Law Review* 7–17, 10.
52   *Ibid*.
53   Thomas Hardy, *Thomas Hardy's Personal Writings*, H Hardy (ed) (University of Kansas Press, 1966), 135.
54   Robin Jacob, "How to write a legal judgment", *Prospect*, 7 December, 2020, www.prospectmagazine.co.uk/philosophy/how-to-write-a-legal-judgment-robin-jacob-court-of-appeal-law.
55   Max Barrett, *The Art and Craft of Judgment Writing* (Globe Law and Business, 2022), 39–42.

writing is that in professional practice, as the abundant references in this book surely show, there is a continuing emphasis on the need for brevity and clarity in writing.

Blinding oneself to the material can yield an appreciation of the ethereal[56]

Essentially, what Hardy has in mind in this regard is 'seeing the wood for the trees', that is, that blinding oneself to some of the detail at play before her, the writer clears his or her mind to see the essential issues presenting. How is one to do this as a legal writer? One author writes that what is required of the legal writer in this regard is "to free your mind up and go for it",[57] to throw paint out like Picasso and then assess whether (and which of) the splashes convey his or her thoughts.

A sympathetic appreciation of life can yield more accurate delineations of life[58]

Here one is back to a point akin to that made by Lord Macmillan and with which I commenced this book, namely that a good lawyer should be well acquainted with the best of literature.[59] However, the point that Hardy makes goes even wider, suggesting that writers (including legal writers) will see their writing enriched if they evince a sympathetic appreciation of life. In a similar vein, it has been said of legal writing (the telling of legal stories) that stories tend to work best when they derive from understanding based on experience.[60] Justice Cardozo makes something of a similar point when he writes that judges (though the point could be made of any legal writer) "ought to be in sympathy with their times".[61]

5. Hardy's observations summarised

When it comes to legal writing, Hardy's observations can perhaps be summarised as follows. First, a legal text should keep as close to reality as

---

56   *Ibid*, 137.
57   Di Ricker, "Verbatim" (1996) 24(6) *Student Lawyer* 6 and 8, 6.
58   Thomas Hardy, *Thomas Hardy's Personal Writings*, H Hardy (ed) (University of Kansas Press, 1966), 137.
59   *Ibid*.
60   Toni Massaro, "Empathy, Legal Storytelling, and the Rule of Law: New Words, Old Wounds" (1989) 87(8) *Michigan Law Review* 2099–2127, 2105.
61   Thomas Hardy, *Thomas Hardy's Personal Writings*, H Hardy (ed) (University of Kansas Press, 1966), 181.

it can. Secondly, there will inevitably be discriminative choice (selection) at play in terms of depicting the reality presenting. Thirdly, it is impossible for a legal writer to replicate the entirety of a reality presenting before her. Fourthly, by blinding oneself to some of the detail at play before her, the legal writer clears his or her mind to see the essential issues presenting. Finally, a legal writer with a sympathetic appreciation of life is perhaps more likely to draft an empathetic legal text.

6. Carelessness in writing

Hardy suggests that in his day the growth in readership had not been joined with a commensurate growth in the ability to discriminate between good and bad writing, the result being an increase in "slipshod writing".[62] Whether there has, since Hardy's day, been an increase in slipshod legal writing is not clear; however, there is certainly an awareness of the perils it poses. Careless writing, it has been suggested, derives from careless thinking[63] and offers a conduit[64] to confusion. There are exceptions to these general rules: one will occasionally find good legal analysis in complex prose.[65] However, experience suggests that poor writing is usually accompanied by poor thinking.

Hardy attributes the growth in slipshod writing to the increase in descriptive reporting in the newspapers of his day,[66] as well as an influx of sensationalist American journals.[67] One finds a similar observation in the writing of Karl Llewellyn, one of the great legal philosophers of the 20th century. Writing in the 1930s, he lamented how the writing of great works had declined to the standard of the *Saturday Evening Post* (a weekly periodical aimed at a mass audience).[68] The visual entertainments that have, to a large extent, replaced the literary entertainments of previous generations have possibly compounded, in our time, the decline identified by Hardy (and, still later, by Llewellyn).

Judge Posner, writing of a perceived decline in the quality of judicial writing from the days of United States Supreme Court Justices Holmes, Cardozo and Jackson, suggests that one negative impact on the writing

---

62   *Ibid*, 147.
63   Mark Mathewson, "Law Students, Beware" (2001–2002) 8 *Scribes Journal of Legal Writing* 141–158, 148.
64   David Mellinkoff, *Legal Writing: Sense and Nonsense* (Charles Scribner's Sons, 1982), 17.
65   Mark Matthewson, "Verbatim" (1988) 16(5) *Student Lawyer* 6–7, 7.
66   Thomas Hardy, *Thomas Hardy's Personal Writings*, H Hardy (ed) (University of Kansas Press, 1966), 147.
67   *Ibid*.
68   Karl Llewellyn, *The Bramble Bush: On Our Law and Its Study* (Oceana Publications, 1996), 151–152.

power of modern judges is the emphasis placed on computers and technology in the education system.[69] Two points, however, might be made in this regard. First, Holmes, Cardozo, and Jackson are among the very best judicial writers; even in their day, there was no one quite to match them (at least on the American side of the Atlantic). Thus, to write of a "decline of great judicial prose (the prose of a Holmes, a Cardozo, a Robert Jackson)"[70] is (I respectfully submit) to set the bar too high – few judges can scale the Olympian heights of prose writing to which that remarkable trio of American judges managed to ascend. Secondly, one has to query (again, respectfully) whether Posner is correct in the point he makes about technology. In the literary world, modern classics continue to be churned out annually by modern authors, written in a style very different from yesteryear but classics nonetheless. Many of these writers will have post-dated the invention of the home computer, and some of them ('digital natives') will have grown up in the age of mass internet availability. So, if there has been a decline in judicial writing (or in writing more generally), it would seem to be a decline that afflicts legal writing but not writing more generally.

Key propositions

- Sincerity is a positive attribute in legal writing.
- Originality in prose is the product of trial and error. Fear of error may hinder advancement in terms of evolving an ever-better system of legal writing.
- The legal writer should constantly aim to tell the plain truth plainly.
- The near-complete absence of spontaneity in legal writing derives from self-censorship.
- Legal writers are generally expected to write legal texts in a detached form that may not best suit the subject at hand.
- A legal text should be as close to reality as it can, though there will inevitably be selection of facts at play in terms of depicting reality.
- It is impossible for a legal writer to describe all the richness of the situation presenting in a case.
- A legal writer with a sympathetic appreciation of life is more

---

69   Richard Posner, "Legal Writing Today" (2001–2002) 8 *Scribes Journal of Legal Writing* 35–38, 36.
70   *Ibid*, 37.

likely to draft a legal text that accurately delineates the human aspects of a case than one with less sympathy.

- Hardy considered that a perceived growth in slipshod writing was due to a decline in the literary standards observed by the newspapers of his day; in our less literary age, it may be that the standards of legal writing have not been immune to a continuation of the trend identified by Hardy.

9. The Hawthornes

On theme, tone, truth, the task of writing and other matters

Nathaniel Hawthorne (1804–1864) was among the most prominent American authors of the early to mid-19th century. His most famous novel is *The Scarlet Letter* (1850). Slightly less well-known is his supernatural tale, *The House of the Seven Gables* (1851),[1] in the preface to which he considers various aspects of the novel. Julian Hawthorne (1846–1934), "[s]eldom remembered now except as Nathaniel Hawthorne's son"[2] was actually a prolific author, albeit one less gifted than his father. His more than 50 titles include a collection of essays, *Confessions and Criticisms*,[3] that touch on aspects of literary theory which are of relevance, I submit, to the task of legal writing.[4]

1.   Plainness and simplicity

Nathaniel Hawthorne contrasts the relative freedom of writing a romantic novel to that of writing a plain and simple novel. The latter form of writing, Nathaniel Hawthorne posits, seeks to adhere faithfully to the ordinary and the probable.[5] Lawyers do not engage, at least in their 'day job', in writing romantic fiction. However, there are notable overlaps between legal writing and fiction writing in general. So, for example, both involve creativity, operate within constraints of format, involve reader-focused communication[6] and often yield detailed works prepared under tight time constraints.[7]

---

1   Nathaniel Hawthorne, *The House of the Seven Gables* (JM Dent & Sons, 1907).
2   Rayburn Moore, "Julian Hawthorne and 'Fortune's Fool'" (2003) 29(2) *Nathaniel Hawthorne Review* 76–83, 76.
3   Julian Hawthorne, *Confessions and Criticisms* (Ticknor & Co, 1887).
4   Julian Hawthorne, "The Moral Aim in Fiction" in Julian Hawthorne, *Confessions and Criticisms* (Ticknor & Co, 1887), 128–139.
5   *Ibid.*
6   Pam Jenoff, "The Self-Assessed Writer: Harnessing Fiction-Writing Processes to Understand Ourselves as Legal Writers and Maximise Legal Writing Productivity" (2013) 10 *Legal Communication and Rhetoric: JAWLD* 187–200, 190.
7   *Ibid*, 189–191.

Plainness and simplicity are virtues of legal writing that have already been discussed in the preceding pages. Plainness is sometimes touted as something that is desirable but not always possible.[8] So, for example, it has been suggested that if a particular form of document is tried and tested, it may be unwise to replace it with plain English.[9] As against this, it surely cannot be that it is beyond the wit of man to express the complex in plain terms. (Lord Denning has shown that legal problems are generally "reducible to fairly clear and certain categories".)[10] As for simplicity, Younger has written in beautiful English of the attractions of this particular virtue, observing that simplicity is a hallmark of masterful writing but that the legal world "has made of simplicity a vice, the shameful badge of a mind too lazy or too weak to be suitably complicated".[11]

The reason simplicity is important is because writing is all about making oneself understood and simple words are the ones most likely to be understood.[12] There are perhaps two 'rules' when it comes to attaining simplicity:

- never use a long word when a short one suffices; and
- favour concrete, familiar and the fewest possible words.[13]

Younger maintains that there are five advantages to the pursuit of simplicity: beauty (of writing), candour, elegance (though this seems but an aspect of beauty), comprehensibility and enhanced efficacy (because legal texts become easier to understand).[14]

2. Tone

Nathaniel Hawthorne observes of the writer of romantic fiction that he or she may manage the atmosphere (tone), lightening or darkening it as the writer sees fit, without doing so to excess.[15] In a similar vein, it is open to the legal writer to amend the tone of his or her legal text so that a piece of prose:

- does not reflect any informality that may exist in the relationship between writer and reader;

---

8 See, eg, David Crump, "'Against Plain English': The Case for a Functional Approach to Legal Document Preparation" (2002) 33(3) *Rutgers Law Journal* 713–744.
9 *Ibid*, 743.
10 Dennis Klinck, "Style, Meaning, and Knowing: Megarry J and Denning MR in *In re Vandervell's Trusts (No 2)*" (1987) 37(4) *University of Toronto Law Journal* 358–388, 388.
11 Irving Younger, "In Praise of Simplicity" (1976) 62(5) *ABA Journal* 632–634, 632.
12 Henry Weihofen, *Legal Writing Style*, 2nd edition (West Publishing Co, 1980), 61.
13 *Ibid*, 63.
14 Irving Younger, "In Praise of Simplicity" (1976) 62(5) *ABA Journal* 632–634, 632.
15 *Ibid*.

- reins in the writer's individual personality and sense of humour; and
- evinces an educational, patient tone.[16]

Tone is important in legal writing. The more professional the tone, likely the greater the initial impression a text will make;[17] conversely, "the breezier you are, the less seriously you will be taken".[18] That said, it does not seem necessary (or advisable) that tone should be allowed to compromise the intellectual goals of clarity and simplicity. So, for example, Floren has observed that he never saw a legal message that required to be pitched at a reading level beyond that of a high school sophomore,[19] that is, a 15- to 16-year-old child.

There are some who contend that plain English diminishes the professional tone of a legal text.[20] However, the concept of a professional legal tone itself presents with a number of inherent difficulties. First, there is a level of assumption (which may not be a correct assumption) that by writing a legal text in a professional tone (rather than plain English) one will be as well understood by the reader of that text as if one had used plain English. Secondly, it has credibly been posited that the legal writer who uses his or her own "authentic voice"[21] will produce writing that is more engaging.[22] Thirdly, there is a question mark as to whether a professional tone can efface a writer's voice,[23] leaving a professional voice that is associated with dominant societal values[24] and which sits ill at ease with the lived experience of many who are served by the legal profession and those within the legal profession who see themselves to be outside its mainstream membership.[25]

Nathaniel Hawthorne points to the significance of tone in romantic fiction. In their own (different) ways, those who contend for writing that

---

16   Shavonnie Carthens, "Watch Your Tone: Aim for Professional and Approachable" (2021) 85(1) *Bench & Bar* 40.
17   Judith Fischer, "Got Issues – An Empirical Study About Framing Them" (2009) 6(1) *Journal of the Association of Legal Writing Directors* 1–27, 25.
18   Katherine Mikkelson, "Better Legal Writing" (2018) 26(2) *GP Solo* 8–12 and 15, 9.
19   M Floren, "Better Legal Writing" (1967) 13(4) *Student Lawyer Journal* 10–21, 11.
20   Allen Hartman, "Legal Writing: A Judge's Perspective" (1991) 79(4) *Illinois Bar Journal* 194–196, 194.
21   Mark Osbeck, "What is 'Good Legal Writing' and Why Does It Matter?" (2012) 4(2) *Drexel Law Review* 417–466, 445.
22   *Ibid.*
23   J Christopher Rideout, "Ethos, Character, and Discoursal Self in Persuasive Writing" (2016) 21 *Legal Writing: The Journal of the Legal Writing Institute* 19–62, 44.
24   Andrea McArdle, "Teaching Writing in Clinical, Lawyering, and Legal Writing Courses: Negotiating Professional and Personal Voice" (2006) 12 *Clinical Law Review* 501–540, 503.
25   *Ibid.*

evinces a professional tone *and also* those who contend that the individual voice should be heard are bringing focus to bear on the importance of tone when it comes to legal writing. Where proponents of the two schools of thought ('single professional tone' versus 'individual voice') appear to differ is on the extent of the individual freedom to vary tone (which is the second aspect of tone to which Nathaniel Hawthorne points: the power that the writer enjoys to vary it). Those who contend for a single professional tone maintain that variation should be done with a view to attaining an impressively professional tone. Those who contend for a greater sphere of freedom for the individual voice see that very individuality as a means of enriching a legal text. At first glance, these two streams of thought seem almost irreconcilable. However, the answer may lie in Floren's observation that the reading level of a suitably professional text is relatively low. If one focuses on reading level, rather than on tone, then it does not matter how one reaches the end goal as regards readability, be that via a perceived professional tone or an actual individual voice.

3.   Morality and writing

Many writers, Nathaniel Hawthorne notes, stress some moral purpose to which they aspire in their works.[26] A generation later, Julian Hawthorne was to make a similar point in his essay, *"The Moral Aim in Fiction"*,[27] in which he observed that a novel aims at a vindication of right over wrong.[28] The literature of law likewise involves "a moral vision of law".[29] It is outside the scope of this book to consider the interrelationship between law and morality. However, one cannot but recall in this regard the analogy once drawn by Adam Smith between (i) the rules of justice and the rules of grammar and (ii) the rules of other virtues and the rules of composition:

> *The rules of justice may be compared to the rules of grammar; the rules of the other virtues to the rules which critics lay down for the attainment of what is sublime and elegant in composition. The one [the rules of grammar] are precise accurate, and indispensable. The other [the rules of composition] are loose, vague, and indeterminate, and present us rather with a general idea of the perfection we ought to aim at, than afford us any certain and infallible directions for acquiring it. A man may learn to write grammatically by rule, with the most absolute infallibility; and so, perhaps,*

---

26   Nathaniel Hawthorne, *The House of the Seven Gables* (JM Dent & Sons, 1907), xii.
27   Julian Hawthorne, *Confessions and Criticisms* (Ticknor & Co, 1887).
28   *Ibid*, 129.
29   Costas Douzinas, "[Book Review] Ian Ward, *Law and Literature: Possibilities and Perspectives*" (1996) 59(2) *Modern Law Review* 315–330, 320.

he may be taught to act justly. But there are no rules whose observance will infallibly lead us to the attainment of elegance or sublimity in writing: though there are some which may help us, in some measure, to correct and ascertain the vague ideas which we might otherwise have entertained of those perfections. And there are no rules by the knowledge of which we can infallibly be taught to act upon all occasions with prudence, with just magnanimity, or proper beneficence; though there are some which may enable us to correct and ascertain, in several respects, the imperfect ideas which we might otherwise have entertained of those virtues.[30]

The analogy and the language are beautiful, not only illustrating the distinction that Smith sought to make between the rules of justice and the rules concerning the other virtues, but also pointing to important features of the rules of grammar and the rules of composition.

Returning, however, to the Hawthornes' point about the moral purpose to which writers aspire in their works, what is the 'moral purpose' (if any) of legal writing? Stone, in an engaging account of law, psychiatry, and morality, makes the following observations of the role of the psychiatrist and psychiatry in the modern world that also apply to the role of the legal writer engaged in the task of legal writing:

We ... are motivated by [a] ... moral enterprise that [is] ... a mixture of compassion, understanding, art, and science ... [O]ur work can never be carried on in a moral and historical vacuum ... We will make mistakes if we go forward, but doing nothing can be the worst mistake. What is required ... is moral ambition ... [with] compassion ... our only guide and comfort.[31]

His idea seems to be that the psychiatrist (for whom one might, it is submitted, substitute the legal writer) should proceed with the moral ambition of identifying truth, doubtless stumbling in the process and constantly informed by compassion in the quest for truth. Compassion, however, is a somewhat controversial word when it comes to legal writing. It has been suggested that the traditional form of legal writing mediates between lawyers and the world, to the point that it stops lawyers from feeling compassion.[32] However, the more contemporary view is that legal writers should be possessed of compassion.[33]

---

30 Adam Smith, *The Theory of Moral Sentiments* (Henry G Bohn, 1853), 250–251.
31 Alan Stone, *Law, Psychiatry, and Morality* (American Psychiatric Press, Inc), 262.
32 Richard Hyland, "A Defense of Legal Writing" (1986) 134(3) *University of Pennsylvania Law Review* 599–626, 605.
33 Stephanie Ledesma, "Compassion: A Critical Skill for Law Students" (2021) 22 *Marquette Benefits and Social Welfare Law Review* 181–206, 183. Ledesma is writing in the quoted text of law students (future professional lawyers); however, her point arguably applies with equal vigour to all legal writers.

There is, Nathaniel Hawthorne suggests, no point in expanding on a single moral because it suffices for the truth to be stated once.[34] It is not just morals that do not bear repetition. One commentator has observed that readers are a fickle lot and will shrink from all unnecessary repetitiveness.[35] Another suggests that lawyers should eschew pleonasm (repetition of the unnecessary).[36] The very notion of 'unnecessary' repetition involves an implicit acknowledgement that some level of repetition may be justifiable. This seems especially the case when it comes to law, when the fear can be that if one does not consistently use the same phraseology or words the reader may assume that different meanings were intended when in truth the writer sought to engage in some sort of elegant variation. And, as mentioned previously, for just this reason elegant variation is now generally frowned upon as a tool of legal writing.[37]

4. Writing models and formulae

Julian Hawthorne is sceptical that it is possible to arrive at a formula whereby a novel might best be written. He found that whenever he attempted to map out what he was going to write he never arrived at his identified end.[38] Legal writing seems somewhat more formulaic: some of the more popular legal writing models (eg, the 'IRAC' and 'FIRAC' models) and some of the more popular frameworks for judgment writing have already been touched upon. The IRAC (Issue–Rule–Analysis–Conclusion) is so popular in the United States that 'to IRAC' is even deployed in some legal writing guides as a verb.[39] However, as a writing model it has also been criticised, for example, for channelling human disputes into a rule-based schema,[40] for being just too simplistic[41] (to the point of obscuring the ethical significance of what is at play in a legal text),[42] and for not indicating what weight to assign to its different parts.[43] A further difficulty with legal writing models such as the 'IRAC' model is

---

34   Nathaniel Hawthorne, *The House of the Seven Gables* (JM Dent & Sons, 1907), xii.
35   Bryan Garner, "Legal Writing" (2009) 38(1) *Student Lawyer* 12–13, 13.
36   David Ross, "Legal Writing" (2005) 1(4) *Original Law Review* 85–102, 96.
37   H Fowler, *A Dictionary of Modern English Usage* (Clarendon Press, 1944), 130–131.
38   Julian Hawthorne, *Confessions and Criticisms* (Ticknor & Co, 1887), 18.
39   Diana Pratt, *Legal Writing: A Systematic Approach* (West Publishing Co, 1990), 175.
40   Oghenemaro Emiri *et al*, "Revisiting the Traditional IRAC Organisational Structure for Legal Analysis: Towards a Multidisciplinary Approach" (2017) 20(1) *Nigerian Law Journal* 31–76, 31.
41   Laura Graham, "Why-Rac – Revisiting the Traditional Paradigm for Writing About Legal Analysis" (2015) 63(3) *University of Kansas Law Review* 681–716, 682.
42   Joel Cornwell, "Legal Writing as a Kind of Philosophy" (1997) 48 *Mercer Law Review* 1091–1136, 1134.
43   Sorna Kedia, "Redirecting the Scope of First-Year Writing Courses: Toward a New Paradigm of Teaching Legal Writing" (2010) 87(2) *University of Detroit Mercy Law Review* 147–178, 150.

a failure among some legal writers to recognise that such models are not set in stone and may be applied in a modified form.[44]

In short, when it comes to legal writing one should not just spew out the applicable issue/s, applicable rule/s, some degree of analysis and a quick conclusion. Rather what is in play is a more sophisticated exercise in which the legal writer:

- identifies all relevant issues and excludes all irrelevant issues;
- considers the sequence in which the relevant issues will be considered;
- brings all the relevant law to bear;
- completely and objectively analyses the relevant law;
- shows where analogies/distinctions exist between the case at hand and previous cases; and
- arrives at a conclusion that derives from that analysis.[45]

Even with this more comprehensive application of the IRAC judgment writing model, there are other aspects of a legal text that require to be addressed, for example:

- choice of language;
- how to select which facts and law to include/exclude; how best to persuade a hostile audience comprising, for example, another lawyer or judge;
- how to gauge what level and length of prose is available in the time available; and
- how best to present one's thoughts – with the modern emphasis on plain English (and all the issues that present in this regard).[46]

5. The steps to writing a text

Julian Hawthorne traces the means whereby one of his novels came into existence (by way of example as to how one might write a novel). In so doing, he identifies the following steps:

- The central idea had been playing for some time on his mind.[47]
- With this central idea came a theme.[48]
- With work he converted the idea into a plausible plot for a novel[49]

---

44   Gertrude Block, *Effective Legal Writing*, 4th edition (The Foundation Press, Inc, 1992), 246.
45   *Ibid*, 245.
46   E Syman Van Deventer and C Swanepoel, "Teaching South African Law Students Legal Writing Skills" (2013) 24(3) *Stellenbosch Law Review* 510–527, 519.
47   Julian Hawthorne, *Confessions and Criticisms* (Ticknor & Co, 1887), 21.
48   *Ibid*.
49   *Ibid*, 21.

– though in hindsight he considered that he had forced the plot to accommodate the central idea rather than allowing it to evolve naturally.[50]

- He sought to retain a sense of proportion in his writing whereby the significant was given weight and the insignificant was given undue weight.[51]

- All the foregoing complete, the writing and publication of the text followed on.

Is it possible to reduce Julian Hawthorne's writing process to a series of precepts that have more direct relevance to writing a legal text? The following suggest themselves:

*A legal writer must bring a central idea/theme to
his or her legal text*

It has been suggested that in order to make written legal submissions stand out it is imperative to have a central idea that underlies all one has to say[52] and which should be stated early and clearly so that it is known to the reader from the beginning.[53] Consistent with the general rules of grammar, it has also been suggested that each paragraph in a legal text should contain no more than one central idea, with an introductory or closing sentence stating the idea and the rest of the paragraph treating with it.[54]

A legal text should be plausible in its reasoning/contentions

The importance of plausibility in the context of legal writing rests in the fact that humans seek to identify historical truths in convincing narratives informed by dependable evidence.[55] To arrive at a text that is plausible it is necessary, when drafting that text to pick between theories, excise weak points and discard whatever does not require to be stated.[56] That said, simply having plausible reasoning does not mean that one is on the side

50   *Ibid*, 26.
51   *Ibid*, 28–29.
52   James McElhaney, "Legal Writing that Works" (2007) 93 *ABA Journal* 30–31, 31.
53   Jim Corkery, *Study of Law* (The Adelaide Law Review Association, 1988), 138–139.
54   Robert Smith, "Making Sense: Some Reflections on Legal Writing" (1985) 56(41) *Oklahoma Bar Journal* 2563–2577, 2568.
55   Robert Burns, *A Theory of the Trial* (Princeton University Press, 1999), 90–91.
56   James McElhaney, "Legal Writing that Works" (2007) 93 *ABA Journal* 30–31, 30.

of right.[57] In fact, the difficulty with legal texts, and the reasons cases go to court for decision, is (as Justice Cardozo once observed) "that reasons plausible … might be found for one conclusion as for another".[58]

Legal writing involves selection

Legal writing necessarily involves the selection of relevant facts and law and emphasising certain aspects of a case,[59] and then using the "poetic quality"[60] of the imagination to see relationships and significance where others do not. Legal writing also involves the patience and skill necessary to select one's words.[61] Part of the task of selection involves choosing words that do not require a reader to look them up in a dictionary – using 'fancy' words, it has been suggested involves sacrificing clarity in a bid to demonstrate cleverness.[62] Nowadays, word selection is not just a question of accuracy but also selecting words that are uncontroversial and inoffensive to the reader.[63]

6. The 'art' of writing

The nature of the novel, Julian Hawthorne writes, is that it combines art and imagination.[64] The artistry (creativity) involved in legal writing is widely acknowledged and has been the subject of much commentary.[65] As White succinctly observes in his groundbreaking text on law and literature, *The Legal Imagination* (1985), the professional life of lawyers and judges involves "an enterprise of … imagination".[66] Imagination, Julian Hawthorne suggests, is the cause of progress.[67] And imagination is

57   HL Mencken, *A Mencken Chrestomathy* (Alfred A Knopf, 1962), 443.
58   Benjamin Cardozo, *Selected Writings of Benjamin Nathan Cardozo*, M Hall (ed) (Fallon Publications, 1947), 177.
59   I Campbell, "Legal Writing" (1999) 30(2) *Victoria University of Wellington Law Review* 427–434, 429.
60   Felix Frankfurter *et al*, "Conditions for and the Aims and Methods of Legal Research" (1930) 6(11) *American Law School Review* 663–681, 666.
61   Alfred Schweppe, "Techniques of Legal Writing" (1963) 9(2) *Student Law Journal* 16–18, 18.
62   Michael Higdon, "The Legal Reader: An Exposé" (2013) 43(1) *New Mexico Law Review* 77–126, 88.
63   Lorraine Bannai and Anne Enquist, "(Un)Examined Assumptions and (Un)Intended Messages: Teaching Students to Recognize Bias in Legal Analysis and Language" (2003) 27(1) *Seattle University Law Review* 1–40, 12.
64   Julian Hawthorne, *Confessions and Criticisms* (Ticknor & Co, 1887), 32.
65   See, eg, Thomas Spahn, "The Art of Legal Writing" (1989) 9(2) *Journal of the National Association of Administrative Law Judges* 137–152; James McElhaney, "The Art of Persuasive Legal Writing" (1996) 82(1) *ABA Journal* 76–82; Tonya Kowalski, "Legal Writing as Art and Science" (2011) 50(2) *Washburn Law Journal* xiii–xiv; Phu Nguyen, "The Art of Legal Writing: How to Find Your Voice" (2016) 44(4) *Student Lawyer* 14–17; Lance Long, "Is There Any Science Behind the Art of Legal Writing?" (2016) 16(2) *Wyoming Law Review* 287–298.
66   James Boyd White, *The Legal Imagination* (University of Chicago Press, 1985), 208.
67   Julian Hawthorne, *Confessions and Criticisms* (Ticknor & Co, 1887), 32.

a necessary element of innovation in writing[68] (though such innovation seems only justified when deployed as an aid to clarity or persuasiveness).[69] In addition to writer imagination, there is also the issue of reader imagination. In this regard, it has been observed that a carelessly crafted document, rather than engaging reader imagination does the opposite,[70] with the legal writer being obliged to enliven legal writing to compensate for the lack of interest that a subject has for reader imagination.[71] Thus, it seems that as part of the imaginative process in which lawyers are engaged it is necessary to 'fire up' their readers' imagination if a piece of prose is to be engaging and to persuade.

7. Writing powerfully

The best literature, Julian Hawthorne suggests, touches the reader deeply because he or she finds in it an "answering ardor".[72] In terms of legal writing, what Julian Hawthorne points to is the desirability of provocative writing, not writing that is rude but writing that manages to sustain the reader's interest through to the end.[73] Provocative writing, it has been suggested, is a "necessary stimulant"[74] to understanding the law (and to making changes to it).[75] Engaging in provocative writing can, of course, require one to be critical of other people's ideas, potentially damaging the sense of community within the legal community,[76] but ultimately acting to the benefit of society by producing ever better ideas.[77] Avoidance of the 'provocative voice', it is submitted, impoverishes the legal writing community (and society more generally).

Legal writing can be profoundly powerful.[78] And there is actually a great deal of commentary on how to make it even more powerful.[79] This

---

68 Scott Longman, "The Architecture of Legal Writing" (2001) 15(3) *CBA Record* 40–66, 45.
69 Edward Re, "Legal Writing as Good Literature" (1985) 59(2) *St John's Law Review* 211–227, 223.
70 Urban Lavery, "Language of the Law" (1922) 8(5) *ABA Journal* 269–274, 270–271.
71 *Ibid.*
72 Julian Hawthorne, *Confessions and Criticisms* (Ticknor & Co, 1887), 36.
73 Alfred Schweppe, "Techniques of Legal Writing" (1963) 9(2) *Student Law Journal* 16–18, 18.
74 David Golden, "G Keeton and G Schwarzenberger (eds), *Current Legal Problems 1950*" (1951) 29(5) *Canadian Bar Review* 566–568, 566.
75 *Ibid.*
76 Linda Berger *et al*, "The Past, Presence, and Future of Legal Writing Scholarship: Rhetoric, Voice, and Community" (2010) 16(1) *Legal Writing: The Journal of the Legal Writing Institute* 521–564, 523.
77 *Ibid*, 538.
78 David Fraser, "The Day the Music Died: The Civil Law Tradition from a Critical Legal Studies Perspective" (1987) 32 *Loyola Law Review* 861–894, 869.
79 A useful text is Edward C Good, *Mightier Than the Sword: Powerful Writing, In Class – On the Job* (Blue Jeans Press, 1989). In what might perhaps be described as something of a 'back to basics' approach, Good emphasises the importance of technical (grammatical) rules as a means to writing powerful prose. See also Richard Andersen, *Powerful Writing Skills* (Barnes & Noble Books, 2001).

commentary suggests that a number of questions can usefully be asked by the legal writer of him or herself when writing a legal text (with a 'yes' answer to each suggesting that one's prose is likely to be more powerful):[80]

- Does the text address all it should?
- Are the issues to be determined identified clearly?
- Does the text resolve (or purport to resolve) all issues presenting?
- Have all relevant/irrelevant facts and law been included/excluded?
- Do all cases cited stand for the asserted propositions?
- Have all quotations been 'pruned back' as much as possible?
- Are foreign language/jargon/dated expressions excised as much as possible?
- Have explanations of the obvious been avoided?
- Are the conclusions clear and supported by law?
- Are factual elements of the text correctly stated?
- Has unnecessary repetition been eliminated?
- Does the text use the active voice where possible?
- Is the punctuation correct and an aid to clarity?
- Has the length/substance of each paragraph been checked?
- Have the cryptic, pompous, and humorous been avoided?
- Is the tone respectful?

More fundamentally, the critical elements of good composition include: *(i) a full mind; (ii) a clear perception of the … weight and value of each part of the subject, (iii) a clear understanding of the relations to each other of each part of the subject, (iv) the power of writing a clear … [and] rhythmical sentence.*[81]

8. Transcendent text

The ideal novel, Julian Hawthorne suggests, should yield an image of a "loftier reality".[82] A legal text typically proceeds by reference to the notion of a 'loftier' society in which law prevails and is as the legal writer states it to be.

Every legal text starts or should start with a transcending vision of what it seeks to achieve: the legal writer who starts with this sense of vision will know what he or she wants to state and will neither forget nor repeat things.[83]

---

80 See generally Max Barrett, *The Art and Craft of Judgment Writing* (Globe Law and Business, 2022), chapter 5, especially 98–99.
81 John Meiklejohn, *The Art of Writing English*, 5th edition (Meiklejohn & Holden, 1905), 17.
82 Julian Hawthorne, *Confessions and Criticisms* (Ticknor & Co, 1887), 37.
83 Gerald Lebovits "Legal-Writing Myths" (2018) 21(2) *Nebraska Lawyer* 39–42, 41.

A clear vision of what comprises good writing has been offered by successive commentators. These include the notions that legal writing should be "plain, active, direct, and verbal", using short sentences and comprehensible words, avoiding the theoretical/abstract (save when such avoidance proves impossible), aiming always for a lively, spontaneous, vigorous and conversational style of writing.[84]

When it comes to the structure of a legal argument, it is not some "transcendent essence"[85] that sits between the lines or beyond the substance of a legal text. The structure must be found, in the language itself. To proceed otherwise would be to understand the law for what it is not: a transcendent theory rather than a vehicle that is a mix of politics and power aimed at the resolution of human problems.[86]

There is another dimension to transcendence, which is the idea of "transcendent values"[87] in legal writing, namely that legal writers should embrace professionalism in their writing.[88] The jurisprudential basis for this notion appears to be the sense that lawyers act as mediators between what the moment demands and the law requires.[89] When it comes to legal writing it embraces the transcendent value of "guileless communication",[90] that is, expressing as clearly as one can what the legal writer wants his or her reader to believe, do, feel and understand.

9. Types of writer

Julian Hawthorne suggests that a novelist should have both an active (theorising) side and a passive (contemplative) side.[91] Bringing this observation into the legal writing context and transforming it into something more practical, it might be submitted that a legal writer should not only have an active side (selecting facts and evidence and then writing up his or her legal text) but should also have a contemplative side (thinking through what has been presented before her, where justice lies, and how that might best be achieved). The process

---

84   Richard Hyland, "A Defense of Legal Writing" (1986) 134(3) *University of Pennsylvania Law Review* 599–626, 602–603.
85   *Ibid*, 620.
86   Soma Kedia, "Redirecting the Scope of First-Year Writing Courses: Toward a New Paradigm of Teaching Legal Writing" (2010) 87(2) *University of Detroit Mercy Law Review* 147–178, 168.
87   Patrick Hugg, "Professional Legal Writing Declaring Your Independence" (1991) 11(2) *Journal of the National Association of Administration Law Judges* 114–143, 118.
88   *Ibid*.
89   William Simon, "Visions of Practice in Legal Thought" (1984) 36(1/2) *Stanford Law Review* 469–508, 469.
90   Joseph Williams, "On the Maturing of Legal Writers: Two Models of Growth and Development" (1991) 1 *Legal Writing: The Journal of the Legal Writing Institute* 1–34, 29.
91   Julian Hawthorne, *Confessions and Criticisms* (Ticknor & Co, 1887), 67.

whereby the critical facts are selected from a factual scenario has been depicted as a "critical aspect"[92] of the field of law that distinguishes it from ostensible sister sciences such as history and sociology. And any selection process will invariably be subjective to some extent.[93]

As to the contemplative side of legal writing, it has been suggested that the accepted manner of thinking about law (as propagated by law schools and the legal profession and in publicly available legal texts such as written judgments) has codified a particular mode of thought, leading ultimately to a waning of ability among lawyers to think beyond 'the way things are thought'.[94] Whether or not that is so, a number of points might be made about the contemplative process that precedes and/or accompanies legal writing:

- A question arises as to just how formulated a legal writer's thoughts are before he or she commits them to writing. As Justice Holmes noted in his judgment in *Chicago, Burlington & Quincy Railway Co v Babcock*:[95] "[M]any honest and sensible judgments … express an intuition of experience which outruns analysis and sums up … unnamed and tangled impressions … which may lie beneath consciousness."[96]

- On a related note a question arises as to the degree of contemplation that goes into legal thinking. Chief Justice Traynor of California, one of the great American judges, has suggested that legal writing is "thinking at its hardest"[97] which suggests that he at least saw the process of contemplation primarily to be done by, not before, committing words to paper.[98]

- In terms of the process of contemplation, it has been suggested that an advocate (and by extension a legal writer) engages in a process akin to that which Wordsworth once described as taking place in the poet's mind before he or she commits thoughts to

---

92   Hilary Charlesworth, "International Law: A Discipline of Crisis" (2002) 65(3) *Modern Law Review* 377–392, 383.
93   Patrick Hugg and Melanie McKay, "Classics Teach Legal Writing" (1985) 2(2) *Journal of Paralegal Education* 13–52, 52. The authors are writing of a different form of selection but the proposition seems to hold true in the above context also.
94   Douglas Litowitz, "Legal Writing: Its Nature, Limits, and Dangers" (1998) 49(3) *Mercer Law Review* 709–740, 728.
95   204 US 585 (1907).
96   *Ibid*, 598. The point was made in the context of the judgment/s involved in the assessment of taxes levelled on certain railroad corporations but seems of wider application, if not indeed born of Holmes's own experience.
97   Roger Traynor, "Some Open Questions on the Work of State Appellate Courts" (1957) 24(2) *University of Chicago Law Review* 211–224, 218. See also Douglas Abrams, "'But Will It Write' – How Writing Sharpens Decision-Making" (2009) 63(9) *Washington State Bar News* 23–27, 24–25.
98   *Ibid*.

writing, namely that what emerges is the product of "emotion recollected in tranquility".[99] (In a similar vein, Judge Voelker – who quit the Michigan Supreme Court in the early 1960s to write successful fiction under the pen name 'Robert Traver' – once observed that serious writing involves concentration, energy, and "finely balanced inner repose".)[100]

- Roark, in a greatly interesting account of the role of loneliness in the formulation of legal thought, suggests that the legal writer must in effect 'blank out' the distractions of the world around him or her in order properly to divine meaning in words[101] and then find a way to express the meaning so divined.[102]

- Literature plays its part in the contemplative process. While it has been suggested that law should disdain literature, the exposure of judges to literature nonetheless creeps into their judgments (and as it is with judges, so it is, I submit, with other legal writers). An example of the pervasive effect of literature on the legal mind is offered by the use of the phrase "deliberate speed" in *Brown v Board of Education*,[103] in which the US Supreme Court ordered (in slightly clunky prose) the doing of all that was "necessary and proper to admit to public schools on a racially non-discriminatory basis with all deliberate speed the parties to these cases".[104] The phrase "all deliberate speed" has been traced back from Chief Justice Warren to previous usage by Justice Frankfurter, to initial usage by Justice Holmes to "The Hound of Heaven" (a poem by Francis Thompson, a 19th/20th-century English poet), though Holmes was wont to claim that the phrase had an even earlier heritage in the English courts.[105]

As can be seen, just as Julian Hawthorne posits that there are active and passive sides to novel writing,[106] there are active and contemplative sides to legal writing, possessed at least of the characteristics considered above.

---

99   John Shepherd and Jordan Cherrick, "Advocacy and Emotion" (2006) 3 *Journal of the Association of Legal Writing Directors* 154–165, 158. For Wordsworth's observations, see his "Preface" to William Wordsworth, *Lyrical Ballads with Pastoral and Other Poems* (TN Longman & O Rees, 1802), vol 1, 1.
100 Quoted in Eileen Kavanagh, "Robert Traver as Justice Voelker – The Novelist as Judge" (2005–2006) 10 *Scribes Journal of Legal Writing* 91–128, 92.
101 Marc Roark, "Loneliness and the Law: Solitude, Action, and Power in Law and Literature" (2009) 55(1) *Loyola Law Review* 45–78, 58.
102 *Ibid*, 59.
103 349 US 294 (1955).
104 *Ibid*, 301.
105 Jim Chen, "Poetic Justice" (2006) 28 *Cardozo Law Review* 581–622.
106 Julian Hawthorne, *Confessions and Criticisms* (Ticknor & Co, 1887), 67.

10. Some common failures in writing

After criticising some fellow American authors, Julian Hawthorne writes that the books those authors had written did not amount to the 'great American novel' because they focused on the lesser to the detriment of the "loftier".[107] What are the common failings in legal writing that tend to yield a deficient text? Perhaps the most common failings discussed in the academic commentary on legal writing are, in no particular order, the following:

Failure to convey accurately what one means

Locke observes in his *Essay Concerning Human Understanding* (1689) that "The chief end of language in communication being to be understood, words serve now well for that end ... when any word does not excite in the hearer the same idea which it stands for in the mind of the speaker". Locke was writing of language generally, but his observation has perhaps an especial resonance when it comes to legal writing.

Excessive precision

Excessive precision can actually be the unwelcome end result of trying to write with maximum clarity.[108] One writer has written of a 'cult of precision' that pervades modern legal drafting yielding prose that can be all but impenetrable to the uninitiated.[109] The goal of the good legal writer, I submit, is not to engage in informal, relaxed and conversational prose, but rather to approach matters as though engaged in polite conversation.[110]

Lack of clarity

Clarity, with brevity and simplicity, comprises something of a 'triple crown' of legal writing.[111] As former Chief Justice McLachlin of Canada once observed, even in a Computer Age when the tools of communication have radically advanced, "clear, concise and organized

---

107   *Ibid*, 69.
108   Thomas Spahn, "The Art of Legal Writing" (1989) 9(2) *Journal of the National Association of Administrative Law Judges* 137–152, 152.
109   Matt Keating, "On the Cult of Precision Underpinning Legalese: A Reflection on the Goals of Legal Drafting" (2018–2019) 18 *Scribes Journal of Legal Writing* 91–122, 91.
110   Gerald Lebovits, "Dress for Success: Be Formal But Not Inflated" (2001) 73(6) *New York State Bar Association Journal* 8–9, 9.
111   Lord Bingham, "What Is the Law?" (2009) 40(3) *Victoria University of Wellington Law Review* 597–612, 609.

legal writing remains the foundation of good advocacy".[112] The reason why clarity is so encouraged is because it minimises the potential for misunderstanding and error.[113] Clarity of writing is thought mainly to proceed from clarity of thought.[114] Charrow, writing in this regard, has formulated 13 guidelines for writing clearly, many of which chime with the themes that pervade this book. They include: writing shorter sentences; avoiding the unnecessary; structuring sentences logically; avoiding complex conditionals; using the active voice; preferring verbs to nouns (eg, 'he admitted' rather than 'he made an admission'); using the positive form; avoiding noun-strings (eg, 'law-case'); avoiding ambiguities; excising verbiage; carefully choosing vocabulary; using parallel structure; and adopting an appropriate tone.[115]

Repetition

Repetition yields redundant words. However, to some extent, it is an understandable aspect of legal writing, for if one uses different words solely to avoid needless repetition one may find a later reader (such as a judge) deciding that the reason a different word was chosen was not merely to avoid repetition but because a different meaning was intended.[116] A distinction falls to be made between deliberate repetition for rhetorical effect (anaphora) and awkward (clumsy) repetition to ill effect. Whether anaphoric repetition is beneficial to legal writing is open to question, with one commentator observing that such repetition is mind-numbing.[117] However, clumsy repetition is invariably undesirable (and the difference between the clumsy and the anaphoric is not always easily discernible in practice).[118]

Prolixity/verbiage

Former Chief Justice McLachlin of Canada has observed that perhaps the worst sin of lawyers is their verbosity.[119] (A relatively recent survey of

---

112   Beverley McLachlin, "Legal Writing: Some Tools" (2001) 39(3) *Alberta Law Review* 695–702, 695.
113   M Floren, "Better Legal Writing" (1967) 13(4) *Student Lawyer Journal* 10–21, 10.
114   I Campbell, "Legal Writing" (1999) 30(2) *Victoria University of Wellington Law Review* 427–434, 434.
115   Veda Charrow, "Some Guidelines for Clear Legal Writing" (1987) 8(2) *Bridgeport Law Review* 405–408, 406.
116   Patrick Barry, "Rhetorical Repetition" (2020) 99(8) *Michigan Bar Journal* 38–41, 38.
117   Wayne Alley, "Effective Legal Writing: One Judge's Perspective" (2015) 86(5) *Oklahoma Bar Journal* 345–348, 345.
118   *Ibid*, 39.

American judges suggested that wordiness was their second 'peeve' when it came to written submissions.)[120] McLachlin suggests that the problem of verbosity is due in part to the use of arcane phraseology and redundant legal phrases.[121] It has also been suggested that wordiness in legal writing may be a cover for unclear thinking,[122] that is, that the writer by 'blathering on' may blind the reader to the fact that in truth not a lot is being said. Wordiness renders writing inferior by adding unnecessarily to the length of a legal text and "diluting analysis".[123] Common forms of prolixity include using words that add nothing, using words to re-state what has already been stated, using three or four words when one word is sufficient, and even a simple failure to use full stops often enough.[124] That said, the flip side of prolixity is that it is possible to be too brief – as one American commentator has observed, if brevity was an absolute virtue then ticker tape would be literature.[125]

Ambiguity

One commentator has referred to ambiguity as one of the "semi-literate sins".[126] The reason for avoiding ambiguity is to avoid misunderstandings arising.[127] By way of a related proposition, it has also long been contended that the same word should have the same meaning throughout the entirety of a legal text if ambiguity is to be avoided.[128] To the extent that ambiguity is said to conceal flaws in substance, this is contentious: it has been suggested that lawyers-as-readers are trained to pierce the linguistic veil[129] (though this does not address the impact of ambiguity on non-lawyers).

119 Beverley McLachlin, "Legal Writing: Some Tools" (2001) 39(3) *Alberta Law Review* 695–702, 697.
120 Their first 'peeve' was the filing of submissions immediately prior to hearings being held. See Chad Baruch, "Legal Writing: Lessons from the Bestseller List" (2009) 43(3) *Texas Journal of Business Law* 593–632, 630.
121 Beverley McLachlin, "Legal Writing: Some Tools" (2001) 39(3) *Alberta Law Review* 695–702, 698.
122 Jim Corkery, *Study of Law* (The Adelaide Law Review Association, 1988), 131.
123 Ginette Chapman, "Apt Phrasing in Legal Writing" (2021) 50(9) *Colorado Lawyer* 10–11, 11.
124 M Floren, "Better Legal Writing" (1967) 13(4) *Student Lawyer Journal* 10–21, 11.
125 G Nicholls, "Of Writing By Lawyers" (1949) 27(10) *Canadian Bar Review* 1209–1228, 1222.
126 C Peairs, "Frank E Cooper, *I Agree Perfectly With What You Say, But I Will Contest to the Death Your Right to Say It: A Review of Effective Legal Writing*" (1954) 34(3) *Boston University Law Review* 404–407, 406.
127 *Ibid*.
128 *Ibid*, 174–175.
129 Richard Dyson, *"Legal Writing Style* by Harry Weihofen" (1963) 11(4) *University of Kansas Law Review* 580–582, 581.

Problems with sentence structure

Clarity in legal writing is aided by simplicity of sentence structure.[130] Poor sentence structure flows from two particular defects: (i) the writer does not know what he or she is writing about, making it impossible to write coherently about it; and (ii) a too-shallow knowledge of the relevant material which has the consequence that the writer cannot restructure the key elements of that material into legal text that is readable and persuasive.[131] Once again, former Chief Justice McLachlin of Canada has been to the fore in addressing the issue of poor sentence structure among lawyers:

> [R]emember your sentence structure. Long sentences filled with subordinate clauses produce headaches, but little else. In their haste to qualify their statements with such clauses, too many lawyers bury the main idea. Sentences beginning with dependent clauses such as "although," "if" or "even if" will tire readers before they get to the main clause. Put dependent clauses at the end of the sentence, not the beginning. Make important points at the beginning or end of the sentence, not in the middle.[132]

Failure to appreciate who one is writing for

The modern concept of legal writing involves the notion that writing is centred on the reader, directed at a particular audience, and written in an unobtrusive style.[133] Lebovits suggests that (in practice) if the audience is a judge it is best to grab his or her attention quickly, writing concisely and to point, whereas if the audience is unknown one should assume that the readers are going to have generalised (non-specialised) knowledge.[134] Judge Posner suggests that it is a good mental discipline for judges to pretend that they are writing for a non-legal audience as it helps them to avoid the worst excesses of legal writing (professional jargon, tedious prose and an excess of quotes and footnotes and citations);[135] his observations also hold true of legal writing more generally. Ultimately, no matter what type of legal writing one is engaged in, a certain

---

130   Adina Radulescu, "The Pitfalls of Simplifying Legal Writing" (2012) 4(2) *Contemporary Readings in Law and Social Justice* 367–372, 370.
131   James Boland, "Legal Writing Programs and Professionalism" (2006) 18(3) *St Thomas Law Review* 711–736, 718.
132   Beverley McLachlin, "Legal Writing: Some Tools" (2001) 39(3) *Alberta Law Review* 695–702, 700.
133   Megan Boyd, "A Gidi and H Weihofen, *Legal Writing Style (3rd ed.)*" (2020) 19 *Scribes Journal of Legal Writing* 198–202, 198.
134   Gerald Lebovits, "Legal-Writing Myths" (2018) 21(2) *Nebraska Lawyer* 39–42, 39.
135   Richard Posner, "Legal Writing Today" (2001–2002) 8 *Scribes Journal of Legal Writing* 35–38, 38.

professionalism of tone is required[136] – though the problematic issue of the (exclusionary) 'professional legal voice' raises its head in this regard.

Poor research

The quality of research raises ethical and service issues for lawyers. When it comes to presenting material before a court, lawyers must present correct, up-to-date information.[137] And when presenting material to clients, lawyers must present up-to-date information that enables a client to make a properly informed decision on whatever it is that has prompted that client to seek legal advice.[138] The great challenge that presents for lawyers is internet research, with lawyers faced with the dilemma that ever more information is online (even though much of that information is unreliable and impermanent).[139] Even so, web-based research is now a necessity, not a luxury.[140] How then are standards to be maintained in terms of producing high-quality legal research using a medium that often offers poor-quality (unchecked) information? This last question seems especially important when private legal database subscriptions are often so expensive and free legal databases may have to be relied upon by smaller law firms who just cannot afford the expense of the private databases.

The University of Toronto is one of many universities whose library teams offer helpful online advice on all internet research that can also usefully be applied to online legal research.[141] It offers the following general guidelines:

- cross-check online information with physical resources (a critical guideline, I submit);
- narrow research scope before doing an online trawl;
- use more than one search engine; and
- record the sites visited and the relevant URLs.

It then proceeds to offer more technical advice as regards: (i) authority (eg, who is the author? what are his or her qualifications? is he or she known?); (ii) affiliation (eg, who owns the website? who is the author? – these may hint at bias); (iii) audience (eg, who is the website aimed at and

---

136 Katherine Mikkelson, "Better Legal Writing" (2018) 26(2) *GP Solo* 8–12 and 15, at 9.
137 Ellie Margolis, "Surfin' Safari – Why Competent Lawyers Should Research on the Web" (2007–2008) 10 *Yale Journal of Law & Technology* 82–119, 118.
138 *Ibid*, 119.
139 *Ibid*.
140 *Ibid*.
141 W Brock McDonald and June Steel, "Research Using the Internet", *Writing Advice*, https://advice. writing.utoronto.ca/researching/research-using-internet/.

is such a site a useful source of information?); (iv) topicality (eg, how topical is the information provided? is the site dated and kept up to date?); and (v) content reliability (this last category is so important that it is worth quoting the relevant guidance):

- *Is the material on the website reliable and accurate?*
- *Is the information factual, not opinion?*
- *Can you verify the information in print sources?*
- *Is the source of the information clearly stated ...?*
- *How valid is the research that is the source?*
- *Does the material as presented have substance and depth?*
- *[A]re given arguments ... based on strong evidence and good logic?*
- *Is the author's point of view impartial and objective?*
- *Is the author's language free of emotion and bias?*[142]
- *Is the site free of* [spelling/grammar] *errors and other ... carelessness in presentation?*
- *Are additional electronic and print sources provided to complement or support the material on the website?*

It is worth noting that these are only guidelines. Adherence to them means that information relied upon will *likely* be useful. However, blind adherence to the guidelines would be unwise, the key being to "think critically"[143] about material found on the Internet.

Readability

Readability is concerned with how difficult/easy it is to read a particular piece of prose. It determines choices as to sentence structure, paragraph length and word choice.[144] The consensus is that the more complex the subject matter, the simpler the prose needs to be if the writer is to stand the best chance of being understood.[145] Readability and style are considered to be interlinked, with readability being commensurate to adherence to a good style.[146] Today, the determination of readability is easier than ever before with readability statistics being built into word processing software such as Microsoft Word® and Word Perfect® and some free websites also offering readability statistics for shorter pieces of prose.

---

142   *Ibid.*
143   *Ibid.*
144   Veronica Finkelstein, "The Importance of Readability" (2021) 332 *New Jersey Lawyer* 10–11, 10.
145   M Floren, "Better Legal Writing" (1967) 13(4) *Student Lawyer Journal* 10–21, 10.
146   Jaro Mayda, "On Style and Form in Legal Writing" (1962) 31 *Revista Jurídica de la Universidad de Puerto Rico* 9–32, 15.

11. Legal texts as national literature

Julian Hawthorne observes that many people believe that national literature should comprise novels, poetry, essays and even statistical literature[147] – the last two categories embracing non-creative writing. By a 'national literature', what he seems to have in mind is literature devoted to local/domestic matters that is possessed of a certain magnificence. In the realm of non-fiction literature, great legal texts, such as great judgments, seem to be an example of such literature *par excellence.*

In the United States, the 'proprietary interest' that the public has in great judges and great judgments of a great democracy seems to be relatively openly acknowledged with, for example, US postage stamps issued to honour US Chief Justices:

- Charles Evans Hughes (a man of "Marshallian stature");[148]
- John Jay (America's first chief justice);
- John Marshall ("the American lawgiver"[149] – though also, to his lasting disgrace, the owner of hundreds of slaves);[150]
- Harlan F Stone (a man who made "vast contributions to multiple fields of law");[151]
- William Howard Taft (who also served as the 27th President of the United States);[152] and
- Earl Warren ("in the front rank of the American judicial pantheon");[153]

as well as Supreme Court Justices Hugo Black (a liberal as a judge, though, disturbingly, a Ku Klux Klan member in his youth),[154] Louis D Brandeis ("one of the Court's truly great Justices"),[155] William J Brennan, Jr ("no other hand contributed more to building a constitutional base for social

---

147   Julian Hawthorne, *Confessions and Criticisms* (Ticknor & Co, 1887), 72.
148   Paul Freund, "Charles Evans Hughes as Chief Justice" (1967) 81(1) *Harvard Law Review* 4–43, 4.
149   Bernard Schwartz, *Some Makers of American Law* (Ajoy Law House, 1985), 26.
150   The fact that Marshall owned large numbers of slaves has understandably caused considerable controversy at certain law schools named after him. (See Sloan, Karen, "Another law school mulls name change over slaveholding Supreme Court Justice", *Reuters*, 13 January 2022, www.reuters.com/legal/legalindustry/another-law-school-mulls-name-change-over-slaveholding-supreme-court-justice-2022-01-13/).
151   Eric Schepard, "Why Harlan Fiske Stone (Also) Matters" (2012) 56(1) *Howard Law Journal* 85–130, 93–94.
152   Stanley Kutler, "Chief Justice Taft and the Delusion of Judicial Exactness – A Study in Jurisprudence" (1962) 48(8) *Virginia Law Review* 1407–1426, 1407.
153   Louis Schwartz, "Justice, Expediency, and Beauty" (1987–1988) 136(1) *Pennsylvania Law Review* 141–182, 143.
154   J Mills Thornton, "Hugo Black and the Golden Age" (1985) 36(3) *Alabama Law Review* 899–914.
155   Edward Purcell, "The Judicial Legacy of Louis Brandeis and the Nature of American Constitutionalism" (2017) 33(1) *Touro Law Review* 5–50, 5.

change"),[156] Felix Frankfurter (a man expected to be a reforming liberal but who proved less radical than expected),[157] Oliver Wendell Holmes, Jr ("as much a part of American legend as law"),[158] Thurgood Marshall ("[he] ranks in the struggles for liberty and justice with the giants in Supreme Court history"),[159] and Joseph Story (a man of "strong convictions as to the role that law should play in a ... republican form of government").[160]

Surprisingly, Justice Cardozo ("among the outstanding American judges")[161] and Judge Learned Hand ("an exceptionally able judge")[162] have not yet been honoured by the US postal service.

In the United Kingdom, the lives and achievements of distinguished judges have never been commemorated by the Royal Mail, despite some British judges – such as Lord Denning – having been prominent figures of international standing in the common law world.

12. Writing engagingly

All writing, Julian Hawthorne suggests, perishes when it merely transcribes facts and is not "organised and vivified"[163] by some emotional or aesthetic influence. Likewise, a legal text becomes mundane and of limited interest unless vivified by a sense of truth and an appetite for justice. Legal writing that is viewed purely as a technical exercise tends to be neither memorable nor engaging for the reader and has been suggested to be indicative of a certain mediocrity on the part of the writer.[164]

One particular issue that presents for legal writers is that they are taught in law school to avoid excessive intrusion of the personal into one's legal writing, the emphasis being on writing analytically, logically and rationally.[165] However, if this excision of the emotional and the personal is taken to the extreme it can yield a "brittle, boring

---

156 Patricia Lucie, "Justice William Brennan Jr: 'Constitutional Visions Take Five Votes'" (1997) 12 *Denning Law Journal* 5–18, 5.
157 Richard Abrams, "The Reputation of Felix Frankfurter" (1985) 3 *American Bar Foundation Research Journal* 639–652, 639.
158 Bernard Schwartz, *Some Makers of American Law* (Ajoy Law House, 1985), 75.
159 Daniel Pollitt, "Thurgood Marshall" (1995) 21(2) *North Carolina Central Law Journal* 179–193, 179. Marshall also enjoys the historical distinction of having been the first African American appointed to the US Supreme Court.
160 Calvin Woodard, "Joseph Story and American Equity" (1988) 45(2) *Washington and Lee Law Review* 623–646, 627.
161 Michael Bernick, "Benjamin Cardozo: A Judge Most Eminent" (1979) 65(5) *American Bar Association Journal* 718–722, 718.
162 David Levy, "Learned Hand: The Man, The Judge: A Review Essay" (1994) 1 *Journal of Supreme Court History* 133–136, 136.
163 Julian Hawthorne, *Confessions and Criticisms* (Ticknor & Co, 1887), 117–118.
164 James Elkins, "What Kind of Story is Legal Writing?" (1996) 20(1) *Legal Studies Forum* 95–136, 118.
165 Andrea Curcio, "Addressing Barriers to Cultural Sensibility Learning: Lessons From Social Cognition Theory" (2015) 15(2) *Nevada Law Journal* 537–565, 537–538.

sensibility".[166] Additionally, it can yield text that evinces a perceived (and perhaps actual) want of empathy/sympathy; and it does not suffice for a legal text to be technically accurate – it needs also to reflect a degree of empathy/sympathy for a client and his or her predicament.[167]

An interesting question arises whether someone of an instinctively artistic predisposition can hope to become a good legal writer. To borrow from Jane Austen, if one is a person of sensibility does that preclude the pursuit of a legal career in which such a premium is placed by so many on sense? One American law professor has written of how he was asked a version of this question by a prospective law student who held a degree in English literature and gave the following insightful answer:

I told him that law and law practice were much like art and artistic practice. Just as an artist finds aesthetic order in the world that he perceives and expresses that order … understanding law and becoming a lawyer requires appreciating the received materials of the legal system and compiling those materials conceptually into a synthesis that appeals to the mind – much as a completed work of art appeals to the eye, the ear, [etc].[168]

As to the enlivenment (vivification) of text, what 'tricks of the trade' might be deployed by the legal writer who wishes to make his or her text more memorable or engaging? The following key points immediately spring to mind:

Be concise

Schiess offers a number of means of achieving greater concision, including avoiding the passive voice, using the possessive form, excising unnecessary detail, avoiding introductory phrases in sentences (eg, 'It should be noted that …'), avoiding nominalisations, that is, nouns used in place of verbs (eg, 'She called X' rather than 'She placed a call to X'), combining and shortening sentences, using shorter/simpler words and employing fewer prepositions.[169] Shortening sentences is an especially useful means of attaining concision, improving clarity and aiding the dynamism of one's writing.[170] In his "Essay on Language", the 18th/19th-

---

166   Frank Pommersheim, "Voice, Values, and Community: Some Reflections on Legal Writing" (1988) 12(4) *Legal Studies Forum* 477–488, 482.
167   Andrea McArdle, "Teaching Writing in Clinical, Lawyering, and Legal Writing Courses: Negotiating Professional and Personal Voice" (2006) 12 *Clinical Law Review* 501–540, 520.
168   Michael Madison, "Writing to Learn Law and Writing in Law: An Intellectual Property Illustration" (2008) 52(3) *St Louis University Law Journal* 823–842, 840.
169   Wayne Schiess, "Editing for Concision" (2017) 20(4) *Nebraska Lawyer* 51–54.
170   Greg Johnson, "Justice Beth Robinson: A Paragon of Good Legal Writing" (2019) 45(4) *Vermont Bar Journal* 24–29, 25.

century English philosopher, Jeremy Bentham, makes various observations as regards concision in language, among which are the following:

- concision saves time spent creating/reading;[171]
- concision contributes to clearness;[172]
- absence of concision contributes to obscurity;[173]
- concision often contributes to impressiveness;[174]
- concision aids in understanding; and[175]
- concision facilitates in retention of knowledge.[176]

Be clear

Justice Cardozo has asserted that "[I]n matters of literary style the sovereign virtue for the judge [and for all legal writers] is clearness". As long ago as the 4th century BCE, Aristotle too was lauding clarity and suggesting that it is best secured by using words that are current and ordinary.[177] In the pursuit of clarity, it is important not to slip into the pitfall of prolixity that aims at clarity but yields confusion. Such efforts at 'perfect perspicuity' have in any event been posited to aim at the impossible,[178] not least because words may have more than one meaning (at least when used in different contexts) and may be understood differently by different readers.[179] One particular impediment to clarity in writing is the excessive use of professional jargon; this may be to some extent inevitable in lawyer-to-lawyer texts but seems best avoided when non-lawyers are among the intended audience.[180] Bentham makes various observations regarding clearness in language, among which are the following:

- to write clearly is to write free from ambiguity and obscurity;[181]

---

171   Jeremy Bentham, "Essay on Language" in Jeremy Bentham, *The Works of Jeremy Bentham*, John Bowring (ed) (William Tait, 1843), vol 8, 290–338, 305.
172   *Ibid.*
173   *Ibid.*
174   *Ibid.*
175   *Ibid.*
176   *Ibid.*
177   Quoted in Stephen Smith, "The Poetry of Persuasion: Early Literary Theory and Its Advice to Legal Writers" (2009) 6(1) *Journal of the Association of Legal Writing Directors* 55–74, 69.
178   Nelson Miller, "Why Prolixity Does Not Produce Clarity: Francis Lieber on Plain Language" (2007) 11 *Scribes Journal of Legal Writing* 107–114, 108.
179   *Ibid*, 110.
180   Mark Mathewson, "Law Students, Beware" (2001–2002) 8 *Scribes Journal of Legal Writing* 141–158, 149.
181   Jeremy Bentham, "Essay on Language" in Jeremy Bentham, *The Works of Jeremy Bentham*, John Bowring (ed) (William Tait, 1843), vol 8, 290–338, 304.

- ambiguity arises where distinguishable positions can be identified in a text, and one cannot determine which applies;[182]
- obscurity arises where no determinate meaning can be settled upon in a text[183] – it can be regarded as the highest level of ambiguity; and[184]
- the greater the number of words, the less clear a text will be.[185]

Be coherent

At its simplest, coherence requires that the conclusion in a legal text should flow from what has been stated before.[186] The task of the legal writer is to offer all the "links of the logical chain"[187] so that what it is sought to convey is coherent, as well as clear.[188] In a legal submission, this process inevitably involves separating the 'wheat' of facts and law from all the 'chaff' that presents in a case and bringing the winnowed material together in a coherent whole.[189] (Excising weaker legal arguments is necessary if the legal writer is to avoid a "mishmash"[190] of legal theory.) In transaction documentation, coherency is necessary if the contemplated contractual arrangements are to work.[191] One contributory factor when it comes to incoherency is unwarranted digression – whereas some level of digression can make for an easier read,[192] digression often yields a 'breeziness' of writing that suggests a want of self-control on the writer's part.[193]

Favour the active voice

The passive voice has a place "but that place is small".[194] An example of the active/passive voice is 'Mr X hit the victim' (active) versus 'The victim

---

182 *Ibid*.
183 *Ibid*.
184 *Ibid*, 305.
185 *Ibid*.
186 Susan Taylor, "Students as (Re)Visionaries: or Revision, Revision, Revision" (2005) 21(2) *Touro Law Review* 265–296, 269.
187 Richard Hyland, "A Defense of Legal Writing" (1986) 134(3) *University of Pennsylvania Law Review* 599–626, 620.
188 Susan Taylor, "Students as (Re)Visionaries: or Revision, Revision, Revision" (2005) 21(2) *Touro Law Review* 265–296, 269.
189 James McElhaney, "Legal Writing that Works" (2007) 93(7) *ABA Journal* 30–31.
190 *Ibid*, 30.
191 Susan Taylor, "Students as (Re)Visionaries: or Revision, Revision, Revision" (2005) 21(2) *Touro Law Review* 265–296, 269.
192 William Wilson, "How I Write" (1993) 4 *Scribes Journal of Legal Writing* 79–81, 81.
193 Gerald Lebovits, "Free at Last from Clarity (continued)" (2003) 75(9) *New York State Bar Association Journal* 60–62, 60.
194 Jim Corkery, *Study of Law* (The Adelaide Law Review Association, 1988), 181.

was hit by Mr X' (passive). The passive voice is considered typically to weaken prose, diminish the sense of motion, evince uncertainty, conceal the actor (yielding ambiguity as to who or what is the actor of the sentence) and lengthen a text.[195] Landau suggests that fundamentally the passive voice is both boring and uneconomical in terms of word length.[196] That said, there may be instances when the passive voice is more appropriate, for example, to deflect culpability:[197] 'Some errors were made by our client' seems somehow less blameworthy than 'Our client made some errors'.[198] Ultimately, whether or not to use the passive voice comes down in any one instance to a question of style, namely whether the sentence flows more smoothly without/with the passive voice.[199]

Remember the reader

The injunction to remember the reader has been described as the most important feature of the process of communication,[200] with vagueness and ambiguity to be eschewed and accuracy, brevity, style and clarity all to be striven for. Littler, in an article on 'reader rights', put matters succinctly but well when he observed:

> *The only object of writing is to produce a pre-determined effect upon the reader … If the reader does not understand, the writing is ineffective. If the reader does not understand easily, the writing is inefficient … The reader, like the customer, is always right.*[201]

Most legal writers, it has been suggested, start out with writing that interests the writer,[202] when the true 'aim of the (legal writing) game' is writing that engages and informs the reader in a manner and style that he or she can readily comprehend.[203] To some extent, one must begin with reader-centred writing in that the writer has to reduce into words what he or she is thinking. However, when the writer rewrites what he or she has to say that is the time to become focused on what the reader

---

195   Mark Cohen, "When to Use Passive Voice" (2019) 48(6) *Colorado Lawyer* 8–9.

196   Jack Landau, "Editing Legal Writing" (1982) 28(2) *Practical Lawyer* 83–88, 86.

197   Katherine Mikkelson, "Better Legal Writing" (2018) 26(2) *GP Solo* 8–12, 11.

198   *Ibid*, 12.

199   K du Vivier, "Problems with the Passive Voice" (1995) 24(3) *Colorado Lawyer* 545–546, 545. For seven instances in which the passive voice is likely preferable, see C Good, "Abolish the Passive Voice? I Don't Think So" (2016) 8(6) *Landslide* 43–48, 46–47.

200   David Sorkin, "Meaning What You Say and Saying What You Mean" (1992) 80(10) *Illinois Bar Journal* 527–528, 528.

201   Robert Littler, "Reader Rights in Legal Writing" (1950) 25(1) *Journal of the State Bar of California* 51–67, 52–53.

202   Karin Ciano, "Legal Writing Notebook: Reader-Centered Writing for Millennials" (2019) 22(5) *Nebraska Lawyer* 68–69, 68.

203   *Ibid*.

needs to know.[204] As the world moves to ever-greater amounts of legal work being done online, an understanding of the particular needs of the online reader seems especially merited. The online experience involves a "new literacy".[205] To take but two examples:

- hypertexts/links create a new environment in which the reader can move in and out of a particular legal text (yielding complications as to the order in which material is read – it may be read in a quite disordered manner);[206] and

- the multimedia potential of electronic communications likewise yields new complications in terms of writer presentation.[207]

Yet for all that the world is changing, much remains the same, not least of which is that it is an error mindlessly to produce documents without regard to who will read them. In this regard, it is perhaps useful for the legal writer always to imagine a dual audience for his or her legal texts, being the person/s to whom that text is primarily addressed and also a second, further audience (such as judges) who may come to read the text in the future.[208] Having this dual audience in mind should aid, I submit, in terms of enhancing the focus, vigour and rigour of one's legal writing.[209]

13. Condescension and children

Writing of children as critics, Julian Hawthorne observes, amongst other matters, that there is a sense that one needs to speak down to children whereas in truth they are forceful literary critics who judge absolutely even if they cannot always fully rationalise their opinions.[210] In this he anticipated the one-time observation of CS Lewis (author of *The Chronicles of Narnia*) on the proper meeting of adult and child as independent personalities:

> *Once, Lewis wrote, in a hotel dining-room I said rather too loudly, "I loathe prunes." "So do I," came an unexpected six-year-old voice from another table. Sympathy was instantaneous. Neither of us thought it funny. We both*

---

204 Angela Campbell, "Teaching Advanced Legal Writing in a Law School Clinic" (1993) 24(2) *Seton Hall Law Review* 653–694, 685.

205 Maria Perez Crist, "The E-Brief: Legal Writing for an Online World" (2003) 33(1) *New Mexico Law Review* 49–94, 77. See also Susie Salmon, "Legal Writing for a Digital Audience (Part I)" (2021) 58(2) *Arizona Attorney* 8–9.

206 *Ibid*, 70.

207 *Ibid*, 77.

208 Wayne Schiess, "The Five Principles of Legal Writing" (2003) 49(3) *Practical Lawyer* 11–20, 13.

209 *Ibid*.

210 Julian Hawthorne, *Confessions and Criticisms* (Ticknor & Co, 1887), 126.

knew that prunes are far too nasty to be funny. That is the proper meeting between man and child as independent personalities.[211]

When it comes to the challenging but rewarding task of writing judgments in child and family law cases that are respectful of the parties to such cases while also acknowledging their particular needs and demands as an audience, the reader is referred to the Appendix to this book which contains relevant extracts from a paper on this subject that was prepared by me for delivery to a colloquium of judges in July 2022.

As to condescension (an attitude of superiority) in legal texts, this, I submit, springs ultimately from a lack of civility,[212] and also an absence of that humility which leads one to recognise personal limitations, value the insights and views of others and aim at continuous self-improvement throughout life.[213]

Kanemoto, in an insightful article, has contended for the importation into courtroom relations between lawyers of the conceptual framework offered by the historical Japanese *bushido* code – which valued politeness, honour, humility, integrity and courage (all recognisable professional values). Treating with condescension in the context of humility, she writes:

Even the slightest air of condescension can appear offensive ... Humility, however, involves much more than the avoidance of a superior attitude ... Humility ... unites the concept of honesty with an attitude of openness and flexibility.[214]

The process of writing requires a certain humility, not just because what one initially seeks to write may be wrong,[215] or because there may be a better way of expressing oneself,[216] but also owing to the possibility that one may simply be wrong in some or all respects of what one contends for or states. Due humility (as opposed to excessive humility) – the very opposite of that sense of superiority which is a necessary predicate for condescension – has even been described as a cornerstone of

---

211   CS Lewis, "On Three Ways of Writing for Children" in CS Lewis, *Of Other Worlds*, W Hooper (ed) (Harcourt, Brace & Jovanovich, 1966), 22–34, 34.

212   On the decline of civility among contemporary (American) lawyers, see, eg, Sophie Sparrow, "Practicing Civility in the Legal Writing Course" (2007) 13 *Legal Writing: The Journal of the Legal Writing Institute* 113–158.

213   On due humility as a professional value (in judges, though many of the observations can be brought to bear in the context of legal writing more generally), see Brett Scharffs, "The Role of Humility in Exercising Practical Wisdom" (1998) 32(1) *UC Davis Law Review* 127–200, 164.

214   Chenise Kanemoto, *"Bushido* in the Courtroom: A Case for Virtue-Oriented Lawyering" (2005) 57(2) *South Carolina Law Review* 357–386, 373.

215   Kenneth Ripple, "Legal Writing in the New Millennium" (1999) 74(3) *Notre Dame Law Review* 925–932, 929.

216   *Ibid.*

legal reasoning.[217] At root, legal writing and speaking should be like good manners: natural and direct (not condescending, obsequious or stiff).[218]

14. What makes a good writer?

Julian Hawthorne writes that it is the poem that begets the poet (not vice versa).[219] By this, he appears to mean that one cannot claim to be a poet until one has written a poem. Presumably, Julian Hawthorne would also contend that it is the task of legal writing that, to some extent, makes a legal writer or – to put matters otherwise – if practice will not make someone a perfect legal writer (perfection is unattainable), legal writing is a skill that certainly benefits from practice. In real life, this practice often manifests in the form of 'rewrites', with the first draft of a legal text being something of a 'dry run' in what the legal writer wants to say and how he or she might manage to say it, with 'perfection' – or as good as one can get a piece of prose – coming in the rewrites, with most legal writers taking more time on rewrites than on the original drafts of their work.[220]

Julian Hawthorne also suggests that it is events (crises and opportunities) that make great people.[221] Events are the predicate for professional legal writing – professional legal texts are produced for a reason (and for a fee). But are great events a necessary predicate for great writing or is it the case that, to borrow from Everett, "Large streams from little fountains flow/Tall oaks from little acorns grow"?[222] It seems to be a characteristic of great writers that they can produce great text even in unexpected situations. If, for example, one takes three great legal phrases penned by Oliver Wendell Holmes, Jr, it is interesting that the events in play in the cases in which those phrases appeared are not always 'great events'. However, aided by natural genius and more than a little hard work, Holmes often espies the kernel of greatness in what is presented before him and polishes it into one or more eye-catching legal insights expressed in the most eloquent of prose. So, for example, in:

- *Lochner v New York*,[223] the issue before the Supreme Court was whether New York law restricting the working hours of bakers

---

217 Gregory Johnson, "Credibility in Advocacy: Humility as the First Step" 39(3) (2013) *Vermont Bar Journal* 22–24, 22.
218 George Gibson, "Effective Legal Writing and Speaking" (1980) 36(1) *Business Lawyer* 1–10, 9.
219 Julian Hawthorne, *Confessions and Criticisms* (Ticknor & Co, 1887), 187.
220 Susan Taylor, "Students as (Re)Visionaries: or Revision, Revision, Revision" (2005) 21(2) *Touro Law Review* 265–296, 265.
221 Julian Hawthorne, *Confessions and Criticisms* (Ticknor & Co, 1887), 137.
222 David Everett, "Lines Spoken By a Boy of Seven Years" in Henry Coates, *The Children's Book of Poetry* (Henry Coates & Co, 1879), 38.
223 198 US 45 (1905).

interfered with the freedom of contract arising under the 14th Amendment. The case had simple origins: Lochner was a New York bakery owner who was prosecuted for breaches of the working hours legislation. The Supreme Court held (5–4) that New York's laws unconstitutionally interfered with individual freedom of contract. Holmes dissented with the following (stirring) words:

> This case is decided upon an economic theory which a large part of the country does not entertain. [A] constitution is not intended to embody a particular economic theory ... General propositions do not decide concrete cases ... I think that the word liberty in the Fourteenth Amendment is perverted when it is held to prevent the natural outcome of a dominant opinion.[224]

- *Towne v Eisner*,[225] the almost dreary focus of the case was whether a stock dividend based on accumulated profits was "income" within the meaning of the Income Tax Law 1913. (It was held not to be.) In his opinion for the court, Holmes observed as follows:

> The government argues that, if such a stock dividend is not income within the meaning of the Constitution, it is not income within the intent of the statute. But it is not necessarily true that income means the same thing in the Constitution and the Act. A word is not a crystal, transparent and unchanged, it is the skin of a living thought, and may vary greatly in color and content according to the circumstances and the time in which it is used.[226]

Though Holmes's observation is beautiful in itself and a statement of what seems but a truism, it also offers an insight into the mind of Holmes, a man for whom "[w]ords ... were vehicles for policy, but their meaning was not fixed".[227]

- *Schenck v United States*,[228] the case arose from the distribution of Socialist Party pamphlets urging potential wartime draftees to resist the draft. As a result of distributing the pamphlets, Schenck and another party member were convicted of offences under the Espionage Act 1917. In his opinion for a unanimous Supreme Court (though he later departed from how *Schenck* came to be applied),[229] Holmes observed as follows:

224　*Ibid*, 75–76.
225　245 US 418 (1918).
226　*Ibid*, 425.
227　Alan Mendenhall, "Dissent as a Site of Aesthetic Adaptation in the Work of Oliver Wendell Holmes" (2012) 1(2) *British Journal of American Legal Studies* 517–550, 524.
228　249 US 47 (1919).
229　See *Abrams v United States* 250 US 616 (1919).

Words which, ordinarily and in many places, would be within the freedom of speech protected by the First Amendment may become subject to prohibition when of such a nature and used in such circumstances as to create a clear and present danger that they will bring about the substantive evils which Congress has a right to prevent. The character of every act depends upon the circumstances in which it is done.[230]

Holmes's words are plain but powerful. The phrase "clear and present danger" (no longer the dominant standard in American free speech cases) has taken deep root in the English language, "used over and over by judges and the public".[231] It was even used as the title of a late-1980s Tom Clancy thriller novel (itself later turned into a movie starring Harrison Ford).

Key propositions

- A legal text should adhere to the ordinary and probable.
- It is open to the legal writer as an author to lighten/darken text and tone in such manner as he or she considers appropriate, though proceeding with moderation.
- It is preferable that a legal text proceeds through understatement and action rather than moralising about truth.
- As a rule, truths need only be stated once – they do not become truer through being repeated.
- One cannot have form without ideas. Ideas create form; when it comes to legal writing one needs to bring ideas and then form will follow.
- A good legal writer will have a nascent style which can be improved – legal writers whose writing styles straddle the heights of genius are uncommon.
- A legal writer must bring a central idea to his or her legal text both as to the outcome and as to what he or she means to say.
- A legal writer will be better equipped to write a legal text if he or she has a central theme.
- With work, it is possible to convert idea and theme into a plausible legal text.

---

230   *Ibid*, 48.
231   Karl Lyon, "The Clear and Present Danger Doctrine" (1949) 1(1) *Hastings Law Journal* 50–65, 50.

- It is important not to get sidetracked into needless detail/digression, placing undue emphasis on the unimportant.
- Although a legal text is an exercise in reason it follows imagination and involves artistry.
- It is typically legal writers who show an imaginative understanding of the law that advance legal knowledge.
- Good legal texts have the power to touch the reader and to provide (or seek to provide) an answer to whatever questions arise.
- A legal text proceeds by reference to a loftier reality in which law reigns supreme.
- Behind the facts/law at play in a case is potentially enlightening factual/legal truth.
- A question arises whether a preference among legal writers for a certain constancy in form has generated a resistance to trying out alternative forms of legal text.
- To the extent that legal writers show reserve, it may be attributable to a sense that the writer is dealing with a great subject.
- A legal writer's reserve runs the risk of rendering a legal text colourless.
- A legal writer should have an active side (selecting facts and evidence and then writing up his or her text) and a contemplative side (thinking through what has been presented to him or her).
- As a legal writer, it is possible to be presented with the opportunity to write a great legal text but to fall short of writing the calibre of text that might otherwise have been written.
- Wisdom in legal texts comes from the pondering and application to life of certain legal truths. Those truths are of great moment and not always complex.
- A legal text such as a judgment seeks to instil a general comprehension of law.
- A legal text becomes mundane and of limited interest unless vivified by a sense of truth and an appetite for justice.
- When writing a legal text it is important to avoid condescension. This may not change the substance of one's legal texts – it may improve their style.
- Legal texts are not intended as vehicles for moralising – to the extent that a legal writer engages in moralising, he or she is likely to be seen not to be presenting some objective morality but his or her own morality.

10. Hazlitt

On pedantry, insight, jargon and other matters

William Hazlitt (1788–1830), "without question one of the greatest writers of prose in the English language",[1] was something of a (belated) 'Renaissance man', being a notably talented critic, essayist, journalist and polemicist. However, in the 21st century, he has declined into some level of obscurity, possibly because "his attitudes have so much become part of the intellectual vocabulary of our own opinions that we no longer see how fine his insights are".[2] In this chapter, Hazlitt's linked essays, "On Pedantry" and "The Same Subject Continued", both drawn from his work, *The Round Table* (1817)[3] – a collection of essays on literature and other matters – are considered and their teachings brought to bear in the context of legal writing.

## 1.	Pedantry

Hazlitt suggests that the characteristic of finding a trifling or painful activity to be interesting is a facet of the human condition. He even suggests that the man who is not a pedant cannot be happy[4] (for he will find the trifling and painful to be trifling and painful). It follows (unexpectedly) that pedantry is not necessarily a vice when found in the legal writer. In fact, given that much legal writing is focused on the painful (and some perhaps on the trifling), a degree of pedanticism is a boon if found in the legal writer. And there are other attributes, such as:[5]

- pedantic focus on a particular specialisation can yield useful expert knowledge of that area;
- enthusiasm for a profession involves an almost pedantic devotion to it;[6]

1	AC Grayling, *The Quarrel of the Age: The Life and Times of William Hazlitt* (Weidenfeld & Nicholson, 2000), ix.
2	*Ibid*, 349.
3	William Hazlitt, *The Round Table* (Longman, Hurst, Rees, Orme & Browne, 1817), vol 2, 27–45.
4	*Ibid*, 28.
5	William Mathews, *"A Plea for Pedants"* (1890) 151(405) *The North American Review* 255–256.
6	*Ibid*, 256.

- people who make their mark on the world tend not to be varied and versatile but to have "some giant faculty developed at the expense of the rest";[7]
- the day of "universal scholars"[8] is gone; pedantry has taken its place;[9]
- pedantry is a natural consequence of a complete love for one's favoured pursuit; and[10]
- only a fool does not rise to some level of pedantry (and fools do not readily become lawyers).

Transplanting these observations on pedantry into the specific context of legal writing, perhaps the following might be posited:

- pedantic focus by a legal writer can yield improvements in his or her writing;
- enthusiasm for one's career in law demands an almost pedantic devotion to legal writing;
- legal writers who make their mark tend to have highly developed writing skills;
- the skill of legal writing should be treated like a (necessary) skill in the legal writer's quiver of skills;
- pedantic devotion to legal writing is the natural result of complete love for the profession of lawyer; and
- only a foolish lawyer would not seek to rise to some level of pedantry in terms of his or her dedication to acquiring ever-finer legal writing skills.

2.   Reading other texts

The chief merit in reading old novels, Hazlitt suggests, is the picture they offer of the various characters and their personalities, their importance to themselves and their self-perceived superiority over the other characters.[11] Something similar presents in legal judgments, as nowadays collated in an abundance of law reports, with the reader being offered (through those reports) a unique and oftentimes intriguing insight into real people and events through the prism of their legal disputes.

Ironically, given the plethora of cases from every major common law

---

7   *Ibid*, 255.
8   *Ibid*.
9   *Ibid*, 256.
10   *Ibid*.
11   William Hazlitt, *The Round Table* (Longman, Hurst, Rees, Orme & Browne, 1817), vol 2, 28.

jurisdiction now readily searchable and available online, as early as the golden anniversary of the publication of the Law Reports in 1915, one Lord Justice of Appeal was heard to complain that the multitude of reports *then* available made the work of judges "infinitely difficult and laborious".[12] One hesitates to think what he would make of the Internet Age – though the exponential increase of case material online does mean that law reporters as creators, editors and headnote writers are now, perhaps more than ever, of critical importance, with their ability to separate the legal wheat (significant case law) from an abundance of chaff and to bring order to bear on the material so harvested.[13]

What the long-term abundance of case reports also means is that it is possible to enter any good English language law library (physically or online) and read cases that are reported in a recognisable form and which date back to the early 13th century. Perhaps because they have "a very practical character"[14] these varied case reports have never appealed to the general public as reading material. Yet if, as Hazlitt suggests, the chief merit in reading old novels is the picture they offer of the various characters and their personalities, a notable merit of old law reports, even those that no longer continue to be of legal significance, are the remarkable insights that they offer into the lawbreaking and litigation of our forebears:

> [A]s a matter of fact, the law reports are a mine of romance. In these musty and dusty volumes lies great wealth of legend and tradition. They faithfully and graphically record all the changes and chances of this mortal life, and probably in no literature are the permutations and combinations of existence more thoroughly worked out. The heights and depths of human vice and folly are here wonderfully illustrated. We have only to turn to a single shelf of law reports to find tersely and graphically recorded the outline of countless tragedies and comedies, which no effort of the imagination could equal, and which prove over and over again the veracity of the old adage that "truth is stranger than fiction". Could we invest with life these puppets of the past, who have played their parts in the melodrama of life, and have left behind them these brief records of their happiness and misery, their frailties and foibles, we should have no need to justify ourselves for speaking of the "Romance of the Law Reports".[15]

12   Josiah Oddy, "The Jubilee of the Law Reports" (1915) 15(1) *Journal of the Society of Comparative Legislation* 208–218, 211.
13   Roderick Munday, "Official Law Reports, Natural Citation and Other Curiosities: Another Visit to the Grand Canon" (2001) 165(18) *Justice of the Peace* 342–345, 345.
14   Thomas Dent, "Of Law Reports as Memorials of History and Biography" (1905) 39(5) *American Law Review* 675–695, 676.
15   Anon., "The Romance of the Law Reports" (1889) 7(1) *Green Bag* 275–278, 275–276.

3.   Jargon

Hazlitt notes that professional jargon is a common butt of ridicule.[16] However, he accepts that it is a natural occurrence,[17] even suggesting that it is a bad sign if a person's profession cannot be discerned from his (or her) conversation.[18] Thus, he writes, "A lawyer, who talks about law, *certioraris, nolle prosequis*, and silk gowns, though he may be a blockhead, is by no means dangerous".[19]

What lessons might be drawn from Hazlitt's observations when it comes to legal writing? First, although it may be the subject of public mockery, there is a natural professional jargon that goes with being a legal writer. Secondly, some professional language is to be expected in a legal text. And finally, even when a legal writer comes spouting legalisms galore that is not necessarily bad (though it might be something for that writer to work on in order to improve comprehensibility).

Godbold cautions against being the lawyer who can give directions if asked for them in the street, but who (when he or she puts pen to paper) engages in the "non-communicative patois" of the legal profession.[20] Rodell identifies various problems with law review prose (though he might just as well be writing of legal writing generally), as well as various possible solutions to these problems that would likely curtail reliance on jargon if deployed.[21] Those solutions might be summarised as follows:

Do not surrender content to style[22]

As Rodell puts it, a good way to "palm off"[23] the inferior is to make it look respectable.[24] However, although the effectiveness of legal communication is all-important, the effectiveness of the legal writer's communication invariably comes second to its content.[25]

---

16   William Hazlitt, *The Round Table* (Longman, Hurst, Rees, Orme & Browne, 1817), vol 2, 29.
17   *Ibid*.
18   *Ibid*, 30.
19   *Ibid*.
20   John Godbold, "Twenty Pages and Twenty Minutes – Effective Advocacy on Appeal" (1976) 30(5) *Southwestern Law Journal* 801–820, 814.
21   Fred Rodell, "Goodbye to Law Reviews" (1936–1937) 23(1) *Virginia Law Review* 38–45, 38.
22   *Ibid*, 38.
23   *Ibid*, 42.
24   *Ibid*.
25   Jaro Mayda, "On Style and Form in Legal Writing" (1962) 31 *Revista Jurídica de la Universidad de Puerto Rico* 9–32, 9.

Do not let clarity yield to dignity[26]

There was a time when a certain pomposity in writing style was (it seems) considered to lend a certain dignity to the legal profession; nowadays that same pomposity is generally considered to be an irritant.[27] As Lord Bingham has observed (of judgment writing, but his observations have a wider resonance) nowadays the ideal judgment is seen to be clear (and brief and simple).[28]

Do not let the "straitjacket of style"[29] constrain what
can be lively literature

If it is not possible to make a piece of legal text exciting then one should at least seek to avoid repeating within it that which is boring.[30] The phrase 'It would seem …' is best avoided.[31] As Levitan observes of this phrase in a notable article entitled "Some Words That Don't Belong in Briefs": "[J]ust what does 'it would seem' mean? Does it mean that the law wishes to appear that way, or persists in so appearing, or that it might do so in the future?"[32] The answer is not clear.

Ignore the taboo surrounding first person pronouns[33]

When I started as a judge I was told never to refer to myself in the first person because no one cares what the judge, as a person, has to say, they care what his or her court has to say. With the benefit of experience, I am not sure that this was great advice, albeit that it was well-intentioned. Probably closer to the truth is that, even for judges if the audience/occasion are suitable (and, eg, a child or family law judgment seems a good example of a case where such suitability presents), one can use first person pronouns without an associated loss of dignity or gravitas and can instead manifest a desirably "warm persona".[34]

---

26   Fred Rodell, "Goodbye to Law Reviews" (1936–1937) 23(1) *Virginia Law Review* 38–45, 39.
27   Robert Littler, "Legal Writing in Law Practice" (1956) 31(1) *Journal of the State Bar of California* 28–36, 32.
28   Lord Bingham, "What Is the Law?" (2009) 40(3) *Victoria University of Wellington Law Review* 597–612, 609.
29   Fred Rodell, "Goodbye to Law Reviews" (1936–1937) 23(1) *Virginia Law Review* 38–45, 41.
30   Robert Fugate, "Redundancy and Wordiness in Legal Writing" (2009–2010) 22(3) *Appellate Advocate* 242–246, 243.
31   Fred Rodell, "Goodbye to Law Reviews" (1936–1937) 23(1) *Virginia Law Review* 38–45, 39.
32   Mortimer Levitan, "Some Words That Don't Belong in Briefs" (1960) 3 *Wisconsin Law Review* 421–429, 425.
33   Fred Rodell, "Goodbye to Law Reviews" (1936–1937) 23(1) *Virginia Law Review* 38–45, 39.
34   Lillian Hardwick, "Classical Persuasion through Grammar and Punctuation" (2006) 3 *Journal of the Association of Legal Writing Directors* 75–107, 103.

> *To be avoided are long sentences, awkwardness and*
> *"fuzzy-wuzzy words"*[35]

In other words, good grammar and vocabulary are always desirable. Legal writing, it has been suggested, should not be perceived as "alien literature"[36] but should proceed like the best of fiction,[37] so with good grammar, good vocabulary and (when written in the English language) good English.[38]

> *Circumlocution (using many words where less would do)*
> *should be avoided*[39]

One commentator has written in this regard of the "verbiage vortex"[40] in which lawyers descend to contrived text that impairs communication and obscures the intended message, sending the implicit message[41] that the reader should not bother wrestling to understand it.

> *Avoid "bombastic pomposity"*[42]

As mentioned, some level of professional jargon seems an attribute of any legal system.[43] Even so, the inspiring and the wise, the memorable and the eternal often come vested in the simplest language.[44]

> *Be conscious that footnotes generate poor thinking/writing*[45]

Footnotes carry the risk of becoming a "sea of verbiage"[46] in which a reader may sink or swim, offering text that distracts the reader from the main body of the text and offers prose that is difficult to read.[47]

---

35   Fred Rodell, "Goodbye to Law Reviews" (1936–1937) 23(1) *Virginia Law Review* 38–45, 39.
36   Herald Fahringer, "Working With Words" (1982) 54(3) *New York State Bar Journal* 140–145, 141.
37   *Ibid.*
38   *Ibid.*
39   Fred Rodell, "Goodbye to Law Reviews" (1936–1937) 23(1) *Virginia Law Review* 38–45, 39.
40   Karen Erger, "Escaping the Verbiage Vortex" (2016) 104(10) *Illinois Bar Journal* 52–53, 52.
41   *Ibid.*
42   Fred Rodell, "Goodbye to Law Reviews" (1936–1937) 23(1) *Virginia Law Review* 38–45, 40.
43   Reed Dickerson, "Toward a Legal Dialectic" (1985) 61(3) *Indiana Law Journal* 315–330, 317.
44   Edward Re, "Legal Writing as Good Literature" (1985) 59(2) *St John's Law Review* 211–227, 224.
45   Fred Rodell, "Goodbye to Law Reviews" (1936–1937) 23(1) *Virginia Law Review* 38–45, 40.
46   Stuart Chase, *The Tyranny of Words* (Harcourt, Brace & Co, 1938), 327.
47   Nancy Rice, "Tips on Legal Writing" (2015) 44(5) *Colorado Lawyer* 61–62, 61.

Avoid the legalistic[48]

Case studies suggest that readers/users prefer plain language in legal documents, are able to understand it more than legalistic language, and are more likely to continue reading it.[49]

Avoid the superficial and stilted[50]

Even complex ideas are capable of being expressed in a manner that is simple, yet neither simplistic nor superficial.[51]

Avoid writing material unfit to read on subjects
not worth writing about[52]

Legal language has traditionally been depicted as the optimal example of language that is "unreadable, often unintelligible".[53] Rodell cautions against this form of writing and is also clearly of the school that legal writing should not come burdened with unnecessary flourishes/ornamentation.[54]

4.   Using foreign words

Hazlitt suggests that the use of Greek and Latin (already in decline in his time) bestowed a certain wonder when it came to religious matters.[55] He was also unconvinced that the widespread abandonment of Greek and Latin was a good thing, suggesting that when books are written in the vernacular everyone becomes a critic and an author is no longer 'tried' by his or her peers.[56]

There is a certain logic to Hazlitt's thinking; after all, the foundations of Western civilisation are to be found in Greek and Latin texts.[57] And use of Latin may not be altogether without purpose. So, for example, Macleod suggests that it enriches legal language and that while a Latin

---

48   Fred Rodell, "Goodbye to Law Reviews" (1936–1937) 23(1) *Virginia Law Review* 38–45, 43.
49   Joseph Kimble, "Flimsy Claims for Legalese and False Criticisms of Plain Language: A 30-Year Collection" (2020) 19 *Scribes Journal of Legal Writing* 1–14, 12.
50   Fred Rodell, "Goodbye to Law Reviews" (1936–1937) 23(1) *Virginia Law Review* 38–45, 43.
51   David Ross, "Legal Writing" (2005) 1(4) *Original Law Review* 85–102, 85.
52   Fred Rodell, "Goodbye to Law Reviews" (1936–1937) 23(1) *Virginia Law Review* 38–45, 45.
53   George Rossman (ed), *Advocacy and the King's English* (Bobbs-Merrill Co, 1960), 766.
54   Edward Re, "Legal Writing as Good Literature" (1985) 59(2) *St John's Law Review* 211–227, 224.
55   William Hazlitt, *The Round Table* (Longman, Hurst, Rees, Orme & Browne, 1817), vol 2, 32.
56   *Ibid*, 33.
57   Various, "Latin and the Lawyer" in *Butterworths South African Law Review* (Butterworths, 1957), 136–150, 137.

phrase may not be more accurate than an English phrase, Latin still is not "necessarily redundant".[58] To this might be added the perceived advantage that Latinisms endow legal texts with a lustre of learning (at least among those unschooled in Latin).

Notwithstanding the possible virtues of occasional use of Latin, the broad consensus in the academic commentary on legal writing is that Latin (Ancient Greek tends not to appear in contemporary legal texts) is best avoided. As one leading American text on effective legal writing observes, the continuing presence of Latin in so many legal texts is a "mind-boggler" when almost nobody understands the Latin language.[59] The solution, the same book posits, is to aid in the gradual disappearance of such foreign language terms from legal writing by avoiding their use in one's own legal writing.[60]

Key propositions

- In a judgment the reader is offered an insight into real people and events of the past.
- There is a natural professional jargon that goes with being a lawyer.
- Some professional language is to be expected in a legal text.
- Even when a lawyer comes spouting legalisms galore that is not necessarily bad (though it might need to be worked upon if the comprehensibility of a text is to be maximised).
- It may be that Latinisms continue to give legal texts a lustre of learning; however, such a practice may also come at the price of comprehensibility.
- Moral principle continues to be a bedrock of legal writing, at least in liberal democracies.

---

58   Peter Macleod, "Latin in Legal Writing: An Inquiry into the Use of Latin in the Modern Legal World" (1997) 39 *Boston College Law Review* 235–252, 251.
59   Gertrude Block, *Effective Legal Writing*, 4th edition (The Foundation Press Inc, 1992), 114.
60   *Ibid*.

11. James

On the art and duty of writing, humour and other matters

Henry James (1843–1916) is one of the greatest English-language novelists: "He looms large in American literature ... but no less large in the ... [longer] history of the modern novel in which he pre-empted such a distinguished and law-giving place".[1] He is famous for such novels as *The Portrait of a Lady* (1881) and *The Ambassadors* (1903), but is perhaps most famous for his horror story *The Turn of the Screw* (1898). James's opus, *The Art of Fiction* (1885)[2] contends for freedom in novel writing and makes various observations that, I submit, are of relevance to the art and craft of legal writing.

1. The 'art' of writing

James notes that art competes with fiction, that their inspiration, process and success is the same and, hence, that they can learn from each other.[3] It is much the same analogy that is made in this text as regards fiction writing and the writing of legal texts. The American philosopher, Joseph Margolis, has also pointed to various shared properties of works of art and aesthetic judgment that can be seen also to point to the artistic/aesthetic character of legal texts. These include the following:

> *A physical product operates as a work of fine art if it*
> *is the result of "deliberate human work"[4] and serves a*
> *"unified human goal"[5]*

A legal text satisfies these criteria: it is the product of deliberate human work and serves the pursuit of truth. That is not to say that all legal texts can amount to fine art but some (judgments are the best example) enjoy

---

1   Leon Edel, *The Life of Henry James* (Penguin Books, 1977), vol 1, 11.
2   Henry James, *The Art of Fiction* (Cupples, Upham & Co, 1885).
3   *Ibid.*
4   Joseph Margolis, "Proposals on the Logic of Aesthetic Judgments" (1959) 9(36) *Philosophical Quarterly* 208–216, 210.
5   *Ibid.*

that potential. There is nothing especially new or radical in this observation. Re, writing in the 1950s about the important role of writing in the legal profession, has described how it "inevitably became a fine art".[6]

> *A work of fine art may also be a useful art if it serves a goal other than "mere design"*[7]

If one accepts that legal writing can constitute a fine art, it is patently a fine art that enjoys a function other than mere design.

Some additional points might be made about the experience arising from, and *vis-à-vis*, a work of art.

- A work of art, including a legal text, destroys in the receiver's consciousness the distance between him or her, the artist (the legal writer) and all others whose minds receive the judgment.[8] The reader sits with the writer, perceiving the world as he or she perceives it.
- If a reader is "infected by the author's condition of soul",[9] then the object which has caused this infection is art, the extent of infectiousness being the benchmark of artistic excellence.[10] Though many legal texts have the potential to be works of art, some rise to the level of superior works of art (as with some of the great judgments). One sign that one is in the hands of a superior legal writer is his or her ability to 'infect' the reader with the feeling that takes hold of the writer as he or she writes.
- This infectiousness itself depends on individuality and clarity of feeling, and also on the sincerity of the legal writer.[11]

How can feeling be excited by words on paper or colours on canvas? The art of painting has been described as "imitating solid objects upon a flat subject by means of pigments".[12] In a similar vein, the art of legal text writing might conceivably be described as 'the art of imagining life through the prism of law by means of words'. Both definitions are relatively simple. But is that all that there is to painting and text writing

---

6   Edward Re, *Brief Writing and Oral Argument*, 2nd edition (Oceana Publications, 1957), 5.
7   Joseph Margolis, "Proposals on the Logic of Aesthetic Judgments" (1959) 9(36) *Philosophical Quarterly* 208–216, 210.
8   Leo Tolstoy, *What is Art?* (Funk & Wagnalls, 1904), 153.
9   *Ibid.*
10   *Ibid.*
11   *Ibid.*
12   Roger Fry, *Vision and Design* (Penguin Books, 1940), 22.

– a scribble of colour, a scramble of words? If so, how can they excite feeling? Perhaps because in an imaginative work, such as a painting or a legal text, one's consciousness is focused on "the perceptive and ... emotional aspects of the experience",[13] with the result that one sees the described event more clearly and notices the emotions roused.

The idea that a text could be art may come as a surprise to lawyers. However, it is, to use a colloquialism, 'old hat' to philosophers of art. So, for example, the American art critic, Arthur Danto, has written (in terms that seem as applicable to legal texts as to other texts):

> *A text is a* Zusammenhang *[context], the principle of whose integrity goes beyond those features of syntax and grammar through which sentences are logically tractable [into] ... the preservation and transmission of truth values.*[14]

Bringing this to bear, for example, in the judgment writing context, what Danto is suggesting is that the text that one sees within a law report is a context whose integrity goes beyond the syntax and grammar of the sentences that the eye sees and becomes a vehicle for the preservation and transmission of truth.

A legal text is a product of intentional activity that expresses a human viewpoint.[15] But it is more. Art in a post-religious age is where an "encounter with transcendence"[16] is sought. This is as true of legal texts (such as judgments and written submissions) as it is of any other form of creative work, with writers seeking – through rational eloquence – to identify truth.

How ought one to read a legal text as a work of art? Perhaps the best guidance to be offered in this regard was given a quarter of a millennium ago by Winckelmann when, in his *Instructions for the Connoisseur*,[17] he outlined various observations as to how one should consider works of art, namely that:

- the great characteristic of works of art is the idea that informs them;[18]
- artists have ideas of their own and also know that beauty is the chief aim of art;[19]

13   *Ibid*, 24.
14   Arthur Danto, "Art and the Text" (1983) 5 *RES: Anthropology and Aesthetics* 5–13, 7.
15   Ruth Lorand, "The Purity of Aesthetic Value" (1992) 50(1) *Journal of Aesthetics and Art Criticism* 13–21, 13.
16   William Desmond, *Art, Origins, Otherness* (SUNY Press, 2003), 1.
17   John Winckelmann, *Instructions for the Connoisseur*, Henry Fusseli (trans) (A Millar, 1765).
18   *Ibid*, 251.
19   *Ibid*, 252.

- to use a modern colloquialism, 'less is more', that is, a work is the best it can be when it is simplest;[20]
- a distinction falls to be made between slavish copying and "reasonable imitation";[21]
- along with the 'Idea', the second characteristic of works of art is beauty;[22]
- no man can act as a connoisseur of beauty who has not dwelled for a time on antiquity;[23]
- execution is a great characteristic of art;[24] and
- undue emphasis on ornament will lead one away from the truth.[25]

Transposing these attributes into the legal context, it might be submitted that:
- the great characteristic of a legal text is the idea that informs it;
- a legal writer (as creator) has his or her own ideas and knows that beauty (harmony with truth) is the chief aim of a legal text;
- a legal text is best when most simple;
- there is a distinction between slavish copying (replication of precedent) and a legal text that is informed by precedent but which proceeds in its own right;
- beauty in a legal text derives from the harmony between its various parts;
- one cannot discern art in a legal text unless one has read great writing;
- the good sense that presents in a legal text is greater than the industry that went into it;
- in identifying the quality of a legal writer, one should look to the clarity, fluency and sensitivity of his or her prose; and[26]
- in a legal text knowledge is of greater value than literary style.

2.   Task of the writer

The task of the writer, James posits, is to represent/illustrate the past and the actions of humanity.[27] Arguably, a not dissimilar process is at play in

---

20   *Ibid*, 273.
21   *Ibid*, 256.
22   *Ibid*, 258.
23   *Ibid*, 265.
24   *Ibid*, 267.
25   *Ibid*, 270.
26   *Ibid*, 267.
27   *Ibid*, 56.

legal texts. Lawyers seek to make "logical propositions and legal arguments"[28] as attractive as possible. They create a scene, time frame and story, and tap into the reader's sentiments.[29] In addition, they reason and decide within a context shaped by cultural myths and models.[30]

3.   Amusement, humour and didacticism in writing

Literature, James posits, should be amusing or instructive.[31] Should legal texts be amusing and are they intended to be instructive? When it comes to humour in legal writing, some view it as: an *enfant terrible* that amuses its creator at the expense of others; as fundamentally disrespectful; and as diminishing the law as a serious-minded field of endeavour.[32] By contrast, there are those who see judicial humour as harmless, even useful, as a means whereby complexity can be addressed, and the (sometimes) boring made more bearable.[33] At a basic level, the appeal of humour is simple, yet notable: it aids communication (and the enjoyability of same).[34] In *Laugh It Off Promotions*,[35] a decision of the South African Constitutional Court in a trademarks case which concerned the production of t-shirts that made a parody of various trademarks, Justice Sachs touched upon the importance of humour in a constitutional democracy in the following memorable terms:

> *Laughter … has its context. It can be derisory and punitive, imposing indignity on the weak at the hands of the powerful. On the other hand, it can be consolatory, even subversive in the service of … marginalised social critics … A society that takes itself too seriously risks bottling up its tensions and treating every example of irreverence as a threat to its existence. Humour is one of the great solvents of democracy. It permits the ambiguities and contradictions of public life to be articulated in non-violent forms. It promotes diversity. It enables a multitude of discontents to be expressed in a myriad of spontaneous ways. It is an elixir of constitutional health.*[36]

In *Russell v The State*,[37] a decision of the Court of Appeals of Georgia,

---

28   Linda Berger, "The Lady, or the Tiger – A Field Guide to Metaphor and Narrative" (2011) 50(2) *Washburn Law Journal* 275–318, 282–283.
29   *Ibid.*
30   *Ibid.*
31   Henry James, *The Art of Fiction* (Cupples, Upham & Co, 1885), 57.
32   Michael Bishop, "Why Must I Cry? Justification, Sacrifice, Loneliness, Madness and Laughter in Post-Apartheid Judicial Decision-Making" (2007) 1 *Pretoria Student Law Review* 33–56, 50.
33   *Ibid*, 51.
34   J Knight, "Humor and the Law" (1993) *Wisconsin Law Review* 897–920, 908.
35   *Laugh It Off Promotions CC v South African Breweries International (Finance) BV t/a Sabmark International* 2006 (1) SA 144 (CC).
36   *Ibid*, paras [108]–[109].
37   188 Ga App 167 (1988).

the issue of whether or not there is a place for humour in court judgments (and, by analogy in legal texts more generally) unexpectedly strode centre stage. The facts of the case were relatively straightforward: an ex-girlfriend of a man committed criminal damage to certain property belonging to the man and his new wife; she was convicted and brought an appeal against her conviction to the Court of Appeals. In the Court of Appeals, the majority judgment struck a surprisingly light tone in a criminal case where the appellant had been imprisoned, fined, and required to undertake a mental health programme. The majority judgment (authored by Judge Deen) commences as follows:

> The events of the instant case dramatically illustrate the stark truth underlying the poetic adage, "… Hell [has no] fury like a woman scorned." Appellant Carol Star Russell, who admittedly believed that "diamonds are a girl's best friend" if and only if they are bought at Tiffany or Maier & Berkele, was rejected by her almost-fiancé, David Roberson, after she had expressed in explicit terms her disdain for the engagement and wedding rings which he had proposed buying for her at Kay Jewelers. Roberson then met and subsequently married another young lady, Tammy, whose taste in jewelry was apparently not so elevated.[38]

This drew the following criticism in a concurring judgment authored by Judge Carley (later a long-time member of the Supreme Court of Georgia, including a brief spell as Chief Justice):

> I agree that the judgment of conviction should be affirmed. However, I cannot join the majority opinion because I do not believe that humor has a place in an opinion which resolves legal issues affecting the rights, obligations, and, in this case, the liberty of citizens. The case certainly is not funny to the litigants. I concur in the judgment only.[39]

Upon motion for rehearing, Judge Deen explained himself as follows:

> [S]ome cases, as here, involve unusual and colorful factual situations. Often, related quotations and expressions are evoked, emphasizing pithy portrayal of the points under consideration. Two famous but innocuous quotations from Alexander Pope and Dorothy Parker were included in the majority opinion here. On rehearing, in deference to appellant attorney's able articulations, and based on the other two judges' vote of "concur in the judgment only," additional comments here are affirmatively advanced.

---

38   *Ibid.*
39   *Ibid*, 169.

Colorful quotes and language of levity

Considerable precedent exists for an array of differing styles of written opinions by judges. This flexibility provides judicial independence for differing views. On page twenty-six of the current history book of the Court of Appeals, unanimously approved by all nine Judges, it is acknowledged: "Books containing compilations of decisions under such titles as 'wit and wisdom in court opinions' always include reprints from the Court of Appeals of Georgia. (See also former Court of Appeals Judge H Sol Clark's 'Judicial Humor (?): A Personal Reminiscence,' 20 Trial 68 *et seq.*, Association of Trial Lawyers of America, June 1984.)"
In the latter cited article, Judge Clark observes, "In all seriousness, Appellate Judges should consider that a little levity lightens their load." He believes "A sense of humor can complement fine judicial standards" and "ward off the highly infectious disease 'blackrobe-itis'," and can immunize Judges to the "abhorrent judicial ailment known as the 'divinity virus'." ... Georgia's most frequently cited Appellate Judge is the illustrious and legendary Chief Justice Logan E Bleckley. Almost every one of his written opinions contains a bit of wit as well as a word of wisdom ...

Various examples of Chief Justice Bleckley's wit are then referenced, including (surprisingly) entire judgments written in verse form. In addition, Judge Deen goes on to point out that the majority judgment in *Russell* included a far more detailed analysis of the facts and law at play before the court than was typically undertaken in criminal cases before the Court of Appeals.[40] And he also criticises the brevity of the concurring opinion with the stinging observation that while concurring in the judgment only was a legitimate manner of proceeding, to proceed so "tells the litigant little or nothing about the case ... This treatment 'certainly is not funny to the litigants' and bodes ill to serious appellate review".[41]

Yet for all that Judge Deen protests, one cannot but wonder whether the original appeals court judgment might have been better (and avoided occasioning an application for rehearing) if it had just struck a consistently more serious tone.

Given the clear difficulties that can emerge from efforts at humour, it is difficult to flaw the view of New York Supreme Court Judge Gerald Lebovits that litigants come to court looking for both justice and

---

40   *Ibid*, 171.
41   *Ibid*.

sensitivity, and that a judge who engages in "biting humor"[42] actually engages in aggressive behaviour,[43] with that aggressiveness unsurprisingly being viewed as offensive (for that is what it is).[44]

James posits that literature should be amusing or instructive.[45] Regardless of being amusing, should a legal text seek to be instructive? Here, it is useful to distinguish between various classes of legal writing, such as:

- legal writing done in practice;
- legal writing done for practice;
- legal writing for education; and
- academic legal writing.

The last three items in this list are clearly intended to be instructive, and sometimes even writing in the first item in the list can be done for the purpose of instruction as, for example, where a practising lawyer prepares a text identifying a client's legal rights or obligations. But what of legal judgments? Are they intended simply to resolve the point at hand or to be more generally instructive? One former lord justice of appeal has drawn a convincing link between the desire to be didactic, the excessive length of many modern judgments, and confusion by judges as to the intended audience of their judgments in the following (convincing) terms:

> *Of course if you think of a judgment as a quasi-PhD thesis it will need to be long ... But a judgment is not meant to be a thesis. It is to explain what the case is about and why the judge is deciding it the way ... she does. That is all. The primary audience is the parties, particularly the "guy who loses," ... Judgments ought not to be written for academics ... – they ... have no need of judges to do their work for them. The legal profession is of course interested ... but that has always been so without judges writing their judgments [for] ... the profession.*[46]

To this might be added the fact that whereas the common law was once revealed in judgments, since the 19th century there has been a creeping "statutorification"[47] of the law across the common law world,

---

42   Gerald Lebovits *et al*, "Ethical Judicial Opinion Writing" (2008) 21 *Georgia Journal of Legal Ethics* 237–310, 272.
43   *Ibid.*
44   *Ibid.*
45   Henry James, *The Art of Fiction* (Cupples, Upham & Co, 1885), 57.
46   Robin Jacob, "How to write a legal judgment", *Prospect*, 7 December 2020, www.prospectmagazine.co.uk/philosophy/how-to-write-a-legal-judgment-robin-jacob-court-of-appeal-law.
47   Guido Calabresi, *A Common Law for the Age of Statutes* (Harvard University Press), 1.

with much of what was once in the common law now contained in statute. As a result, the law-revealing task of judges has surely become more constrained. The task of the judgment writer is to explain (especially to the losing party) why the judgment went the way it did,[48] not to embark upon an academic excursus. Legal judgments are not the place to answer the great questions of the day.[49] It may sometimes be appropriate for an appellate court to opine upon the law beyond the immediate facts at play[50] so as to bring clarity to a particular area – though it is best for a court to recall even in this context the view offered by Lord Macmillan in *Read v J Lyons and Co Ltd*[51] that the task of a court "is to decide particular cases between litigants … not to rationalise the law".[52]

4. Superabundant judgments

When it comes to the superabundance of novels that emerged in the 19th century, James makes a number of observations that, it is submitted, can be applied as regards the superabundance of judgments that exist in the common law world and its composite jurisdictions today. Thus, when considering the notion that the novel is a superior form of art, James writes:

> [T]his might sometimes be doubted in presence of the enormous number of works of fiction that appeal to … our generation, for it might easily seem that there could be no great substance in a commodity so quickly and easily produced. It must be admitted that good novels are somewhat compromised by bad ones, and that the field at large suffers discredit from overcrowding, I think, however, that this injury is only superficial, and that the superabundance of written fiction proves nothing against the principle [that it is a superior form of art] … It has been vulgarized, like all other kinds of literature, like everything else to-day, and it has proved more than some kinds accessible to vulgarization. But there is as much difference as there ever was between a good novel and a bad one; the bad is swept … into some unvisited limbo or infinite rubbish-yard … and the good subsists and emits its light and stimulates our desire for perfection.[53]

Bringing these observations to bear in the context of legal writing,

48 Roslyn Atkinson, "Judgment writing", *Supreme Court Library Queensland*, 6 February 2010, https://archive.sclqld.org.au/judgepub/2010/atkinson060210.pdf, 3.
49 Debbie Mortimer, "Some Thoughts on Writing Judgments in, and for, Contemporary Australia" (2018) 42(1) *Melbourne University Law Review* 274–297, 285.
50 Mirko Bagaric and James McConvill, "The High Court and the Utility of Multiple Judgments" (2005) 1(1) *High Court Quarterly Review* 13–43, 42.
51 [1947] AC 156 (HL).
52 *Ibid*, 175.
53 Henry James, *The Art of Fiction* (Cupples, Upham & Co, 1885), 59–60.

what might be stated? Perhaps that the sheer number of judgments now available at the touch of a button (as opposed to the position that presented well into the 20th century when only a limited number of legal texts were available via the law reports) has diminished the value of the judgment as a commodity.[54] As one anonymous wag once observed in the *South African Law Journal*, "Too many judgments spoil the broth".[55] On a more serious note, Lord Diplock, writing in the 1980s, complained that so many authorities were even then being cited before the English courts as to present the risk of "so blinding the court with case law that it has difficulty in seeing the wood of legal principle for the trees of paraphrase".[56] The problem has only become worse in the Internet Age, one English High Court judge observing at the turn of this century (when computer databases were, to some extent, still in their nascency) that the problem they presented was a want of pre-selection:

> In this case reference was made to a number of unreported decisions which have been obtained from legal database ... This is not new, but the recent growth of computerised databases has made it an ever more frequent and extensive occurrence ... Until ... recently, this was not a substantial problem. The courts were only taken to cases which had been published in a limited number of sets of law reports after selection by legally qualified editors ...
>
> Now there is no preselection. Large numbers of decisions, good and bad, reserved and unreserved, can be accessed. Lawyers frequently feel that they have an obligation to search this material. Anything which supports their clients' case must be drawn to the attention of the court ... A number of consequences flow from this. First ... it is the client who ... has to pay ... [Second] ... sometimes courts go wrong ... A poor decision of, say, a court of first instance used to be buried silently by omission from the reports. Now it may be dug up and used to support a cause of action or defence which, without its encouragement, might have been allowed to die a quiet death. Thirdly, it is a common experience that the courts are presented with ever

---

54   *Ibid*, 59.
55   The observation was made in the context of the reasons given by Lord Diplock in *National Dock Labour Board v John Bland & Son Ltd* [1972] 2 AC 222, 236 (HL), as to why he would join in the reasoning of Lord Cross of Chelsea, rather than offering separate reasoning of his own:
     The reasons for dismissing the appeal on both points which I had drafted were in substance the same as those which will be expressed by ... Lord Cross ... although the actual words that I had used to express them inevitably differed from those which appear in his speech. Lest unintended seismological distinctions between the wording of our speeches should be used in future cases to cloud the meaning of the statute or the Scheme, I am content to adopt as my own the reasoning of my noble and learned friend, Lord Cross.
56   *Lexmead (Basingstoke) Ltd v Lewis* [1982] AC 225, 274–275.

larger files of copied law reports ... extending the duration and cost of trials, to the disadvantage of the legal system as a whole.[57]

In the same year, Lord Bingham (then the Lord Chief Justice of England and Wales) was expressing concern that "[the] availability of vast new swathes of [online] material ... presents a ... risk to the system which may ... simply succumb to the weight of the materials presented".[58]

Lord Judge, another former Lord Chief Justice of England and Wales, has suggested that the solution is to require that counsel refer only to those judgments to which it was necessary to refer. (In making this suggestion he noted that a similar suggestion had been made as long ago as 1641 but not acted upon – which may point to a difficulty in discerning what is necessary and what is not.) Writing extrajudicially, Lord Carnwath, a former 'law lord' has pointed to what is the most sensible means of curtailing excessive citation of precedent (and thereafter excessive mention of precedent) in court judgments, emphasising the discussion of the law (and the related distillation of case law) in a reputable textbook or law review article as a substitute for the citation of multiple authorities:

In one case in the Court of Appeal the answer turned ultimately on the application to the facts of a proposition of law stated by Cockburn CJ as long ago as 1864, and confirmed by citation in the textbooks. Yet we had been taken through some twenty-four authorities dating back more than 100 years. I said (with the support of my colleagues):

One of the curses of the common law method in the 21st century is unlimited accessibility to authorities, reported and unreported, and apparently unlimited resources for copying them ... On the other hand, one of the blessings is the availability of up-to-date and authoritative textbooks on almost every relevant subject, in which the material cases have been sorted out and digested ... Of course, that is only the starting point. Authorities may be needed to qualify, expand, or merely illustrate the basic principle. However, it is important to be clear for which of those purposes any case is being advanced. Furthermore, where the purpose is to qualify or expand, it is not enough simply to cite an authority, without being able to articulate with reasonable precision the proposition which it is said to support.[59]

---

57 See the postscript to the judgment of Laddie J in *Michaels v Taylor Woodrow Developments Ltd* [2001] Ch 493, 519–520.

58 As referred to in the judgment of Lord Judge LCJ in *R v Erskine* [2010] 1 WLR 183, 203.

59 Lord Carnwath, "Judicial Precedent – Taming the Common Law" (2012) 12 *Oxford University Commonwealth Law Journal* 261–272, 271. The judgment that Lord Carnwath quotes from is his own judgment (as a member of the Court of Appeal) in *CEL Group Ltd v Nedlloyd Lines UK Ltd* [2003] EWCA Civ. 1716; [2004] 1 All ER (Comm) 689, 697, [25].

As to James' other observations,[60] his closing observation also has a ring in the field of judgment-writing, namely that there is as much difference as there ever was between a good judgment and a bad judgment, with better judgments retaining their allure and casting the same illumination as ever. The tell-tale signs of a bad legal judgment are much the same as the tell-tale signs of any bad legal writing:

Bad grammar, punctuation and sentence structure

Legal writing is meant to be precise:[61] bad grammar, punctuation and sentence structure can each introduce imprecision. Sentence structure is a critical (if sometimes unappreciated) feature of legal writing: while sentences are typically created when the author is thinking about content (rather than sentence structure), a more deliberate approach to sentence structure is merited; after all, word order establishes emphasis, "heralding the hierarchy"[62] that helps readers to understand the relative importance of sentence components.

Poor word choices

For example: archaisms, doublets/triplets (eg, 'give, devise, and bequeath'), formality to the point of pomposity, 'here and there' words (eg, 'herein' and 'thereafter'), language that is excessively legalistic and lawyerly, and nominalisations (converting verbs to nouns, eg, 'he placed reliance upon' instead of 'he relied on').[63]

Wordiness

As Younger observes, "[l]anguage is as precious as any coinage and as easily debased".[64] It follows that words should be used sparingly and that an unnecessary abundance of words dilutes the potency and effect of what the legal writer is striving to state.

---

60   Henry James, *The Art of Fiction* (Cupples, Upham & Co, 1885), 59.
61   Betsy Brand Six, "Bad Grammar Examples: What Amusing Grammar Errors Can Teach Us" (2017) 86 *Journal of the Kansas Bar Association* 19–21, 19.
62   Terri LeClercq, "Deliberate Sentence Structure" (1991) 54(2) *Texas Bar Journal* 151–156, 151.
63   Kevin Collins, "The Use of Plain-Language Principles in Texas Litigation Formbooks" (2005) 24(2) *Review of Litigation* 429–472, esp 432–437.
64   Irving Younger, "Skimming the Fat Off Your Writing" (2001–2002) 8 *Scribes Journal of Legal Writing* 121–140, 125.

Excessive citations

There are different views on the proper use of citations. For example, on the one hand, it is arguably preferable to focus on principles over authorities, that fewer citations make for shorter (and hence more comprehensible prose), and that too many citations involve the repetition of what is already well-settled, while, on the other hand, sometimes extensive citation is unavoidable if the law on a particular point or in a particular respect is properly to be documented.[65]

Excessive quotations

When it comes to the proper use of quotations there is something of a divergence between the literature on legal writing (which typically advises that quotes should be used sparingly)[66] and what happens in practice (eg, judgments frequently issue that have an abundance of quotations).[67] Why this divergence continues is unclear. Even in the early 20th century, Benjamin Cardozo railed against deploying a "dreary succession of quotations".[68] (He was writing of judgments but the point arguably has a more general resonance.) Yet legal texts continue habitually to issue trailing a 'security blanket' of unnecessary quotations.

Excessive footnotes

Landau, though not a "footnote abolitionist"[69] has suggested that the practice of footnoting in legal articles, briefs and judgments is "running amok",[70] with the number and length of footnotes increasing, and their increased usage in appellate court judgments being (he suggests) an ominous trend. The problem with excessive (discursive) footnoting is that it is distracting, often serves no real purpose (other than showing how clever one is) and can be used as a means of advancing or retreating from contentious ideas to the point of yielding uncertainty.[71] Landau also

---

65   Russell Smyth, "Judicial Citations – An Empirical Study of Citation Practice in the New Zealand Court of Appeal" (2000) 31(4) *Victoria University Wellington Law Review* 847–896, 855–857.
66   Maureen Johnson, "To Quote or Not to Quote: Making the Case for Teaching Law Students the Art of Effective Quotation in Legal Memoranda" (2014) 56(2) *South Texas Law Review* 283–312, 284.
67   *Ibid.*
68   Benjamin Cardozo, *Selected Writings of Benjamin Nathan Cardozo*, Margaret Hall (ed) (Fallon Publications, 1947), 352.
69   Jack Landau, "Footnote Folly" (2006) *Oregon Appellate Almanac* 199–207, 199.
70   *Ibid*, 200.
71   *Ibid*, 203–205.

advances a couple of ideas aimed at stemming the modern flood of footnotes, namely that a writer should: (i) pause before using them and ask if an intended footnote is truly necessary; and (ii) decline to join the 'footnote bandwagon' of simply including footnotes because that is the way things are done, rather than asking if they could be done better.[72]

5. Writing engagingly

James offers but one law of novel writing, namely that a novel be interesting. What is it that makes a legal text interesting? The following characteristics spring immediately to mind:

It is based on scrupulous research

Perhaps to an extent unappreciated by those who have only ever seen lawyers in operation on television or in movies, professional legal practice involves "primarily researching the law and writing about it".[73] As with the societies in which they operate, laws are in a constant state of flux and clients require continuously to be advised on the exact state of the law at any one time. In fact, research – and related writing – skills are so important a part of the lawyer's professional armoury that, in the United States, declining reading experience and writing skills among incoming law students has fuelled a debate as to how legal pedagogy should be reshaped to ensure that law graduates emerge well prepared to discharge these vital professional functions.[74]

It offers good and correct legal analysis

For legal writing to be effective it needs to set its author apart as someone whose position is both sensible and legally sustainable.[75] Getting legal analysis right is not as easy a task as might be supposed: the amount/rate of change in the law makes keeping pace with such changes profoundly challenging.[76]

---

72   *Ibid*, 206–207.
73   Mark Cooney, "Get Real About Research and Writing" (2004) 32(9) *Student Law* 18–25, 20.
74   See, eg, Cathaleen Roach, "Is the Sky Falling? Ruminations on Incoming Law Student Preparedness (and Implications for the Profession) in the Wake of Recent National and Other Reports" (2005) 11 *Legal Writing: The Journal of the Legal Writing Institute* 295–328.
75   Megan Boyd and Adam Lamparello, "Legal Writing for the Real World: A Practical Guide to Success" (2013) 46(2) *John Marshall Law Review* 487–532, 531.
76   M Furmston, "Ignorance of the Law" (1981) 1 *Legal Studies* 37–45, 46.

It distils the necessary from the dense

Most legal research still focuses on the ancient task of identifying and elucidating what the law is and how it falls to be applied in any one instance. A primary task of the lawyer is to distil a few clear, critical issues from what MacCormack has described as the "infinitely complex continuum of facts and events"[77] – and, in instances of doubt, to gauge how a court would decide the issue presenting.[78]

It contributes to the solution of practical problems

A legal text is not simply an aesthetic product. Thus, while it should be elegant and graceful, legal prose is fundamentally functional ("primarily instrumental")[79] either aiding in the resolution of a particular problem or adding to the repository of knowledge from which solutions may be drawn.[80]

It is brief/concise

What is aimed for in this regard is not an unnatural shortness of form but adequate detail joined with an avoidance of the superfluous.[81] Concision has become an especially important objective in the Computer Age, with online usability experts positing the need for 'chunking' of electronically provided information, that is, breaking up long paragraphs into shorter ones, yielding more on-screen white space and making the on-screen reading experience more enjoyable.[82] Achieving desirable concision in the time allowed the busy practising lawyer is, one commentator suggests, a matter of excising wordy stock phrases, weak verbs and nominalisations.[83] This can be a time-consuming process: writing short is more difficult than writing long.[84] As Steven Spielberg has the character

---

77   Neil MacCormick, *Legal Reasoning and Legal Theory* (Clarendon Press, 1978), 47. See also Charles Maechling, "Legal Research and the Problems of Society" (1968–1969) 21(1) *Journal of Legal Education* 86–88, 87.
78   See Maechling, *ibid.*
79   Samuel Murumba, "Good Legal Writing: A Guide for the Perplexed" (1991) 17(1) *Monash University Law Review* 93–105, 94.
80   *Ibid.*
81   Mark Osbeck, "What is 'Good Legal Writing' and Why Does It Matter?" (2012) 4(2) *Drexel Law Review* 417–466, 437.
82   Maria Perez Crist, "The E-Brief: Legal Writing for an Online World" (2003) 33(1) *New Mexico Law Review* 49–94, 76.
83   Tenielle Fordyce-Ruff, "Cutting the Clutter: Three Steps to More Concise Legal Writing" (2011) 54(1) *Advocate (Idaho State Bar)* 41–46, 41.
84   Gerald Lebovits, "Legal-Writing Myths" (2015) 16 *Scribes Journal of Legal Writing* 113–122, 117.

of Lincoln tell his Cabinet in the eponymous biopic of the greatest American President: "As the preacher said, I could write shorter sermons but once I start I get too lazy to stop."[85]

It is clear

As Justice Cardozo observes of good judicial writing, though the point holds good as regards legal writing more generally, clarity is its supreme value.[86] Why is clarity so important? At its most fundamental because legal writing is about communication and it is only with due clarity that what it is sought to communicate can duly be communicated.[87] That said, clarity alone does not suffice: as Cardozo himself acknowledges also required are "persuasive force ... sincerity and fire ... the mnemonic power of alliteration and antithesis, or the terseness and tang of the proverb and the maxim".[88]

It is simple

As Coleridge once exclaimed, "If men would say what they have to say in plain terms, how much more eloquent they would be!"[89] Coleridge also gives some pointers on how a desirable simplicity of style might be attained in practice. Thus he counsels that one should: (i) "not ... attempt to express [oneself] ... in language before ... thoroughly know[ing] our own meaning"; (ii) strive for "preciseness in the use of terms"; and (iii) consistently bring to bear on one's writing the litmus-test "whether you can translate the phrase adequately into simpler terms, regard being had to the feeling of the whole passage" (the idea being that if you can, you should).[90] Why is simplicity important? Because the principal object when one writes is to be understood and simple words are more likely to be generally understood (and to come across as sincere).[91]

---

85 Extracted from the online version of the screenplay at https://imsdb.com/scripts/Lincoln.html.
86 Benjamin Cardozo, *Selected Writings of Benjamin Nathan Cardozo*, Margaret Hall (ed) (Fallon Publications, 1947), 341.
87 Mark Osbeck, "What is 'Good Legal Writing' and Why Does It Matter?" (2012) 4(2) *Drexel Law Review* 417–466, 428.
88 Benjamin Cardozo, *Selected Writings of Benjamin Nathan Cardozo*, Margaret Hall (ed) (Fallon Publications, 1947), 342.
89 Samuel Coleridge, *The Literary Remains of Samuel Taylor Coleridge* (William Pickering, 1836), vol 1, 240.
90 *Ibid*.
91 Henry Weihofen, *Legal Writing Style*, 2nd edition (West Publishing Co, 1980), 61.

It is elegant

It is a strange person who would contend that legal writing should be other than elegant – though not every form of legal writing is entirely conducive to elegance. So, for example, a handsomely worded discovery request may not be necessary or desirable.[92] Even so, elegance in legal prose (or eloquence – the two terms are used interchangeably by commentators) is touted as a virtue. A fixed definition of what exactly constitutes elegance in writing is hard to come by: as one commentator has observed, it is more "know-it-when-you-see-it".[93] However, as a rough guide to what is involved, it has been suggested that elegant writing is memorable, poetic, and striking, with all due attention to imagery, rhythm, and sound.[94] I submit, however, that care is required when it comes to elegance in legal prose, not to surrender clarity to style: as a rule of thumb, 'when in doubt, clarity should win out'.[95]

It avoids vagueness

The fundamental objection to vagueness (and the related 'sin' of ambiguity) is that the principal object when one writes is to be understood and ambiguity/vagueness can obscure what it is meant to convey.[96] However, vagueness in the use of words (words themselves tend not to be vague)[97] is not an evil always to be avoided in legal writing. For example, a writer may seek to 'future-proof' a contract/statute by deliberately introducing a certain vagueness into the language deployed so as to allow for future technological developments. There can also be a certain refuge to be found in vagueness; after all, a desire for precision may yield a greater risk of error.[98] And being able to view a precedent in macro (more abstract) terms and then apply it by analogy to the different facts of a specific case is a key skill for practising lawyers.[99] To be avoided,

---

92   Collyn Peddie, "Improving Legal Writing: The Triumph of Hope Over Experience" (1993) 13(1) *Review of Litigation* 83–104, 84.
93   Stephanie Melnick, "Hamilton's Legal Writing Lessons" (2017) 90(1) *Wisconsin Lawyer* 28–32, 32.
94   Laurel Oates *et al*, *The Legal Writing Handbook* (Aspen Law & Business, 2002), 721.
95   On the potential for conflict between the demands of style and clarity, see Mark Osbeck, "What is 'Good Legal Writing' and Why Does It Matter?" (2012) 4(2) *Drexel Law Review* 417–466, 454–456.
96   Richard Neumann, *Reasoning and Legal Writing*, 5th edition (Aspen Publishers, 2005), 25.
97   J Austin, *Sense and Sensibilia* (Oxford University Press, 1979), 125.
98   *Ibid*.
99   Mark Cooney, "Analogy Through Vagueness" (2019) 16 *Legal Communications and Rhetoric* 85–110, 109.

however, is raising unsupported or poorly supported "airy assertions"[100] – and raising in the process a suspicion that the writer does not really understand whatever point he or she is seeking to make.[101]

It avoids wordiness

Among the most common criticisms of the lawyer in practice is that his or her writing is poor, uncertain, vague – and wordy.[102] The great risk that attaches to wordiness is that the writer may dilute the force/logic of what he or she is seeking to state.[103] Writing over half a century ago, Floren offered as a 'golden rule' of clear legal writing that one should seek to avoid using an excess of words; and he offered four steps whereby such excess might be avoided by the legal writer: avoid words that say nothing; avoid repetition; avoid using multiple words when a single word will do; and use full stops.[104] Mellinkoff points to four common explanations for wordiness: there is not enough time in practice to be concise; it is better to say too much than too little; when text is dictated, often what is longer sounds better (even if it reads worse); and while one may aim for brevity. sometimes a text just comes out long.[105] However, he does not consider these explanations to be justifications and notes three particular downsides to wordiness: the more one says, the greater the potential there is for error; wordiness defeats clarity; and the longer a sentence, the more a piece of prose is exposed to reader/writer forgetfulness.[106] Fundamentally, reading unduly wordy text is a waste of reader time.[107]

It avoids grand flourishes

Along with legalese, legal writers are often encouraged to avoid grand and fancy words.[108] Of course, there will always be the occasional Holmes (a man of "wonderful writing skill")[109] or Denning (a man of "glorious legal

---

100   Bryan Garner, "Know Thy Reader: Writing for the Legal Audience" (2009) 38(1) *Student Lawyer* 12–13, 13.
101   *Ibid.*
102   George Gibson, "Effective Legal Writing and Speaking" (1980) 36(1) *Business Lawyer* 1–10, 1.
103   Robert Smith, "Making Sense: Some Reflections on Legal Writing" (1985) 56(41) *Oklahoma Bar Journal* 2563–2577, 2564.
104   M Floren, "Better Legal Writing" (1967) 13(4) *Student Lawyer Journal* 10–21, 11.
105   David Mellinkoff, *Legal Writing: Sense and Nonsense* (Charles Scribner's Sons, 1982), 127–128.
106   *Ibid*, 129–132.
107   *Ibid.*
108   See, eg, Michael Hyman, "Go Easy on the Legalese" (2018) 106(9) *Illinois Bar Journal* 48–49, 48.
109   Gerard Hogan, "Holmes and Denning: Two 20th Century Legal Icons Compared" (2007) 42 *Irish Jurist* 119–135, 134.

talents").[110] They are lawyers whose writings will likely be read by future generations for pleasure long after the particular issues that confronted them have been overtaken by time. However, such writers are a mix of the natural-born and the self-made.[111] For the great mass of legal writers, "[c]arefully tailored craftsmanship"[112] suffices to persuade. Good legal writing ought not to be confused with writing that is pedantic, pompous, and ponderous, punctuated with "irrelevant flourishes".[113] The most memorable legal writing is often the simplest.[114]

It is engaging

If a piece of legal text is to persuade, it must first be read, and to do this it must be engaging. Lord Denning perhaps captured best what is required in this regard with his observation that it is only when legal writing is "presented in a lively and attractive setting … [that readers] will read you with engrossment".[115]

6.   **Avoiding ornamental writing**

James defines the novel as "a personal definition of life … which is greater or less according to the intensity of the impression".[116] A legal text, it is submitted, is not so very different. It involves a perception of life through the prism of law and it is a creative work in which intensity plays a part – at least when the author subscribes to the tenets of the 'plain English' movement which seeks to make legal prose accessible to and understandable by the so-called 'ordinary' person.[117]

This last goal has been likened to achieving in legal prose what Hemingway managed in the literary world – and Hemingway's style was marked not just by its accessibility but also by an intense discipline on Hemingway's part, both in terms of plot and the most carefully chosen un-ornamental prose.[118]

---

110   *Ibid.*
111   *Ibid.*
112   *Ibid.*
113   Edward Re, "Legal Writing as Good Literature" (1985) 59(2) *St John's Law Review* 211–227, 224.
114   Thomas Spahn, "The Art of Legal Writing" (1989) 9(2) *Journal of the National Association of Administrative Law Judges* 137–152, 138. So, eg, Lincoln's Second Inaugural Address comprises 701 words, of which 505 contain one syllable (Spahn, *ibid*), while Justice Holmes' renowned dissent in *Lochner v New York* 198 US 45 (1905) runs to a mere 622 words (including citations), of which 388 are monosyllabic.
115   Lord Denning, *The Family Story* (Butterworths, 1981), 216.
116   Henry James, *The Art of Fiction* (Cupples, Upham & Co, 1885), 60–61.
117   Helen Leskovac, "Legal Writing and Plain English: Does Voice Matter?" (1988) 38(4) *Syracuse Law Review* 1193–1222, 1196.
118   Eric Bennett, "Ernest Hemingway and the Discipline of Creative Writing, or, Shark Liver Oil" (2010) 56(3) *Modern Fiction Studies* 544–567, 557.

Hemingway's aversion to writing that was heavy in adjectives and verbs was not unique to him. It is a trend that can be traced back to Ezra Pound and, through him, to the writings of the late 19th/20th-century art historian, Ernest Fenollosa.[119] But Hemingway's fame is such that he is repeatedly mentioned in the academic commentary on legal writing as an author whose style bears repeating. To give but three examples:

- Floren observes, in an article on better legal writing notes, how "in successful writing from the Bible to Ernest Hemingway, you'll find the same wise use of plain language".[120]
- Mayda, having touted the virtues of variety in the length and form of sentences, offers a quote from Hemingway's Men Without Women as an example of what he means.[121]
- Furey, in an article on the desirability of concision, clarity and coherence in legal writing, suggests that the reader take a look at Hemingway's prose, "if you can stand his machismo".[122]

Whether these appeals to Hemingway's hallmark style[123] are altogether fair to legal writers is perhaps open to question. After all, Hemingway writes with a remarkable intensity, eschews the transcendent, and chips away at abstraction until all that remains is detail.[124] Yet lawyers are typically expected to manifest some level of professional detachment,[125] to treat with the "analytic concepts"[126] that underpin the common law system, and to treat also with matters both abstract and concrete by "expressing the objective relation of ideas".[127] All that said, when one looks more closely at the references to Hemingway in the academic literature on legal writing, it is clear that the authors of that literature are not canvassing for an adoption of every aspect of Hemingway's style but rather for the attributes of clarity, concision, and simplicity[128] for which –

---

119 *Ibid*.
120 M Floren, "Better Legal Writing" (1967) 13(4) *Student Lawyer Journal* 10–21, 19.
121 Jaro Mayda, "On Style and Form in Legal Writing" (1962) 31 *Revista Jurídica de la Universidad de Puerto Rico* 9–32, 16. The text quoted by Mayda appears in Ernest Hemingway, *Men Without Women* (Charles Scribner's Sons, 1955), 13.
122 Linda Furey, "To Write Well: A Primer on Concision, Clarity and Coherence in Legal Writing" (1992) *New Jersey Lawyer* 18–26, 19.
123 Richard Hyland, "A Defense of Legal Writing" (1986) 134(3) *University of Pennsylvania Law Review* 599–626, 611.
124 *Ibid*, 612.
125 Kathryn Stanchi, "Moving Beyond Instinct: Persuasion in the Era of Professional Legal Writing" (2005) 9 *Lewis & Clark Law Review* 935–950, 938.
126 Julie Ann Interdonato, "The Consummate Legal Education: Teaching Analysis as Doctrine" (2019) 4 *Concordia Law Review* 68–100, 70.
127 Daniel Mandelker, "Legal Writing – The Drake Program" (1951) 3(4) *Journal of Legal Education* 583–586, 586.

rightly or wrongly – Hemingway is understood generally to stand. Those are the basic attributes of good legal writing and operate to yield that intensity of prose which James touts as a virtue.

7. Writing engagingly, recounting facts

To James, the quality of reality is the supreme virtue of the novel. Legal texts, of course, seek to deal solely with reality. However, the ability of a legal writer to capture the vivacity of the facts presenting before him or her – the facts typically being the first substantive limb of a legal text – can be a sign that one is in the hands of a gifted legal writer who has written an insightful legal text. If ever there was a legal writer whose greatest works establish the truth of this proposition, it is surely Lord Denning, "possibly the most important English judge of the twentieth century".[129] As a judge, Denning was renowned for his recitations of fact (and clearly enjoyed reciting them).[130] Harvey has traced the evolution of Denning's writing style, pointing to the absence of his classic staccato form in his earliest judgments, its sudden entrée in a nascent state in *James v Minister for Pensions*[131] ("Gunner James joined the army on July 24, 1941, at the age of thirty-two. In January 1943, he had a swelling on the right side of his neck"), and its evolution into the classic Denning 'openers', which Harvey divides into nine categories, namely:

- the intriguing opener (eg, "It was a fine Chinese carpet worth £900, but it needed cleaning");[132]
- the historical opener (eg, "The village has an attractive name, Dibden Purlieu. It goes back to the times of the Norman French");[133]
- the fatal opener (eg, "A man's head got caught in a propeller. He was decapitated and killed");[134]
- the 'This is the case' opener[135] (eg, "This is the case of the Birmingham bombers");[136]

---

128 Richard Hyland, "A Defense of Legal Writing" (1986) 134(3) *University of Pennsylvania Law Review* 599–626, 611.
129 Robert Stevens, "Judicial Legislation and the Law Lords: Four Interpretations – II" (1975) 10(2) *Irish Jurist* 216–254, 237.
130 For a fuller consideration of Lord Denning's judgments, see Max Barrett, *The Art and Craft of Judgment Writing* (Globe Law and Business, 2022), 231–243.
131 [1947] KB 867 (CA).
132 *Levinson v Patent Steam Carpet Cleaning Co Ltd* [1978] QB 69, 77 (CA).
133 *Jennings Motors Ltd v Secretary of State for the Environment* [1982] 2 WLR 131, 134 (CA).
134 *Allen v Jambo Holdings Ltd* [1980] 1 WLR 1252, 1254 (CA).
135 Cameron Harvey, "It All Started with Gunner James" (1986) 1 *Denning Law Journal* 67–84, 78.
136 *McIlkenny v Chief Constable of West Midlands Police Force* [1980] 2 All ER 227 (CA). As later history would show it was not actually the case of the Birmingham bombers: error had infused the underlying criminal proceedings (see generally Chris Mullin, *Error of Judgment* (Chatto & Windus, 1986)).

- the editorial opener (eg, "This case ought to have been simple, but the lawyers have made it complicated");[137]

- the *non sequitur* opener (eg, "Many years ago Sir Edward Coke had a case about six carpenters. Now we have a case about six car-hire drivers");[138]

- the 'This is an interesting case' opener (ie, "This is an interesting case ...");[139]

- the whimsical opener (eg, "A gigantic ship was used for a gigantic fraud"); and[140]

- the picturesque opener (eg, "In 1962 life was peaceful in Buckinghamshire").[141]

To these nine categories a further category might be added: the occasionally disappointing opener, such as Denning's observation in *Rank Film Distributors Ltd v Video Information Centre*:[142]

> *"It is, it is a glorious thing, to be a Pirate King," said WS Gilbert ... But he was speaking of ship pirates. Today we speak of film pirates. It is not a glorious thing to be, but it is a good thing to be in for making money.*[143]

Even geniuses, it seems, have their 'off days'.

If nothing else Denning's remarkable abilities as a storyteller point to the importance of facts in the legal process[144] and why the manner in which facts are portrayed can dictate results.[145] Legal disputes often turn on disputed facts. So lawyers must be able to describe facts, identify potentially determinative facts, and see the possible ambiguities in a given pattern of facts.[146] To James, the quality of reality is the supreme virtue of the novel. In law, factual reality is likewise of critical importance. For James, if a literary author fails adequately to capture reality, then, to James, that author's work is a failure.[147] In a similar way, if lawyers fail to understand thoroughly the facts at play in a matter that

---

137   *Marsden v Regan* [1954] 1 All ER 423, 436 (CA).
138   *Cinnamond v British Airports Authority* [1980] 1 WLR 582, 585 (CA).
139   *Southam v Smout* [1964] 1 QB 308, 319 (CA).
140   *Shell International Petroleum Ltd v Gibbs* [1982] 2 WLR 745, 771 (CA).
141   *Myers v Milton Keynes Development Corporation* [1974] 1 WLR 696, 699 (CA).
142   [1982] AC 380 (CA).
143   *Ibid*, 403.
144   Erika Abner and Shelley Kierstad, "A Preliminary Exploration of the Elements of Expert Performance in Legal Writing" (2010) 16(1) *Legal Writing: The Journal of the Legal Writing Institute* 363–410, 382.
145   Michelle Simon, "Teaching Writing Through Substance: The Integration of Legal Writing with all Deliberate Speed" (1993) 42(2) *DePaul Law Review* 619–630, 626.
146   Soma Kedia, "Redirecting the Scope of First-Year Writing Courses: Toward a New Paradigm of Teaching Legal Writing" (2010) 87(2) *University of Detroit Mercy Law Review* 147–178, 173.
147   Henry James, *The Art of Fiction* (Cupples, Upham & Co, 1885), 66.

is placed before them, they will produce a legal analysis that is fundamentally flawed. This is because it is the organisation/ systematisation of "collected facts"[148] that brings the lawyer "bounding ... into the region of fundamental principles".[149] That bound can only be as sure-footed as the facts on and from which the lawyer springs forward.

8. Types of writing

James sees only two classes of novel: the bad novel and the good novel.[150] Nor is he prepared to countenance a distinction between the modern English novel and previous classes of novel, observing that one writes the novel of one's time,[151] with that novel being either good or bad. Aspects of what makes good and bad legal writing have already been considered above. Also of interest, however, is James' notion that one writes the novel of one's time.

What characteristics might be identified in modern legal writing such that one could point to a legal text as a product of its time? Perhaps the single greatest change in recent decades has been the evolution of the legal writing firmament from one in which legalese was all-pervasive to one in which the demand and desire for plain English have taken hold. The modern 'Plain English Movement' began in the 1970s, originally as a US-based movement aimed at ensuring that consumer-friendly documentation issued in the consumer insurance/sales contexts.[152] (In England, the 16th-century king, Edward VI, may have stolen something of an advance on the Americans in this regard, having apparently once said that "I would wish that ... the superfluous and tedious statutes were brought into one sum together, and made more plain and short, to the intent that men might better understand them".)[153] Ultimately, the American 'Plain English Movement' eventually morphed beyond its original purely consumer-oriented context into a campaign that canvassed for general good communication in the law.[154] This brought to the fore a number of issues, such as:

---

148 Walter Kennedy, "Principles or Facts" (1935) 1 *Current Legal Thought* 55–57, 57.
149 *Ibid*.
150 Henry James, *The Art of Fiction* (Cupples, Upham & Co, 1885), 68.
151 *Ibid*, 70.
152 J Christopher Rideout and J Ramsfield, "Legal Writing: A Revised View" (1994) 69(1) *Washington Law Review* 35–100, 40; Carl Felsenfeld, "The Plain English Movement in the United States" (1982) 6(4) *Canadian Business Law Journal* 408–421.
153 Committee on the Preparation of Legislation, *The Preparation of Legislation* (HMSO, 1975, Cmnd 6053), 6.
154 Carl Felsenfeld, "The Plain English Movement in the United States" (1982) 6(4) *Canadian Business Law Journal* 408–421, 412.

Could legal language be rephrased in plain English?

A concern sometimes raised in this regard is that the desire for plain English encounters difficulty when it comes to the common law convention whereby the precise meaning of a word or phrase may become the subject of a particular judicial interpretation.[155] Two points might usefully be made in this regard. First, there are actually quite few judicially defined terms. Secondly, there is no evidence to suggest that plain English would actually end up requiring judicial interpretation. (Statistically, there are few terms of art in any one legal document and a desire for plain English does not, in any event, require that they all be avoided.)[156]

How could the clarity of legal writing be improved?

The various attributes of good and bad legal writing (and related suggestions as to improved and effective legal writing have already been considered above).

Could Latin and 'Law French' terms be reduced to plain English?

When it comes to Latin, the general consensus is that while some Latin words are unavoidable, they should only be used when no English alternative exists (and when writers completely understand the meaning of whatever Latin is used).[157] As one American commentator colourfully observes of Latin, "like drug store aftershave a little goes a long way".[158] As to 'Law French' this was a legacy from the Norman ancestry of the common law. Many 'Law French' words have graduated to full membership of the English language, for example, 'agreement', 'appeal' and 'contract'. However, many remain specialist legal terms that have no place in everyday English, for example, 'choses in action', 'estoppel' and

---

155   Peter Tiersma, "Some Myths About Legal Language" (2006) 2(1) *Law, Culture and the Humanities* 29–50, 49.

156   Hwee Ying Yeo, "Plain English for Lawyers" (1996) 8(2) *Singapore Academy of Law Journal* 303–322, 312.

157   Elizabeth Frost, "Latin in Legal Writing: When to Use It, How, and What It Means" (2015–2016) 76 *Oregon State Bar Bulletin* 13–18. See also Peter Macleod, "Latin in Legal Writing: An Inquiry into the Use of Latin in the Modern Legal World" (1997) 39 *Boston College Law Review* 235–252. Macleod seems better disposed to Latin than some commentators; even so, he too indicates that Latin should always be used with care (*ibid*, 251).

158   Elizabeth Frost, "Latin in Legal Writing: When to Use It, How, and What It Means" (2015–2016) 76 *Oregon State Bar Bulletin* 13–18, 13.

'laches'. Obviously, those words that have become everyday English words typically present no issue from a legal writing perspective. As to those 'Law French' words/phrases which have crept into legal English but gone no further, a distinction falls to be made between those terms which have become legal terms of art and those which are neither clear nor precise.[159] The continuing use of the latter type of phraseology is difficult to justify. Perhaps the best advice when it comes to deploying 'Law French' or Latin in legal writing is offered by Mellinkoff, namely that in all instances the aim should be to make matters intelligible to one's audience.[160] If that objective is frustrated by the use of Latin or Law French then alternative wording requires to be considered.

Should plain English in legal texts be mandated by statute?

This is a matter for individual legislatures to determine. However, the American experience has been that plain English laws – the principal value of which seems to be their symbolic value[161] – even when coupled with readability requirements do not altogether eliminate the problem of 'legalese' in standard-form legal documentation.[162] Thus, it has been observed in the insurance law context (and there is no reason to suspect that there is a contrary trend in other commercial fields) that legalese will not be vanquished until 'offending' companies want to end it.[163] Plain English statutes may represent a step in the right direction in terms of maximising the accessibility and comprehensibility of the law and legal texts. However, general 'buy-in' from the legal profession is required if the plain English movement is to triumph.[164]

Should there be 'plain English' precedent libraries?

Lawyers tend not to draft entirely original documents; their efforts involve something of a 'cobbling together' of text, often drawn from encyclopaedias of forms and precedents. In *Whishaw v Stephens*,[165] Lord

---

159 Donald Layh, "Plain English: Increasing the Power of Our Writing" (1992) 56(1) *Saskatchewan Law Review* 1–22, 4.
160 David Mellinkoff, "Plain English and the Law" (1994) 73(1) *Michigan Bar Journal* 22–25, 24.
161 F Reed Dickerson, "Should Plain English Be Legislated?" (1980) 24(7) *Res Gestae* 332–334, 334.
162 George Hathaway and Peter Marroso, "Plain English in Insurance Papers" (1994) 73(2) *Michigan Bar Journal* 196–199, 198.
163 *Ibid.*
164 Michael Friman, "Plain English Statutes – Long Overdue or Underdone?" (1995) 7(3) *Loyola Consumer Law Reporter* 103–112, 108–109.
165 [1968] 3 WLR 1127 (HL).

Reid adverted to the dangers of blindly relying on such encyclopaedias, noting how the "botched clause"[166] at issue in that case had "somehow found its way into a standard book of precedents".[167] At one time, there was also a perception that such encyclopaedias were impeding the more widespread usage of (innovative) plain English. However, one commentator, writing in the Singaporean context (though his observations, I submit, have a wider resonance) has observed that there has been progress in this regard, with more recent editions of forms and precedents seeking to adopt a modern simplicity of layout/style.[168]

Should there be requirements as to the design/readability of text?

As mentioned previously above, Lord Denning has pointed to how legal reasoning "if it is presented in a dull and turgid setting" will prove off-putting to readers,[169] but if "presented in a lively and attractive setting"[170] will excite an interest in readers. Denning was writing of style but his observations have an equal relevance when it comes to design, one more recent commentator pointing to how well-designed text will attract readers (and noting how many modern legal texts are ugly and off-putting to readers).[171] Design is important to legal text writers and there are many texts dedicated to the design of legal documents.[172] And design and readability have acquired particular importance in the Computer Age as people shift from paper-based reading to on-screen reading – a new format that entails new opportunities and challenges. The temptation is to copy, paste and use block quotes. However, the sheer abundance of information (and innovations such as hyperlinks – as well as footnotes being notably challenging to read online) places new demands on lawyers when it comes to the synthesis and organisation of on-screen text.[173] As Crist observes (and it seems but a truism), an effective lawyer must understand e-communications and the use of hypertext (which he

---

166   *Ibid*, 1130.
167   *Ibid*.
168   Hwee Ying Yeo, "Plain English for Lawyers" (1996) 8(2) *Singapore Academy of Law Journal* 303–322, 306.
169   Lord Denning, *The Family Story* (Butterworths, 1981), 216.
170   *Ibid*.
171   C Edward Good, "Ugly Legal Writing" (2018) 11(2) *Landslide* 55–ii. Good identifies a number of practical steps that can be taken by legal writers when preparing legal texts on a computer.
172   For a brief but useful commentary see Scott Moise, "Architecture and Legal Writing" (2010) 22(3) *South Carolina Lawyer* 42–46.
173   Scott Longman, "The Architecture of Legal Writing" (2001) 15(3) *CBA Record* 40–66, 40.

describes as the "key characteristic"[174] of such communications). The introduction of legal requirements as to design/readability seem almost redundant: computers and the Internet are here to stay and lawyers must be able to use both technologies well.

9. Style and freedom in writing

In his closing remarks, James returns to the freedom that novel writing offers, encouraging would-be novelists to seek to capture life's full colour.[175] His point as to vivacity has already been touched upon. However, James's point as to literary freedom bears closer examination: to what extent is the author of a legal text free as to how and what he or she writes (subject to an overriding commitment to present law and facts truthfully)? The truth is that the legal writer is not very free. Thus, the writer cannot change facts or deliberately misstate legal principles and must generally eschew novelty, save when innovation will aid the clarity/effectiveness of whatever point he or she seeks to make.[176] The above constraints are particular to legal writers. They are also subject to the constraints that apply to all good English-language writers such as coherency, diction, and style.[177] Yet through the observation of all of the various constraints to which they are subject the freedom to attain excellence in his or her writing presents for the legal writer. As Justice Cardozo has observed:

> There are those who have perceived that the highest measure of condensation, of short and sharp and imperative directness, a directness that speaks the voice of some external and supreme authority, is consistent, none the less, with supreme literary excellence … [A] French novelist used to say that "there was only one example of the perfect style, and that was the Code Napoléon; for there alone everything was subordinated to the exact and complete expression of what was to be said".[178]

For all that the constraints identified above present for judgment writers, they do still enjoy some freedom to seek/fashion new causes of action and forms of relief.[179] Viewed so, at least some legal writing can be

---

174 Maria Perez Crist, "The E-Brief: Legal Writing for an Online World" (2003) 33(1) *New Mexico Law Review* 49–94, 49.

175 Henry James, *The Art of Fiction* (Cupples, Upham & Co, 1885), 85.

176 Edward Re, "Legal Writing as Good Literature" (1985) 59(2) *St John's Law Review* 211–227, 223–224.

177 *Ibid*, 224.

178 Benjamin Cardozo, *Selected Writings of Benjamin Nathan Cardozo*, Margaret Hall (ed) (Fallon Publications, 1947), 339.

179 Douglas Litowitz, "Legal Writing: Its Nature, Limits, and Dangers" (1998) 49(3) *Mercer Law Review* 709–740, 722.

seen to be "a highly creative act ... akin to painting or literary creation".[180] This last concept of legal writing as a creative act akin to painting (and hence of the legal writer as an artist with the freedom of mind that the artist has traditionally enjoyed in Western culture) seems notable. Schlegel has observed that "[w]hat men are among the other creatures of the earth, artists are among men".[181] Yet there is a strange hesitation to treating legal writers as engaged in any level of artistry, perhaps because of the tradition that artists belong to a fanciful class to which a legal writer could not conceivably belong.[182]

The process of creating 'art', as that concept is popularly understood, is in some ways similar to that of formulating a creative legal text, as can be seen, for example, in Danto's description of how the American minimalist artist, Robert Mangold, approaches the creation of his 'column paintings':

> *Mangold typically begins his pieces with small studies on paper. In these, he is able to experiment with the curves in their relationship to one another, and to the edges of the shape that contains them. The figures are in pencil, but not single pencil lines: they are like thin ribbons, with their own boundaries. In a given piece, one of the "ribbons" is filled in, while the other is left empty. After the drawing has been achieved, Mangold covers it with pastel which, when smoothly smudged, leaves the drawing visible through the chalk. When satisfied with the study, he repeats the procedure on a larger scale, this time with acrylic. The paint is put on with rollers, in perhaps three thin coats. Once more, the drawing remains visible. The work is a single entity, suffused with lightness and grace ...*[183]

It is not hard to translate this into a description of the process of writing a legal text such as a judgment:

> *Judge X typically begins her judgments with small studies on paper. In these she is able to experiment with the facts and law in their relationship to one another, and to the judgment form that contains them. Her observations are like thin ribbons, with their own boundaries. In a given judgment, one of the "ribbons" is rich with detailed references, while the other is more stark. After the shape of the judgment has been achieved, Judge X attends to the finer detail and enters it into her computer. She prints what she has typed, then repeats the procedure of adding, removing,*

---

180   *Ibid.*
181   J Bernstein, *Classic and Romantic German Aesthetics* (Cambridge University Press, 2012), 263.
182   Arthur Danto, "Art, Evolution, and the Consciousness of History" (1986) 44(3) *Journal of Aesthetics and Art Criticism* 223–233, 225.
183   Arthur Danto, "Robert Mangold's 'Column Paintings'" (2004) 8(5) *Art on Paper* 60–63, 63.

and finessing the detail. Throughout the essence remains visible, suffused with lightness and grace …

Tolstoy, the great Russian author, sees true artistry and the true artist as a rarity: men of little enough talent, he suggests, can produce works that pass for art but are not.[184] In this, he might almost be addressing a key difference between competent legal writers and great legal writers. But what precisely is the characteristic that makes a legal text great? What exactly is one seeking when looking for greatness, even beauty in works of the mind? Such beauty, the 17th/18th-century French philosopher, Père André maintains, appeals to reason by virtue of its "excellence … light … exactness, and … intrinsic pleasantness".[185] A great/beautiful legal text is possessed of like characteristics. Re neatly brings the artistic and utilitarian functions of legal writing together when he observes that law must be learned, read, and written carefully and thoughtfully, adding that by observing the rules of English (and the rules of English composition) "legal writing can not only be literature, but … good literature of obvious excellence and enduring value".[186] Each time the legal writer sits down to write, he or she enjoys that freedom to which James refers to produce just such literature.

Key propositions

- Legal texts offer a worldview peculiar to a given legal writer at a given time.
- The task of the writer, James posits, is to represent/illustrate the past and the actions of people.[187] As a summary of what is often at play in a legal text, this is as good as any, save that the law falls also to be brought to bear.
- Legal texts should not be unduly frivolous or serious.
- A number of points might be made when it comes to the present abundance of judgments in the common law world, namely that: the sheer number of judgments now available has diminished the value of the judgment as a commodity; that the field of judgments is crowded and not all legal texts are equally good; and that there is as much difference as ever between a good/bad

184   Leo Tolstoy, *What is Art?* (Funk & Wagnalls, 1904), 114.
185   Yves Marie André, "Essay on Beauty", A Cain (trans), https://archive.org/details/EssayOnBeauty/page/n1/mode/2up, 31.
186   Edward Re, "Legal Writing as Good Literature" (1985) 59(2) *St John's Law Review* 211–227, 227.
187   Henry James, *The Art of Fiction* (Cupples, Upham & Co, 1885), 56.

judgment (with better judgments retaining their allure and casting the same illumination as ever).

- James observes of novels that they are as varied as men's temperaments and successful in proportion to the extent that they reveal a particular mind.[188] The same observation might be made of legal writers and legal texts.
- A legal text involves the view of one or more legal writers on the sliver of life on which they are asked to opine or decide. However, their greatness has less to do with intensity of impression than with clarity of expression and analysis.
- With legal texts the criterion of worth is truth.
- The mental acuity of the legal writer is directly proportional to the quality of the legal texts that he or she is likely to produce. Truth is the fundamental determinant of a legal text's quality, but from an aesthetic perspective, a legal text is just as capable of beauty as any other prose work.
- The first duty of the legal writer is to be as complete as possible in his or her writing and to make as perfect a work as possible.

---

188   *Ibid*, 60.

12. Stevenson

On composition, pattern, sound and other matters

Robert Louis Stevenson (1850–1894) was a relatively short-lived Scottish essayist, novelist and poet whose most famous works include *Treasure Island* (1883), *The Strange Case of Dr Jekyll and Mr Hyde* (1886) and *Kidnapped* (1886). Though his works are now firmly ensconced in the canon of Western literature, up until the late 20th century the general view among literary scholars was that Stevenson's works "were not quite 'literary' enough to study"[1] – an unexpected fate for a man who, in his own time, was seen as a literary star and a "stylist of giddying promise"[2] who generated aphorisms as abundantly as Wilde minted epigrams.[3] In his *Essays on the Art of Writing* (1905),[4] Stevenson published essays entitled "On Some Technical Elements of Style in Literature"[5] and "A Note on Realism".[6] Both essays, I submit, are of interest to the legal writer minded to improve the quality of his or her legal writing.

1. Vocabulary, word choice and grammar

Stevenson suggests that the first merit one encounters in good writing is a fitting choice/contrast of terminology.[7] Words, he suggests, are rough building blocks and it takes art to turn words that are created for use at the market or in the pub and give them the finest meanings and distinctions.[8] That said, he notes that it is a skill which is not equally present in all great writers.[9] Nor do they deploy words to the same effect.[10] What lessons might be drawn from this for the legal writer? Two lessons,

---

1   Claire Harman, *Robert Louis Stevenson: A Biography* (HarperCollins, 2005), xv.
2   *Ibid.*
3   *Ibid.*
4   Robert Louis Stevenson, *Essays on the Art of Writing* (Chatto & Windus, 1919).
5   *Ibid*, 3–43.
6   *Ibid*, 93–107.
7   *Ibid*, 6.
8   *Ibid*, 7.
9   *Ibid.*
10   *Ibid.*

it is contended. First, that a merit of good legal texts is that they are written well. Second, that not all great legal writers will be equally skilled in their deployment of words. Word choice in the context of legal writing is something of a subject in itself; however, the following general points might be made.[11]

Words are an important persuasive tool[12]

Language is a "tool of wonderful power"[13] whereby a good legal writer can change the perception of a particular set of facts through the "selective use"[14] (and careful deployment) of adjectives, adverbs, nouns and verbs. However, it is important to remember that words are not just persuasive tools but have real-life consequences,[15] so care is needed in their use.

Words have meaning and additional connotations[16]

As the English legal philosopher, HLA Hart indicated as long ago as the late-1950s,[17] it is impossible to define legal concepts precisely; one needs to look at the context in which a word is used. Words, Hart posits, have a core meaning, as well as a peripheral meaning (which may be very wide when it comes to everyday words).[18] So again, word choice is of necessity a matter of some care.

There is a distinction between useful/possible word choices[19]

In discerning words that might usefully be used from those that may possibly be used, it is necessary to consider the purpose of the text in which those words will feature.[20] In this regard it is important to be a 'conscious' writer, deliberately choosing words (and revising word

---

11 Stephen Smith, "A Rhetorical Exercise: Persuasive Word Choice" (2014–2015) 49 *University of San Francisco Law Review Forum* 37–40.
12 *Ibid*, 37.
13 Robert Barr Smith, "[Book Review] *A Dictionary of Modern Legal Usage* by Bryan A Garner" (1989) 42(1) *Oklahoma Law Review* 183–185, 184.
14 Jennifer Jolly-Ryan, "Four Tips for Persuasive Legal Writing" (2016) 80(2) *Bench & Bar* 31.
15 Adam Lamparello and Charles MacLean, "Legal Writing – What's Next? Real World, Persuasion Pedagogy from Day One" (2013–2014) 38 *New England Law Review on Remand* 85–95, 89.
16 Stephen Smith, "A Rhetorical Exercise: Persuasive Word Choice" (2014–2015) 49 *University of San Francisco Law Review Forum* 37–40, 38.
17 HLA Hart, "Scandinavian Realism" (1959) 17 *Cambridge Law Journal* 233–240, esp 239–240.
18 Frank Maher, "Words, Words, Words" (1984) 14(3) *Melbourne University Law Review* 468–511, 475.
19 Stephen Smith, "A Rhetorical Exercise: Persuasive Word Choice" (2014–2015) 49 *University of San Francisco Law Review Forum* 37–40, 38.
20 *Ibid*.

choices) not simply by reference to a particular word or sentence but to the text as a whole,[21] having regard also, for example, to audience and stance.

Word choice raises ethical issues (eg, as to biases/stereotypes)[22]

Legal writing, to use a colloquialism, needs to be 'woke', in the sense of being empathetic, sympathetic and tolerant. As Justice Anthony Kennedy, formerly of the United States Supreme Court, has observed, "[T]he law lives through language, and we must be very careful about the language that we use",[23] not just so as to express precisely what one is thinking but also to avoid causing avoidable offence when so doing. Being 'woke' in the manner described above also involves being alive to the fact that Western canons of rhetoric are presently dominant, even exclusive, but that there is a case for 'decolonisation' of dominant rhetorical practices and the dominant canon.[24]

Beautiful words are the light of thought[25]

While words may be the light of thought, there is a constraint presenting in the legal writing context that does not affect literary writing, which is that one cannot escape the facts and the law: whatever words are chosen they must illuminate the truth of the facts and law presenting, not distort it. While good legal writing is a fine art,[26] the most important task of the legal writer is surely to create a clear, comprehensive, detailed and effective text,[27] and no amount of beautiful words can be allowed to get in the way of producing such a statement.

---

21   Christopher Anzidei, "The Revision Process in Legal Writing: Seeing Better to Write Better" (2002) 8 *Legal Writing: The Journal of the Legal Writing Institute* 23–58, 51.
22   Stephen Smith, "A Rhetorical Exercise: Persuasive Word Choice" (2014–2015) 49 *University of San Francisco Law Review Forum* 37–40, 38. See also Sha-Shana Crichton, "What Happens When the Media Gets Ahead of Your Client's Story? An Attorney's Duty to Use Conscious Word Choice" (2019) 47(1) *Southern University Law Review* 155–176, 172.
23   Bryan Garner, "Justice Anthony M Kennedy" (2010) 13 *Scribes Journal of Legal Writing* 79–98, 97.
24   Teri McMurtry-Chubb, "Still Writing at the Master's Table: Decolonizing Rhetoric in Legal Writing for a 'Woke' Legal Academy" (2019) 21(2) *Scholar: St Mary's Law Review on Race and Social Justice* 255–292, 288.
25   Stephen Smith, "A Rhetorical Exercise: Persuasive Word Choice" (2014–2015) 49 *University of San Francisco Law Review Forum* 37–40, 39.
26   J Tim Willette, "Memo of Masochism (Reflections in Legal Writing)" (1993) 17(2) *Nova Law Review* 869–882, 869.
27   *Ibid.*

Word choice should be deliberate/precise to convey
the intended meaning[28]

The principal aim of legal writing is to communicate thoughts accurately.[29] Accuracy aids both reading and understanding and requires care.[30] All that said, the desire for accuracy should not be surrendered to an excess of detail. As Justice Cardozo has observed: "There is an accuracy that defeats itself by the over-emphasis of details ... [A] sentence may be so overloaded with all its possible qualifications that it will tumble down of its own weight."[31]

Words evoking positive images are useful[32]

Positive/negative writing is more/less attractive to the reader (with the attractive more likely to win favour).[33] Writing has been described as involving an "interplay of images".[34] Thinking, it has been suggested, even presupposes image (because otherwise there is nothing to think).[35] Facts likely create visual images in a way that arguments cannot.[36] However, it has been suggested that even when it comes to arguments each principal argument should be reduced by the legal writer to "good visual imagery"[37] so as to have a lasting effect.

Concrete nouns are better than abstract nouns[38]

A concrete noun identifies something that is material and non-abstract (eg, a chair). An abstract noun identifies an idea, quality or state (eg,

---

28   Sha-Shana Crichton, "What Happens When the Media Gets Ahead of Your Client's Story? An Attorney's Duty to Use Conscious Word Choice" (2019) 47(1) *Southern University Law Review* 155–176, 166.

29   Henry Weihofen, *Legal Writing Style*, 2nd edition (West Publishing Co, 1980), 41.

30   Edward Re, "Legal Writing as Good Literature" (1985) 59(2) *St John's Law Review* 211–227, 223.

31   Benjamin Cardozo, *Selected Writings of Benjamin Nathan Cardozo*, M Hall (ed) (Fallon Publications, 1947), 341.

32   Sha-Shana Crichton, "What Happens When the Media Gets Ahead of Your Client's Story? An Attorney's Duty to Use Conscious Word Choice" (2019) 47(1) *Southern University Law Review* 155–176, 165.

33   Kathryn Stanchi, "Feminist Legal Writing" (2002) 39 *San Diego Law Review* 387–436, 394.

34   Joel Cornwell, "Legal Writing as a Kind of Philosophy" (1997) 48 *Mercer Law Review* 1091–1136, 1094.

35   *Ibid*, 1095.

36   Scott Longman, "The Architecture of Legal Writing" (2001) 15(3) *CBA Record* 40–66, 42.

37   *Ibid*, 43.

38   Sha-Shana Crichton, "What Happens When the Media Gets Ahead of Your Client's Story? An Attorney's Duty to Use Conscious Word Choice" (2019) 47(1) *Southern University Law Review* 155–176, 167.

happiness). The choice between concrete and abstract nouns is a critical task when crafting effective legal writing. This is because a legal writer can make positive facts tangible by way of concrete nouns (or transform unfavourable facts into neutral or even favourable facts by way of abstract nouns).[39]

Concrete verbs are better than abstract verbs[40]

A concrete verb describes literal action (eg, a ball 'bounces'). An abstract verb is concerned with less literal actions (eg, the court 'investigates'). Concrete verbs are generally preferred to abstract verbs in legal writing because they engage the reader by showing action rather than describing it.[41] They are viewed as enhancing persuasiveness by enlivening a text, appealing to the senses/emotions and accentuating clarity.[42]

The active voice is better than the passive voice[43]

In a sentence written in the active/passive voice, the subject performs/ receives the action. So, for example, 'Mr X attacked the victim' is a sentence that uses the active voice; 'the victim was attacked by Mr X' is a sentence that uses the passive voice. As a general rule, academic commentators prefer an active voice in legal writing. This is because sentences using the active voice are typically shorter, the active voice is seen to eliminate uncertainty (and so aid clarity), and portray confidence (with the passive voice being perceived to betray uncertainty).[44] That said, the choice of active/passive voice is a stylistic one, that is, it is not a question of being grammatically right or wrong. So there may be instances where a legal writer may legitimately prefer the passive voice, not least because it often helps to make sentences move and read more smoothly.[45]

---

39 Justin Kishbaugh, "Rolling Off the Tongue: Structuralist Legal Writing and Keith Richards" (2020) 33(2) *Second Draft* 40–48, 46.
40 Sha-Shana Crichton, "What Happens When the Media Gets Ahead of Your Client's Story? An Attorney's Duty to Use Conscious Word Choice" (2019) 47(1) *Southern University Law Review* 155–176, 168.
41 See, eg, Wayne Schiess, "What Plain English Really Is" (2003–2004) 9 *Scribes Journal of Legal Writing* 43–76, 72.
42 Sha-Shana Crichton, "What Happens When the Media Gets Ahead of Your Client's Story? An Attorney's Duty to Use Conscious Word Choice" (2019) 47(1) *Southern University Law Review* 155–176, 168.
43 *Ibid*, 169.
44 See, eg, Mark Cohen, "When to Use Passive Voice" (2019) 48(6) *Colorado Lawyer* 8–9; Brandy Johnson and Brian Bartels, "Keep It Conversational: Use Active Voice" (2021) 24(4) *Nebraska Lawyer* 45–46.
45 Benjamin Halasz, "Activate Your Prose By Using the Passive Voice" (2019) 73(5) *NWLawyer* 16–17.

Excessive adjectives and adverbs should be avoided[46]

Excessive deployment of adjectives/adverbs generates unnecessarily wordy text;[47] it also moves the focus of a sentence away from the all-important nouns and verbs.[48] The elimination of unessential adjectives/adverbs ('qualifiers') is seen as an aid to concision[49] – in a writing context where concision and precision are viewed as positive attributes.[50] Adjectives and adverbs have a place:[51] lawyers are sometimes asked to opine/pronounce on matters in respect of which no certainty presents and thus a qualifier may be needed to ensure accuracy;[52] the downside is that they create an impression of uncertainty.[53] The aim is for an appropriate level of usage, to yield the sense that the writer is offering "the gospel truth"[54] on whatever issue is in play.

Words should humanise a client[55]

By humanising a client the hope is to generate sufficient empathy for the client to win sympathy for his or her cause. This may not mean that a client will always prevail but, as one judge has observed, when presented with a case which yielded empathy it always prompted him to want to look more closely at a matter.[56] That said, lawyers need to be careful not simply to craft a tale aimed at winning sympathy. Yes, lawyers tell stories, but a good lawyer separates the facts of legal relevance and brings the rule of law to bear upon them.[57] As an advocate, it is an error to cultivate judicial sympathy, yet leave judges to discern which facts are legally

---

46   Sha-Shana Crichton, "What Happens When the Media Gets Ahead of Your Client's Story? An Attorney's Duty to Use Conscious Word Choice" (2019) 47(1) *Southern University Law Review* 155–176, 171.

47   Mary Dunnewold, "Ten Ways to Spruce Up Your Legal Writing" (2005) 74(3) *Hennepin Lawyer* 18–23, 20.

48   K du Vivier, "A Thousand Probabilities" (1994) 23(9) *Colorado Lawyer* 2082.

49   Mark Osbeck, "What is 'Good Legal Writing' and Why Does It Matter?" (2012) 4(2) *Drexel Law Review* 417–466, 440.

50   Bridget Meeds, "Precision and Concision: Lawyering Program Teaches Skills and Values" (2010) 36(2) *Cornell Law Forum* 16–19, 16.

51   K du Vivier, "A Thousand Probabilities" (1994) 23(9) *Colorado Lawyer* 2082.

52   *Ibid.*

53   *Ibid.*

54   Alan Dworsky, *The Little Book on Legal Writing*, 2nd edition (Fred B Rothman & Co, 1992), 138.

55   Sha-Shana Crichton, "What Happens When the Media Gets Ahead of Your Client's Story? An Attorney's Duty to Use Conscious Word Choice" (2019) 47(1) *Southern University Law Review* 155–176, 171.

56   Wallace Jefferson, "Reflections on Legal Writing for the Supreme Court" (2020) 92 *Advocate* 49–52, 51.

57   Richard Hyland, "A Defense of Legal Writing" (1986) 134(3) *University of Pennsylvania Law Review* 599–626, 613.

relevant without those facts being identified and presented by that advocate in the manner which best aligns with his or her client's interests.[58]

Undue reliance on emotional words may suggest a case
has no legal merit.[59]

When it comes to deployment of emotional language in United States Supreme Court briefs, it has been suggested that the members of the court are "unfazed" by such efforts,[60] that usage of such language runs the risk of "diminished credibility",[61] and that appeals to emotion do not help a party to escape an inevitable loss.[62] This accords with the general consensus in the commentary on legal writing that it is best to avoid using unduly emotional language.[63]

Word choice can increase speed of comprehension[64]

Ease of understanding is an objective that good legal writers strive to achieve.[65] That said, it has been noted that a certain formality in legal writing is part and parcel of life in a complex society,[66] and that professional lawyers (if they are to earn an income) must be competent at producing such writing, but that – mindful of the downsides of undue formality – they should not deploy complex language "unreflexively".[67]

Word choice can better ensure accuracy[68]

Lawyers do a lot of writing and presumably wish generally for that writing to be understood as they intend it to be understood. The more

---

58   *Ibid*, 620.
59   Sha-Shana Crichton, "What Happens When the Media Gets Ahead of Your Client's Story? An Attorney's Duty to Use Conscious Word Choice" (2019) 47(1) *Southern University Law Review* 155–176, 174.
60   Ryan Black *et al*, "The Role of Emotional Language in Briefs Before the US Supreme Court" (2016) 4(2) *Journal of Law and Courts* 377–408, 396.
61   *Ibid*, 396.
62   *Ibid*.
63   *Ibid*, 397.
64   Patrick Hugg, "Professional Legal Writing Declaring Your Independence" (1991) 11(2) *Journal of the National Association of Administration Law Judges* 114–143, 128.
65   *Ibid*, 131.
66   Douglas Litowitz, "Legal Writing: Its Nature, Limits, and Dangers" (1998) 49(3) *Mercer Law Review* 709–740, 738.
67   *Ibid*.
68   Patrick Hugg, "Professional Legal Writing Declaring Your Independence" (1991) 11(2) *Journal of the National Association of Administration Law Judges* 114–143, 128.

accurate one's writing, the less risk there is of misunderstanding in this regard.[69] When it comes to the modern demand for plain English in legal writing, it has been suggested that (to ensure accuracy) it is preferable to use tried and tested legal jargon, rather than plain English; however, the international experience is that statutes and contracts have been 'translated' into plain English without any loss of accuracy.[70] Lawyers, it has been suggested, should not simplify to the point of inaccuracy.[71] However, a lot of legal writing can likely be improved with (amongst other matters) more simple vocabulary[72] that enhances readability without diminishing accuracy.

Proper word choice yields clarity[73]

Speaking in 1823, Judge Marks (a New York judge) observed of legal submissions (though he could have been speaking of legal writing more generally) that clearly stated and deeply considered thought is "a formidable weapon in legal warfare".[74] In essence, what Marks points to is that words in a legal text should reflect the thoughts of a legal writer and to that end, word choice is critical to clarity. Clarity is, of course, more than a matter of word choice: it involves "a firm grasp on ... meaning ... an acute ambiguity radar ... fine editorial techniques ... [and] careful organisation of text".[75] But word choice plays its part.

Proper word choice yields writing purpose[76]

Writing was invented to facilitate more complex and enduring communication[77] and control of meaning[78] is still at the core of writing. Word choice involves a form of control over writing and must be carefully deployed if the meaning which the legal writer seeks to express

---

69   David Ross, "Legal Writing" (2005) 1(4) *Original Law Review* 85–102, 85.
70   Joseph Kimble, "Notes Toward Better Legal Writing" (1996) 75(10) *Michigan Bar Journal* 1072–1075, 1072.
71   Jennifer Romig, "Improving Legal Writing – Quantifiably" (2012) 18(1) *Georgia Bar Journal* 64–67, 65.
72   *Ibid.*
73   Jessica Ronay, "A Mother Goose Guide to Legal Writing" (2014) 36(1) *University of La Verne Law Review* 119–144, 134.
74   Various, *Lectures on Legal Topics* (Macmillan, 1923–1924), 17.
75   Mark Cooney, "The Architecture of Clarity" (2016) 95(9) *Michigan Bar Journal* 40–43, 40.
76   Jessica Ronay, "A Mother Goose Guide to Legal Writing" (2014) 36(1) *University of La Verne Law Review* 119–144, 134.
77   Mary Barnard Ray, "Writing on the Envelope: An Exploration of the Potentials and Limits of Writing in Law" (2011) 49(3) *Duquesne Law Review* 573–612, 581.
78   *Ibid.*

and control is to be conveyed accurately.[79] All writing (legal and non-legal) communicates meaning by arranging facts and thoughts in a particular combination of the writer's devising.[80] For the legal writer, this task of arrangement involves aligning facts to create the most relevant meaning.[81] Again, word choice is critical to the precise expression of meaning and the attainment of whatever end is desired.

The quirks of on-screen reading make word choice especially important[82]

Technology has made good legal writing skills more important than ever before; this is because technology presents the legal writer with a vast amount of information that requires organisation and synthesis at levels not previously known[83] – with physical design (not least in terms of space, though also as regards capitalisation, font, headings, and spacing) having a role to play.[84] A well-structured on-screen legal text balances design, structure and word choice so that the reader is provided with the needed in an understandable and useful manner.[85]

Consistent word choice is important;[86] *elegant variation is best avoided*[87]

Emerson once remarked that "foolish consistency is the hobgoblin of little minds".[88] However, the overwhelming consensus among commentators on legal writing is that 'elegant variation' (consciously finding different ways to say the same thing in a single piece of writing merely to avoid repetition) is best avoided by legal writers. As one leading American commentator on effective legal writing observes, in the legal writing world clarity trumps the desire to avoid monotony.[89] In short,

---

79 Sha-Shana Crichton, "What Happens When the Media Gets Ahead of Your Client's Story? An Attorney's Duty to Use Conscious Word Choice" (2019) 47(1) *Southern University Law Review* 155–176, 166.

80 Carolyn Amadon, "When Fact Becomes Meaning" (2011) 25(8) *CBA Record* 44–52, 44.

81 *Ibid.*

82 Susie Salmon, "Legal Writing for a Digital Audience (Part I)" (2021) 58(2) *Arizona Attorney* 8–9, 8.

83 Scott Longman, "The Architecture of Legal Writing" (2001) 15(3) *CBA Record* 40–66, 40.

84 *Ibid,* 58.

85 Dave Pettit, "What is Plain Language?" (2019) 44(2) *LawNow* 57–58, 58.

86 Debra Cohen, "Competent Legal Writing – A Lawyer's Professional Responsibility" (1999) 67(2) *University of Cincinnati Law Review* 491–526, 521.

87 Mark Osbeck, "What is 'Good Legal Writing' and Why Does It Matter?" (2012) 4(2) *Drexel Law Review* 417–466, 434.

88 Ralph Waldo Emerson, *The Essay on Self-Reliance* (The Roycrofters, 1908), 23.

89 Gertrude Block, *Effective Legal Writing*, 4th edition (The Foundation Press, Inc, 1992), 90.

what Emerson perceived to be foolish in writing generally is seen to be prudent when it comes to legal writing.

Sentence structure is more important than word choice[90]

Effective legal communication has traditionally been perceived as a matter of word choice and placement.[91] Traditionally, the view was that word choice was the more important of the two.[92] However, there is a school of thought that word placement is actually more important. So, for example, Gopen posits that readers get most of their "interpretive clues"[93] in a sentence from structural location rather than word choice.[94]

2.   Composing a text

In terms of composition, Stevenson suggests the following:

Each phrase employed by an author should be "comely"
(apt),[95] varied,[96] and with a pleasant "equipoise of sound"[97]

Settling on the correct words and mix of words has been described as a "key element" of good legal writing.[98] Cooney suggests that what is typically apt is a formulation of words in "a calm, teaching tone", with histrionics best avoided.[99] Additionally, while – as discussed previously above – there is no need for elegant variation in legal writing, it is generally accepted that "shifting sentence length and syntax variation"[100] aid in keeping an audience engaged. As to sound, there is a sense that by reading a draft legal text aloud during the revising stage and having regard to the acoustics of what one has written it can only be improved. This is doubly the case with legal texts that are written to be (or as if to be) read aloud.[101]

---

90   George Gopen, "CCISSR: The Perfect Way to Teach Legal Writing" (2007) 13 *Legal Writing: The Journal of the Legal Writing Institute* 315–330, 324–325.
91   K du Vivier, "Proper Words in Proper Places" (1995) 24(1) *Colorado Lawyer* 27–28, 27.
92   *Ibid.*
93   George Gopen, "CCISSR: The Perfect Way to Teach Legal Writing" (2007) 13 *Legal Writing: The Journal of the Legal Writing Institute* 315–330, 324–325.
94   *Ibid.*
95   Robert Louis Stevenson, *Essays on the Art of Writing* (Chatto & Windus, 1919), 10.
96   *Ibid*, 11.
97   *Ibid.*
98   Ginette Chapman, "Apt Phrasing in Legal Writing" (2021) 50(9) *Colorado Lawyer* 10–11, 10.
99   Mark Cooney, "Do the Opposite for Better Legal Writing" (2007) 36(4) *Student Lawyer* 14–17, 17.
100   Jillian Singer, "Four Principles to Help Guide Your Legal Writing" (2016) 8(2) *Solo & Small Firm* 4–6, 5.
101   Gerald Lebovits, "Legal-Writing Myths" (2015) 16 *Scribes Journal of Legal Writing* 113–122, 120.

*Whatever the intricacies/obscurities of a point, the polish of
one's prose ought not to suffer*[102]

Polishing the rough edges of a piece of legal text is a task that typically
falls to be undertaken at the proofreading stage. One commentator has
observed, in this regard, that there is always time for a final proofread.[103]
However, in a busy professional world, it sometimes seems that not many
lawyers can afford the time necessary.[104] And there is also a 'flip side' to
producing polished text: having taken the time to edit and polish his or
her text the legal writer must remain ever ready to excise entire sections
of a legal text if that aids the effectiveness/persuasiveness over the writing
overall.[105]

*No form of words should be selected or phrases
employed that do not advance an argument and illuminate
the reader*[106]

This is hardly a new idea. The Book of Ecclesiastes contains the
injunction, "Let thy speech be short, comprehending much in few
words".[107] When it comes to legal writing, it has been suggested that if
sentences are to be kept clear and comprehensible, the legal writer needs
to eliminate needless words and phrases – such redundant words and
phrases being compared to the physical tic of throat-clearing when
speaking.[108] In public life, Abraham Lincoln offers perhaps the best
example of a leader, lawyer and "master prose stylist"[109] who understand
the value of concision,[110] that is, getting the greatest number of thoughts
into the fewest number of words.[111] That said, clarity in writing seems
ever to be preferred, even over concision, for fear of ambiguity.[112]

---

102 Robert Louis Stevenson, *Essays on the Art of Writing* (Chatto & Windus, 1919), 11.
103 Patrick Hugg, "Professional Legal Writing Declaring Your Independence" (1991) 11(2) *Journal of the National Association of Administration Law Judges* 114–143, 124.
104 James Raymond, "Legal Writing: An Obstruction to Justice" (1978) 30(1) *Alabama Law Review* 1–19, 17.
105 James McElhaney, "Legal Writing that Works" (2007) 93 *ABA Journal* 30–31, 30.
106 Robert Louis Stevenson, *Essays on the Art of Writing* (Chatto & Windus, 1919), 11.
107 Ecclesiastes 32:8.
108 Lisa Hatlen, "Conciseness in Legal Writing" (2009) 82(8) *Wisconsin Lawyer* 21–23, 21.
109 Marshall Myers, "'Rugged Grandeur': A Study of the Influences on the Writing Style of Abraham Lincoln and a Brief Study of His Writing Habits" (2004) 23(4) *Rhetoric Review* 350–367, 350.
110 *Ibid*, 361. In a consideration of the edits made by Lincoln to the drafts of the First Inaugural Address that were prepared for him, Oseid shows how Lincoln clearly understood the power of brevity in communication, generally (though not invariably) shortening the text that was prepared for him (and offering something of a masterclass in effective communication in the process). See Julie Oseid, "The Power of Brevity: Adopt Abraham Lincoln's Habits" (2009) 6(1) *Journal of the Association of Legal Writing Directors* 28–54, esp 37–39.

A meaningless/weak phrase deployed merely to achieve a
balance in sound should be avoided[113]

Having a good ear has long been touted as an essential attribute of a good author. Justice Jackson of the United States Supreme Court once wrote as follows on the potency in the sound of language:

The effective advocate ... will read and reread the majestic efforts of leaders of his profession on important occasions, and linger over their manner of handling challenging subjects. He will stock the arsenal of his mind with tested dialectical weapons ... He will rejoice in the strength of the mother tongue [sic] as found in the King James version of the Bible, and in the power of the terse and flashing phrase of a Kipling or a Churchill.[114]

It has been suggested that with the best prose one can hear the author talking as one reads.[115] And it has even been contended – though this is not a commonly held view – that given the oral/acoustic dimension to good writing, the modern trend of dictating legal texts is fundamentally conducive to better writing.[116] (There is, however, an alternative view which holds that dictation yields prolixity).[117] Returning, however, to the notion that a good ear is critical to being a good writer, what Stevenson points to is that the ambition to produce good legal writing should not be sacrificed on the altar of acoustics. Clarity is the "supreme virtue"[118] of effective legal writing.

3. Style

As to style, which he contends to be the foundation of literature,[119] Stevenson suggests that what is at play in this regard is the process

---

111   Gerald Lebovits, "Off With their Heads: Concision" (2001) 73(9) *New York State Bar Association Journal* 64.
112   C Scott Pryor and Jeremy Pryor, "Watertight – Royalty Indemnity Ruling Is Not: Ambiguity Often Results When Concision Trumps Clarity" (2011) 38(2) *VBA News Journal* 22–24, 22.
113   Robert Louis Stevenson, *Essays on the Art of Writing* (Chatto & Windus, 1919), 12.
114   Robert Jackson, "Advocacy Before the United States Supreme Court" (1951) 25(2) *Temple Law Quarterly* 115–130, 129. Jackson is something of a product of his age in pointing unblushingly to a religious text and the prose of two renowned imperialists as a source of good English. (Kipling's public reputation came to be seen as synonymous with the "outspoken jingoistic Imperialistic tradition" (H Varley, "Imperialism and Rudyard Kipling" (1953) 14(1) *Journal of the History of Ideas* 124–135, 124); and Churchill, though one of the saviours of western democracy (a profound achievement), was also *"always an imperialist"* (see Maurice Ashley, "Churchill and History" (1966) 42(1) *International Affairs* 87–94, 90).)
115   Thomas Spahn, "The Art of Legal Writing" (1989) 9(2) *Journal of the National Association of Administrative Law Judges* 137–152, 148.
116   *Ibid.*
117   Francis Leach, "Length of Judicial Opinions" (1911–1912) 21(2) *Yale Law Journal* 141–146, 144.
118   Catherine Langlois, "Power of the Pen: Brief Writing in Appellate Court" (1992) 2 *New Jersey Lawyer* 33–38, 36.
119   Robert Louis Stevenson, *Essays on the Art of Writing* (Chatto & Windus, 1919), 14.

whereby the artist takes various elements of a subject and places them in such an arrangement as to yield an enriched meaning or to have done the work of two sentences into one.[120] Unexpectedly perhaps, Stevenson does not consider natural style ("disjointed babble")[121] to be the best style but prefers instead a style which (unobtrusively) attains an elegance rich in meaning or (obtrusively) yields a richness and vigour of meaning.[122]

What might be said about style in legal writing? For starters, style matters. It 'separates the wheat from the chaff', making the difference between a legal text that is memorable and likely to be quoted from in the future. When it comes to judgment writing – though also to other legal texts – it seems but a truism to acknowledge the significance of style.[123] This is because judges and other legal writers, when they write legal texts, are seeking to persuade, and persuasion is closely and inexorably linked to style.[124] Style is not a matter of dressing or ornamentation. As Justice Cardozo has observed, "Form is not something added to substance as a … protuberant adornment. The two are fused into a unity".[125] This does not mean that the legal writer must descend to purple prose. It means merely that style is an "essential element" of any successful legal text if only because people cannot act/think without it.[126]

Lord Macmillan once observed that the style of a text is "dominated by its purpose".[127] Legal writing is informed by a seriousness of aim and a desire for clarity. Given these constant objectives, it is in one sense surprising that legal texts present in so many styles, but then choice of style is a personal matter, be that a terse, technical approach or a style that shows knowledge beyond the particular facts and law in issue.[128] Pickering offers some practical tips on the cultivation of style which bear repeating:[129]

- Practice and study are the keys to cultivating an attractive style.
- When the task of writing beckons, it is as important to think as

---

120 *Ibid*, 12.
121 *Ibid*, 13.
122 *Ibid*.
123 Andrea Bianchi, "International Adjudication, Rhetoric and Storytelling" (2018) 9 *Journal of International Dispute Settlement* 28–44, 30.
124 *Ibid*. See also Roderick Macdonald, "Legal Bilingualism" (1997) 42(1) *McGill Law Journal* 119–168, 144.
125 Benjamin Cardozo, *Selected Writings of Benjamin Nathan Cardozo*, M Hall (ed) (Fallon Publications, 1947), 340.
126 P Horwitz, "Law's Expression: The Promise and Perils of Judicial Opinion Writing in Canadian Constitutional Law" (2000) 38(1) *Osgoode Hall Law Journal* 101–142, 113.
127 Lord Macmillan, "The Writing of Judgments" (1948) 26(3) *Canadian Bar Review* 481–499, 491.
128 Katrina Banks-Smith, "More than Just Precedent: Perspectives on Judgment Writing" (2019) 21 *University of Notre Dame Australia Law Review* 1–17, 4. Banks-Smith is writing of judicial authors but her comments have a resonance when it comes to legal writing more generally.
129 Harold Pickering, "On Learning to Write: Suggestions for Study and Practice" (1955) 41(12) *American Bar Association Journal* 1121–1124.

much about the craft of writing as it is to think about the topic under consideration.

- It is useful to read a book (or judgment) that is in the selected style and to do so "until you feel yourself in the mood of the style".[130]
- It is beneficial to keep a thesaurus to hand and to use synonyms when appropriate (subject to the caveat as to 'elegant variation' considered above).
- A legal writer should retain and read good books written by masters of prose.[131]

Academic commentary discusses a number of stylistic issues to which any legal writer determined to improve his or her writing style might usefully have regard:

- A legal writer cannot communicate ideas in writing except by writing well.[132]
- A legal writer has failed if his or her words do not convey thoughts or meaning to readers: writing has as its purpose the conveying of thoughts precisely.[133]
- The central rationale for a legal text is to explain the law "candidly, openly, and precisely".[134]
- A legal writer should try to write in a way that is accessible to intelligent non-lawyers, avoiding any lawyerly inclination to "mandarin obscurity".[135]
- Being interesting is not the same as being entertaining, with the evangelical/flamboyant[136] having no place in legal writing.
- Language should be rhetorically effective and should not reflect a contrived effort on the part of the author.[137]
- Greater concision is generally desirable.[138] However, undue concision is to be avoided; it yields a text that is terse, abrupt and potentially incomplete.

130　*Ibid*, 1123.
131　*Ibid*.
132　Linda Furey, "To Write Well: A Primer on Concision, Clarity and Coherence in Legal Writing" (1992) *New Jersey Lawyer* 18–26, 18.
133　Gibson Witherspoon, "The Importance of Legal Writing to Young Lawyers" (1960) 6(1) *Student Lawyer Journal* 20–24, 21.
134　Robert Keeton, "How I Write" (1993) 4 *Scribes Journal of Legal Writing* 31–37, 34. Judge Keeton is writing of judgments; however, his observations arguably apply to legal writing more generally.
135　Richard Posner, "How I Write" (1993) 4 *Scribes Journal of Legal Writing* 45–49, 47.
136　Ivor Richardson, "The Role of an Appellate Judge" (1981) 5(1) *Otago Law Review* 1–10, 10.
137　Matthew Salzwedel, "The Lawyer's Struggle to Write" (2015) 16 *Scribes Journal of Legal Writing* 69–90, 72.
138　Michael Frost, "Ethos, Pathos & Legal Audience" (1994) 99(1) *Dickinson Law Review* 85–116, 95.

- The superfluous should be excised if wordiness is to be avoided.[139] (The superfluous also poses a problem when it comes to judicial interpretation thanks to the "judicial fancy"[140] that no words fall to be read as "verbal fat".)[141]
- Editing is critical to good writing/style; it is the rare writer who can achieve a completeness of style at the first go.[142]
- It is important not to use a style that excludes. This comes back to the Aristotelian notion of *ethos* (character) as an attribute of persuasive rhetoric. One may write what is otherwise a great piece of legal text yet fail *ethos*-wise through the use of non-inclusive language.[143]
- A good legal writer should always have a style guide to hand.[144]

4. Key elements of style

Stevenson identifies the following key elements of style:

> *Prose writers must keep phrasing pleasing/rhythmical,*[145] *but not metrical*[146]

Aristotle identifies two problems with a descent into metre. First, it smacks of contrivance.[147] Secondly, it is distracting, prompting the audience to focus on cadence, rather than substance.[148] (Rhythm, however, *is* important because diction/prose without rhythm is displeasing and lacks clarity. So a sentence should be possessed of rhythm but not metre – if it has metre it will have become verse.)[149]

---

139   Ginette Chapman, "Apt Phrasing in Legal Writing" (2021) 50(9) *Colorado Lawyer* 10–11, 11.
140   Maurice Kelman, "Is the Constitution Worth Legal Writing Credit?" (1994) 44(2) *Journal of Legal Education* 267–272, 269.
141   *Ibid*.
142   Mary Dunnewold, "Ten Ways to Spruce Up Your Legal Writing" (2005) 74(3) *Hannepin Lawyer* 18–23, 18.
143   Heidi Brown, "Inclusive Legal Writing" (2018) 104(4) *ABA Journal* 22–25, 23.
144   Harold Pickering, "On Learning to Write: Suggestions for Study and Practice" (1955) 41(12) *American Bar Association Journal* 1121–1124, 1123–1124.
145   Robert Louis Stevenson, *Essays on the Art of Writing* (Chatto & Windus, 1919), 42.
146   *Ibid*.
147   Aristotle, *Treatise on Rhetoric*, T Buckley (trans) (Henry G Bohn, 1850), 226.
148   *Ibid*.
149   *Ibid*, 227.

The prose writer's task is artfully to combine ordinary
language into musical phraseology[150]

Just as the musicians remembered in the popular memory tend to be those who make a deep connection with their audiences,[151] lawyers succeed by connecting with their audiences.[152] The better legal text (like music) tends to involve fused passion/reason.[153] And a lawyer without conviction, just like music without inspiration, seems unlikely to impress.[154]

A prose writer must weave an argument, using wording that
is "apt, explicit, and communicative"[155]

Settling on the correct words and mix of words in a legal text has been described as a critical element of good legal writing.[156] By "explicit"[157] what Stevenson appears to have in mind is clarity and Justice Cardozo, as mentioned previously, has touted clarity as the prime virtue in judgments. (The same is true in legal writing more generally.) Effective communication is what legal writers and texts are all about: good legal writing involves communicating effectively following on considered legal thinking.[158]

5.   Patterns in writing and writing models

Stevenson points to how in beautiful prose one finds heightened organisation, concision, balance and counterpoise.[159] This process of synthesis also occurs in legal writing, with one commentator observing that the legal writer in his or her actions is arranging/combining pieces into a pattern that was not clearly discernible beforehand.[160] In some ways, what lawyers do in this regard may not always be terribly original – because legal writers spend so long reading judgments (as well of course

---

150   Robert Louis Stevenson, *Essays on the Art of Writing* (Chatto & Windus, 1919), 42.
151   Sandra Day O'Connor, "Music and the Law" (2005) 18 *Western Legal History: The Journal of the Ninth Judicial Circuit Historical Society* 41–48, 44.
152   *Ibid.*
153   *Ibid,* 46.
154   *Ibid.*
155   Robert Louis Stevenson, *Essays on the Art of Writing* (Chatto & Windus, 1919), 42.
156   Ginette Chapman, "Apt Phrasing in Legal Writing" (2021) 50(9) *Colorado Lawyer* 10–11, 10.
157   Robert Louis Stevenson, *Essays on the Art of Writing* (Chatto & Windus, 1919), 42.
158   Adina Radulescu, "The Pitfalls of Simplifying Legal Writing" (2012) 4(2) *Contemporary Readings in Law and Social Justice* 367–372, 368.
159   Robert Louis Stevenson, *Essays on the Art of Writing* (Chatto & Windus, 1919), 19.
160   Jim Corkery, *Study of Law* (The Adelaide Law Review Association, 1988), 133.

as other legal prose) it may be that their patterns, rhythms and words begin to enter one's head and (for better or worse) a legal writer begins to think and write like the works that he or she reads.[161] That said, the process of arrangement and combination in which lawyers engage when writing is a technical skill that goes beyond the mere alignment of facts[162] and bringing a quality of coherence/congruity to bear, that is, finding a word pattern that properly reflects one's thought pattern,[163] with words and thoughts moving to a common end.

Just as no work of art can be produced without some technical skill, no competent legal text can be wrought without a degree of technical skill (including but not limited to knowledge of law). That said, it is not always the case that the greater the technical skill, the better any ensuing work of art. Thus, it is not always the best-qualified lawyer who makes the finest legal writer. Just as what made Ben Jonson a great poet was not his ability at constructing patterns but rather "his imaginative vision",[164] what distinguishes great legal writers from their lesser compeers is, their imaginative vision. (In fact, there has been criticism in the United States of law school teaching that requires particular forms of analysis – such as 'TEC' (Topic, Sentence, Elaboration, Conclusion), 'IRAC' (Issue, Rule, Application, Conclusion) and 'PS' (Problem, Solution) – and makes insufficient room for the imaginative self.)[165]

6.   'Sound' in writing

Every phrase in prose comprises sounds, each of which harmonises to a greater/lesser extent with each other.[166] The art of combining those sounds, in a harmonious whole, is what Stevenson considers to be the essence of literary art.[167] In fact, this may be something of a misuse of the musical concept of harmony, which when listened to in isolation is often not euphonious or pleasing;[168] what Stevenson actually appears to have in mind is tonality (which offers a set of principles by reference to which

---

161   Wayne Schiess, "Legal Writing Is Not What It Should Be" (2009) 37(1) *Southern University Law Review* 1–24, 8–9.

162   Joel Modiri, "The Time and Space of Critical Legal Pedagogy" (2016) 27 *Stellenbosch Law Review* 507–534, 527.

163   George Gibson, "Effective Legal Writing and Speaking" (1980) 36(1) *Business Lawyer (ABA)* 1–10, 3.

164   R Collingwood, *The Principles of Art* (Clarendon Press, 1938), 27.

165   See, eg, Philip Meyer, "Convicts, Criminals, Prisoners, and Outlaws: A Course in Popular Storytelling" (1992) 42(1) *Journal of Legal Education* 129–138, 130.

166   Robert Louis Stevenson, *Essays on the Art of Writing* (Chatto & Windus, 1919), 31.

167   *Ibid.*

168   Ian Gallacher, "Count's Dilemma: Or, Harmony and Dissonance in Legal Language" (2012) 9 *Legal Communication and Rhetoric* 1–20, 2.

music is organised).[169] Be that as it may, flow, rhythm and tone (all essential elements of music) have likewise been touted as "essential components"[170] of good prose and fall, as a consequence, to be "consciously incorporated"[171] by legal writers into their texts – at least if those writers wish to write an engaging and enjoyable text with which readers find themselves in agreement.

Having commended assonance and alliteration and having reiterated the importance of variation,[172] Stevenson turns to consider how literature is written by and for two senses: the auditory sense (attuned to melody in prose)[173] and the visual sense (which guides the writer in writing and the reader in reading).[174] There are a couple of points to be made in this regard. First, when it comes to assonance and alliteration, all words have an aural dimension: good writers harness/direct these sounds so as to produce the intended meaning.[175] Secondly, the good legal writer will deploy the auditory and visual potential of a legal text so as to appeal to the reader's senses;[176] the great legal writer will craft his or her legal text so that it appeals to a particular sense in a particular way.[177]

Few writers, Stevenson suggests, are aware of how much they are involved in arranging the "melody of letters",[178] that is, unconsciously substituting one phrase for the other so as to achieve the melodious. The notion of melody, though not perhaps at the top of the legal writer's 'to do' list when drafting a legal text, nonetheless presents as an attribute of what is in play in the legal writing process – not in the form of rhymed poetry (this is unlikely to occur in most legal texts and has been the subject of strong criticism from lawyers when it has occurred in judicial prose)[179] but rather in the form of prose that brings the reader through "the uncouth noise of legal materiality … to … the harmonious melody of justice".[180]

---

169 *Ibid*, 19.
170 Bret Rappaport, "Using the Elements of Rhythm, Flow, and Tone to Create a More Effective and Persuasive Acoustic Experience in Legal Writing" (2010) 16(1) *Legal Writing: The Journal of the Legal Writing Institute* 65–116, 68.
171 *Ibid*.
172 Robert Louis Stevenson, *Essays on the Art of Writing* (Chatto & Windus, 1919), 31–32.
173 *Ibid*, 32.
174 *Ibid*.
175 Justin Kishbaugh, "Living in a Material Word: The Applications of Poetic Form to Legal Writing" (2016) 29(1) *Second Draft* 4–7, 6.
176 Elizabeth Frost, "On the Subject of Subjects: Here's a Concrete Way to Avoid Abstract Writing" (2021) 81(4) *Oregon State Bar Bulletin* 13–15, 13.
177 Justin Kishbaugh, "Living in a Material Word: The Applications of Poetic Form to Legal Writing" (2016) 29(1) *Second Draft* 4–7, 6.
178 Robert Louis Stevenson, *Essays on the Art of Writing* (Chatto & Windus, 1919), 40.
179 Aaron Strickland, "Poetic Justice: An Interpretation of Lawyers' Reactions to Verse Judgments" (2016) 29(3) *International Journal for the Semiotics of Law* 643–666, 643.
180 Thomas Giddens, "Institution and Abyss" (2020) 2(2) *Law, Technology and Humans* 150–171, 167.

In his "Essay on Language", the 18th/19th century English philosopher, Jeremy Bentham, makes various observations as regards "melodiousness"[181] and "harmoniousness"[182] in language, among which are the following:

- by harmony/melody is meant the property of producing "an agreeable cast in the mind";[183]
- there is both positive and negative melodiousness;[184]
- the right degree of melodiousness depends on "the nature of the discourse";[185]
- there is a connection between the efficiency and harmoniousness of a text;[186] and
- Shakespeare's great strength is the harmony of his writing.[187]

To be avoided at all costs is writing in which (to borrow from Stevenson) one finds "cacophony supreme"[188] – a particular 'sin' in a common law system which has seen generations of lawyers strive to establish a functioning legal system from "a cacophony of texts".[189]

7.   What to include or omit

The matter of what to put in and what to leave out can preoccupy the author. Stevenson writes that in every case a critical task of the author is one of suppression and omission. Among the issues that Stevenson sees as falling to an author to decide in this regard are the following:

The inclusion of a fact may be necessary/ornamental

This process of fact selection finds echo in the legal writing process, Judge Posner pointing in this regard (in the context of judgment writing but his observations have a wider resonance) to a degree of freedom akin to that of a literary prose writer.[190]

---

181   Jeremy Bentham, "Essay on Language" in Jeremy Bentham, *The Works of Jeremy Bentham*, John Bowring (ed) (William Tait, 1843), vol 8, 290–308, 305.
182   *Ibid.*
183   *Ibid.*
184   *Ibid*, 306.
185   *Ibid.*
186   *Ibid.*
187   *Ibid.*
188   Robert Louis Stevenson, *Essays on the Art of Writing* (Chatto & Windus, 1919), 41.
189   Thomas McSweeney, "English Judges and Roman Jurists: The Civilian Leaning Behind England's First Case Law" (2012) 84(4) *Temple Law Review* 827–862, 845–846.
190   Richard Posner, *Cardozo: A Study in Reputation* (University of Chicago Press, 1990), 46.

The inclusion of a fact may weaken/obscure
the general design

Legal writing "demands absolute integrity".[191] Facts must be stated accurately,[192] and even unwelcome facts must be included when they are relevant.[193] At the same time, the legal writer needs to be careful to avoid the pedantic and the pedestrian – what Justice Cardozo has referred to as "an accuracy that defeats itself by the overemphasis of details".[194]

Text may be boring/irrelevant (and hence excisable)

Being boring is not perhaps as great a flaw in legal writing as it is in literary writing: staid language may actually suggest careful consideration of (and a real commitment to) the point being addressed/canvassed.[195] That said, the general consensus in the commentary on legal writing is that the more engaging a legal text is to the reader, the more persuasive it is likely to be.[196]

As to the inclusion of irrelevant material, when it comes to:

- judgments, it has been suggested that judges tend to include irrelevant material because they consider that the next court up in the hierarchy cannot be trusted with a judgment that gets directly to the point;[197]
- visual evidence, it has been suggested that an opponent is unlikely to object to a 'cropping out' of the irrelevant;[198]
- written submissions, it has been suggested that legal writers must be careful to excise the irrelevant.[199] So across the gamut of legal writing, one can see an emphasis on the inclusion of the relevant and the exclusion of the irrelevant.

---

191   I Campbell, "Legal Writing" (1999) 30(2) *Victoria University of Wellington Law Review* 427–434, 428.
192   *Ibid*, 434.
193   *Ibid*, 428.
194   Benjamin Cardozo, *Selected Writings of Benjamin Nathan Cardozo*, M Hall (ed) (Fallon Publications, 1947), 341.
195   Susan Bartie and John Gava, "Some Problems With Extrajudicial Writing" (2012) 34 *Sydney Law Review* 637–658, 644.
196   See, eg, Mark Osbeck, "What is 'Good Legal Writing' and Why Does It Matter?" (2012) 4(2) *Drexel Law Review* 417–466, 440.
197   James Raymond, "Legal Writing: An Obstruction to Justice" (1978) 30(1) *Alabama Law Review* 1–19, 3.
198   Steve Johansen and Ruth Anne Robbins, "Articulating the Analysis: Systemizing the Decision to Use Visuals as Legal Reasoning" (2015) 20 *Legal Writing: The Journal of the Legal Writing Institute* 57–108, 105.
199   Heidi Brown, "Breaking Bad Briefs" (2017) 41(2) *Journal of the Legal Profession* 259–300, 270.

Key propositions

- Good legal texts are written well.
- Not all legal writers are equally skilled in their deployment of words.
- Style is a quality of writing whereby a legal writer as author may improve him or herself. ('Style' means the dexterous use of writing skill, having regard to the proportion of one part of a text to another and to the whole, excision of useless words, the emphasis of important words and having a uniform form/style.)
- What to put in and leave out of a legal text is a constantly presenting question; among the issues arising are whether the inclusion of some fact is necessary or will weaken/obscure the general design of a particular legal text.
- A legal writer may commence with rough thoughts that then become refined thoughts. It is when the writer sits down to actually write that he or she will begin to determine the scale, spirit, particularity, style, etc of the intended text.
- Realising imagined text is challenging. Less dedicated authors stick to a style that they settle upon early. Better authors (and those who seek to be better) see new texts as a prompt for fresh style.
- In a legal text it may be necessary to include the tedious, but there seems no reason why the irrelevant cannot be omitted and the tedious kept to a minimum. Unnecessary detail and carelessness in writing are to be avoided.
- Each phrase must be apt, varied, satisfying to the ear and possessed of "ingenious neatness".[200]
- Whatever the intricacies/obscurities of a point, the polish of one's prose should not suffer.
- No form of words should be selected or phrases employed that do not advance an argument and enlighten the reader.
- Meaningless/weak phraseology is to be avoided.
- It is by the brevity/charm/clarity/emphasis of argument that the aptness and fitness of prose falls to be judged.
- Natural style ("disjointed babble")[201] is not the best style. To be preferred is a style which (unobtrusively) attains an elegance rich in meaning or (obtrusively) yields a richness and vigour of meaning.

---

200   Robert Louis Stevenson, *Essays on the Art of Writing* (Chatto & Windus, 1919), 11.
201   *Ibid*, 13.

- Sometimes reversing the natural order of phrases can be conducive to clarity.
- In the best prose the text shows a superior degree of organisation/concision/fluidity.
- Each phrase of each sentence should comprise a mix of long and short, and of the emphasised and understated, such as to gratify the inner ear.
- Prose should be rhythmical; it should not, however, be metrical – if metrical it becomes verse.
- Prose quality rests on sound. A legal writer determined to write impactful legal text will be attentive to the sounds within/between words.
- Good writers, in ordinary moments, content themselves with avoiding what is harsh (occasionally rising to alliteration or assonance); in bad writing, one finds "cacophony supreme".[202]

---

202   *Ibid*, 41.

13. Trollope

On literary quality, truth and the 'rules' of writing

Anthony Trollope (1815–1882) was one of the most prominent English novelists of the 19th century, as well as an accomplished essayist, short-story and non-fiction writer. He is perhaps best known for his novel, *Barchester Towers* (1857). In his autobiography (and he was sufficiently famous in his day that his autobiography sold well), Trollope devotes a chapter to the subject of "Novels and the Art of Writing Them",[1] in which he makes various observations that, I submit, are also relevant when it comes to legal writing.

1. Artistry and writing

In Trollope's day, there was a continued perception that fiction was a low form of literature. People in their millions read novels but, as Trollope observes, there was a prejudice which denied them their due.[2] In a similar vein, there continues to be a general reluctance to recognise the artistry in much legal writing. Some legal writers are great artists, capable of ensuring that what they write is beautifully suited to the situation presenting.[3] As in all free arts, in the writing of legal texts there is something of the mechanical ("skill without beauty")[4] without which the spirit which informs art would remain unembodied. However, for all good legal writers, artistry is at the heart of their endeavour.[5]

If one accepts the creation of a legal text to involve some element of artistry, what qualities might it be expected to possess as a text? Perhaps the following: that it is susceptible to "heightened … perception",[6]

---

1   Anthony Trollope, *An Autobiography* (William Blackwood & Sons, 1883), vol II.
2   *Ibid*, 27.
3   Louis Schwartz, "Justice, Expediency, and Beauty" (1987–1988) 136(1) *Pennsylvania Law Review* 141–182, 142.
4   John Rist, "Aesthetics and Ethics: Some Common Problems of Foundationalism" in *Natural Moral Law in Contemporary Society*, Holger Zaborowski (ed) (The Catholic University of America Press, 2010), 335.
5   Karl Llewellyn, "On the Good, the True, the Beautiful, in Law" (1942) 9 *University of Chicago Law Review* 224–265, 230.
6   Roger Fry, *Vision and Design* (Penguin Books, 1940), 33.

offering a vista of the writer's thought; that it satisfies in terms of drawing together different things naturally in a coherent manner ("unity ... is necessary for ... restful contemplation");[7] and that it possesses rhythm, feeling, motion, proportion, colour and draws the mind's eye to closer appreciation,[8] making the final legal text a "unified whole".[9]

Nobody, Trollope suggests, can labour long at any trade without eventually considering whether their work tends to produce good or evil.[10] Legal texts, I submit – at least when devoted to the vindication of individual freedoms – incline towards the good. And public legal texts, such as judgments, can aid in the formation of a due concept of justice from generation to generation.[11]

One does not need to look far to find renowned judgments that have perpetuated injustice and those which have secured justice. Offhand one thinks, for example, of the (disappointing) judgment of the United States Supreme Court in *Bowers v Hardwick*[12] which upheld the constitutionality of a Georgia law that criminalised certain forms of sexual intercourse done in private between consenting, competent adults (in that case, between two homosexual men), and the (more impressive) judgment of the Court in *Lawrence v Texas*,[13] overruling *Bowers* and reaffirming the right to privacy and the traditional view that the state has no place regulating private sexual behaviour between consenting competent adults.

2. Honesty in writing

Trollope points to the necessity/virtue of truth in novel writing.[14] In a legal text, truthfulness falls likewise to be lauded. A number of general points might usefully be made in this regard:

---

7   *Ibid*, 34–35.
8   *Ibid*, 36–37.
9   *Ibid*.
10   Anthony Trollope, *An Autobiography* (William Blackwood & Sons, 1883), vol II, 28.
11   Mary Ellen Maatman, "Justice Formation from Generation to Generation: Atticus Finch and the Stories Lawyers Tell Their Children" (2008) 14 *Legal Writing: The Journal of the Legal Writing Institute* 207–248, 211.
12   478 US 186 (1986).
13   539 US 558 (2003).
14   Anthony Trollope, *An Autobiography* (William Blackwood & Sons, 1883), vol II, 44.

Truth in time

Like any creative work, a legal text presents matters "in this moment",[15] that is, giving its version of the truth at a moment in time. I submit that lawyers as storytellers:

- can learn much from creative artists who are likewise required to fuse a moment into "a frozen glimpse of what was, and ... will be",[16] not least by focusing on discovering, capturing, presenting, and enhancing images in place of the traditional focus on words;[17] and

- need to acquire an "artist's eye"[18] in terms of determining what imagery might best be used as a means of communication.[19]

Unity of writer/reader

Tolstoy has provided a useful working definition as to what a work of art comprises, writing that:

If a man ... on reading ... another man's work, experiences a mental condition which unites him with that man and ... other people who ... partake of that work of art ... the object evoking that condition is a work of art.[20]

It is a rare lawyer who cannot, for example, recall reading a judgment and experiencing a mental moment which united him or her with the judge who wrote the judgment. And there can be few lawyers unable to recall a moment when a colleague said that he or she had just the same experience when reading that same judgment. In this unity/commonality lies hard evidence that a particular legal text involves true artistry. Stephen King writes of what is at play in this regard as a form of telepathy,[21] a meeting of minds,[22] suggesting that all art relies to some extent on telepathy but that "writing offers the purest distillation".[23]

---

15 Friedrich von Schelling, *The Philosophy of Art: Plastic Arts and Nature* (John Chapman, 1845), 11.
16 James Eyster, "Lawyer as Artist: Using Significant Moments to Obtuse Objects to Enhance Advocacy" (2008) 14 *Legal Writing: The Journal of the Legal Writing Institute* 87–126, 88.
17 *Ibid*, 92.
18 Michael Murray, "*Mise en Scène* and the Decisive Moment of Visual Legal Rhetoric" (2019) 68 *University of Kansas Law Review* 241–314, 246.
19 *Ibid*.
20 Leo Tolstoy, *What is Art?* (Funk & Wagnalls, 1904), 152.
21 Stephen King, *On Writing* (Hodder & Stoughton, 2001), 113.
22 *Ibid*, 117.
23 *Ibid*, 113.

Conscious/unconscious

In writing a legal text, one often encounters the moment when a thought leaps from the mind onto the page. It has even been suggested that finding the right words to express a particular thought is mostly unconscious.[24] Justice Holmes's dissent in *Lochner v New York*[25] has been touted as an example of such unconscious thought at play, with Holmes offering "a window into his interior monologue ... [his] unconscious thought"[26] when he begins into the most famous part of his (brief) dissent, observing:

> *This case is decided upon an economic theory which a large part of the country does not entertain. If it were a question whether I agreed with that theory, I should desire to study it further and long before making up my mind. But I do not conceive that to be my duty, because I strongly believe that my agreement or disagreement has nothing to do with the right of a majority to embody their opinions in law.*[27]

In writing this text, Holmes has clearly seized on a truth which he offers to the reader in a burst of "cultivated spontaneity".[28] In proceeding with the "effortless confidence"[29] that the above text so clearly possesses, Holmes leaves the reader with the comforting sense that he or she is reading the views of the very best of judges.

Transcendence

A legal text is a product of intentional activity that expresses a human viewpoint.[30] But it is more. Art in a post-religious age is where transcendence is sought.[31] This is as true of legal texts as it is of any other form of artwork, with better writers managing sometimes to afford an aspect of truth which flows from what the great 18th-century English painter, Sir Joshua Reynolds, once described as "poetical enthusiasm ...

---

24   Stephen Maurer, "Beauty Is Truth and Truth Beauty: How Intuitive Insights Shape Legal Reasoning and the Rule of Law" (2018) 42(1) *Seattle University Law Review* 129–160, 145.

25   198 US 45 (1905).

26   Andrew Kerr, "The Perfect Opinion" (2020) 12(2) *Washington University Jurisprudence* 221–266, 249.

27   198 US 45, 75 (1905).

28   Andrew Kerr, "The Perfect Opinion" (2020) 12(2) *Washington University Jurisprudence* 221–266, 250.

29   *Ibid*, 257.

30   Ruth Lorand, "The Purity of Aesthetic Value" (1992) 50(1) *Journal of Aesthetics and Art Criticism* 13–21, 13.

31   William Desmond, *Art, Origins, Otherness* (SUNY Press, 2003), 1.

[ie] Inspiration".[32] That said, a cautionary note should perhaps be sounded: that a legal argument should not be considered a transcendent essence floating between or beyond the lines: "[P]ersuasiveness of a legal text appears on the surface."[33]

The great whole

Within the whirl of inspiration/imagination/information to be found in any legal text a glimpse of real truth is sometimes to be found – even if that truth is that law's path does not always lead to truth but also to "discovery of infinite complexity".[34] This is akin to a feature of what Moritz once observed of beauty, *viz* that "[e]very instance of beauty ... is beautiful only insofar as ... the great whole is more or less revealed in it".[35] (And this gives a means of distinguishing between legal texts that are great [beautiful] and those that are not, namely whether 'the great whole' or some aspect of it is more or less revealed in it.)

3. 'Laws' of writing

After making the above and other general observations regarding novels, Trollope turns to identify some rules for novel writing:[36]

- The writer who sits down to write a novel, Trollope posits, should do so because he or she has a story to tell (not because he or she has to tell a story).[37] Through storytelling the legal writer seeks to invoke the reader's empathy, seeking to persuade him or her to see things the way the writer wants them to be seen.[38] And like any good story it must contain:
  - a theme;
  - a structure;
  - an awareness of audience;
  - a definite beginning point;
  - a point of view;
  - points of emphasis;

---

32 Joshua Reynolds, *Seven Discourses Delivered in the Royal Academy by the President* (Cambridge University Press, 2014), vol 3, 70.
33 Richard Hyland, "A Defense of Legal Writing" (1986) 134(3) *University of Pennsylvania Law Review* 599–626, 620.
34 Grant Gilmore, "For Arthur Leff" (1981) 91 *Yale Law Journal* 217–218, 218.
35 J Bernstein, *Classic and Romantic German Aesthetics* (Cambridge University Press, 2012), 143.
36 Anthony Trollope, *An Autobiography* (William Blackwood & Sons, 1883), vol II, 45.
37 *Ibid*.
38 Marcia Canavan, "Using Literature to Teach Legal Writing" (2004) 23(1) *Quarterly Law Review* 1–22, 12.

- a comprehensive narrative;
- good word choice and vocabulary; and
- selected facts (and law).

In addition, it must:
  - avoid the intrusion of self;
  - involve good sequencing;
  - be understated;
  - let the facts make the case;
  - address such contrary points as might be made;
  - deploy emotion and imagery appropriately;
  - aim for brevity, clarity and simplicity; and
  - proceed confidently.[39]

- Trollope emphasises the importance of character over plot,[40] suggesting that if a novelist does not intimately know his or her characters, then the ensuing tale will be wooden.[41] Character also plays an important role in legal writing. Just as literature has a protagonist and an antagonist, in legal writing the legal writer is the protagonist (and any opponent the antagonist).[42] Thus, it has even been suggested that because humans respond intuitively to certain standard plotlines and characters ("character archetypes")[43] lawyers should seek consciously to weave such plotlines and archetypes into their 'storytelling'.[44]

- Language, Trollope suggests (though the point is perhaps self-evident), is the critical element by which a novelist tells a tale. The legal profession has been described as a "profession of words",[45] with language being described as "an indispensable skill for success"[46] as a lawyer. Language involves the re-creation of a writer's thoughts.[47] When it comes to good legal writing (as with

---

39 Jonathan van Patten, "Storytelling for Lawyers" (2012) 57(2) *South Dakota Law Review* 239–276.
40 Anthony Trollope, *An Autobiography* (William Blackwood & Sons, 1883), vol II, 49 *et seq.*
41 *Ibid*, 50.
42 Bret Rappaport, "Tapping the Human Adaptive Origins of Storytelling by Requiring Legal Writing Students to Read a Novel in order to Appreciate How Character, Setting, Plot, Theme, and Tone (CSPTT) are as Important as IRAC" (2008) 25 *Thomas M Cooley Law Review* 267–302, 288–289.
43 Ruth Anne Robbins, "Harry Potter, Ruby Slippers and Merlin: Telling the Client's Story Using the Characters and Paradigm of the Archetypal Hero's Journey" (2006) 29 *Seattle University Law Review* 767–804, 768.
44 *Ibid*, 769.
45 Edward Re, "Increased Importance of Legal Writing in the Era of the Vanishing Trial" (2005) 21(3) *Touro Law Review* 665–688, 670.
46 *Ibid.*
47 Samuel Murumba, "Good Legal Writing: A Guide for the Perplexed" (1991) 17(1) *Monash University Law Review* 93–105, 98.

literary writing) it has been contended that one of the two critical features to this process is skilful language use[48] (the other being good structure/organisation) – though that 'skilful use' falls to be deployed in an age when writers tend to use fewer and simpler words[49] and when, as a consequence, "the image of the world"[50] (as viewed by legal authors) is increasingly beyond their "communicative grasp".[51]

- One of the tasks of a writer, Trollope posits, is to be intelligible.[52] In a similar vein, legal writers should:
  - take care in their choice of words;
  - mean precisely what they state and state precisely what they mean; and
  - avoid the temptation to keep a passage in a text that is less than entirely clear to both themselves and the reader.

  In terms of pitching a legal text at the right level of intelligibility, it has been suggested that legal documents should be as comprehensible to the intelligent layperson as they are to a person competent in matters legal.[53]

- Trollope also points to the need for a sentence to be harmonious to the ear.[54] With legal texts, which continue to be crafted as though they are to be read out in court (and sometimes are) this need for harmoniousness is all the greater. In legal writing (as in literary writing), rhythm flow and tone (all "acoustic devices")[55] are all-important. As a result, one frequently finds it suggested that lawyers should, in effect, listen to themselves by reading aloud.[56] That said, some level of caution is required in this regard. This is because prose is never fully heard (as the transmutation from written words to spoken words leads to "acoustic qualities that do not exist in words on a page").[57] If authors know in advance how each sound in their sentences will affect the force of their text they will (Trollope

---

48   *Ibid.*
49   George Steiner, *Language and Silence: Essays on Language, Literature and the Inhuman* (Atheneum, 1970), 25.
50   *Ibid.*
51   *Ibid.*
52   Anthony Trollope, *An Autobiography* (William Blackwood & Sons, 1883), vol II, 52–53.
53   Wayne Schiess, "What Plain English Really Is" (2003–2004) 9 *Scribes Journal of Legal Writing* 43–76, 66.
54   Anthony Trollope, *An Autobiography* (William Blackwood & Sons, 1883), vol II, 53.
55   Bret Rappaport, "Using the Elements of Rhythm, Flow, and Tone to Create a More Effective and Persuasive Acoustic Experience in Legal Writing" (2010) 16(1) *Legal Writing: The Journal of the Legal Writing Institute* 65–116, 107.
56   Gerald Lebovits, "Legal-Writing Myths" (2017) 96(2) *Michigan Bar Journal* 50–53, 52.
57   *Ibid.*

maintains) charm their readers.[58] Even the best of lawyers have done this (and there is surely a lesson in that): "[Justice] Holmes ... read ... to his law clerks all of his opinions before they ... issued. He did not care, surely, what his law clerks thought ... He wanted to know ... how they [his opinions] sounded."[59]

- When it comes to the length of a novel, Trollope cautions against 'padding', writing that every word and sentence should "tend to the telling".[60] Similarly, it has been posited that the golden rule of clear legal writing is to avoid excess words, albeit that there is a difference between inadvertently using too many words (an excusable error) and 'padding' ("there is no excuse for padding sentences deliberately").[61] Instead of padding sentences, the aim of the effective legal writer is to tighten up the wording, avoiding the "stuffy ... and fluffy".[62]

- When writing dialogue Trollope cautions, amongst other matters, against "long speeches".[63] Likewise, when quoting the oral testimony or affidavit evidence of witnesses, a legal writer should take care to quote only that which is strictly necessary to advance the substance of the legal text. Steed suggests not just avoiding block quotations but avoiding quotations altogether, or at least using fewer quotations (and only memorable ones). To proceed otherwise, he suggests, risks leading to "clutter on the page".[64]

Key propositions

- There is a general failure to recognise the literary quality of legal texts and the high literary quality to which many legal texts can stake a claim.
- If the inherent literary potential that legal texts entail is not duly recognised, legal writers seem less likely to attain that potential.
- Legal texts as a form of prose seem not just suited but dedicated to promoting the highest values to society's benefit.
- In writing legal texts, a legal writer is engaged in promoting a

---

58   Anthony Trollope, *An Autobiography* (William Blackwood & Sons, 1883), vol II, 55.
59   Robert Sack, "Hearing Myself Think: Some Thoughts on Legal Prose" (1993) 4 *Scribes Journal of Legal Writing* 93–100, 98.
60   Anthony Trollope, *An Autobiography* (William Blackwood & Sons, 1883), vol II, 56.
61   *Ibid.*
62   Robert Benson, "Plain English Comes to Court" (1986) 13(1) *Litigation* 21–25, 23.
63   Anthony Trollope, *An Autobiography* (William Blackwood & Sons, 1883), vol II, 56.
64   Jason Steed, "Cleaning Up Quotations in Legal Writing" (2017) 37(1) *Appellate Practice* 16–20, 16.

peaceable system of dispute resolution within a society grounded on common ethical standards. There is no reason why legal texts cannot be written in an interesting style and every reason why they should be.

- In a legal text dedicated to the promotion/realisation of truth, legal writers should not succumb to selectivity in facts/law in a bid to maximise a legal text's persuasiveness.
- Legal writers should approach their task not out of a sense that they have to write but because they have a story of fact and law to tell.
- A legal text in which the legal writer has taken care to familiarise him or herself closely with the facts and law will be a superior form of legal text.
- A legal text is likely to be better appreciated the better it is written.
- Authors should take care in their choice of words so that they mean precisely what they state and state precisely what they mean.
- With legal judgments – which continue to be crafted as though they are to be read out in court (and sometimes are) – the need for harmony of expression is clear. If a judge pays regard to how the sound of each sentence will affect the force of his or her text, then his text is likely to prove more engaging.
- A question arises whether there is ever much desire for especially long legal texts; certainly, it seems safe to assert that a legal text should never be any longer than it needs to be. In a legal text, as in a novel, every sentence and every word should be necessary and, if unnecessary, disregarded.
- When including quotes a legal writer should take care to quote only that which is strictly necessary to advance the substance of the legal text.
- A legal writer must steer a course between "absolute accuracy"[65] and "slovenly inaccuracy".[66]

---

65   Anthony Trollope, *An Autobiography* (William Blackwood & Sons, 1883), vol II, 60.
66   *Ibid*.

14. Woolf

On quality in writing, 'rules' of writing and other matters

Virginia Woolf (1882–1941) was one of the greatest authors of the 20th century. Starting out with a reputation as "the delicate lady authoress of a few experimental novels",[1] she has come to be recognised as among "the most professional, perfectionist, energetic, courageous and committed of [English] writers",[2] the brilliant author of such renowned works as *Mrs Dalloway* (1925) and *Orlando* (1928). Woolf suffered from poor mental health (possibly bipolar disorder) and tragically took her own life in 1941 by drowning herself in the River Ouse. This chapter considers Woolf's essays on "Modern Fiction"[3] ("one of Woolf's most famous essays"[4]) and "The Modern Essay"[5] from the perspective of what the legal writer might glean from them.

1. Weaknesses of modern writing

Woolf suggests that the history of modern fiction does not suggest that humanity has learned to write any better.[6] However, she qualifies this by suggesting that it is hard to get a proper vantage on one's own era.[7] Although she may be correct in this, when it comes to legal writing there does seem to be a general sense that legal writing has disimproved in recent times. Thus, it has been suggested that contemporary legal writing is:

> *flabby, prolix, obscure, opaque, ungrammatical, boring, redundant, disorganized, gray, dense, unimaginative, impersonal, foggy, infirm, indistinct, stilted, arcane, confused, heavy-handed, jargon and cliché-*

---

1. Hermione Lee, *Virginia Woolf* (Vintage Books, 1996), 4.
2. *Ibid.*
3. Virginia Woolf, *The Common Reader* (The Hogarth Press, 1948), 184–195.
4. Laura Ma Lojo Rodríguez, "'A New Tradition': Virginia Woolf and the Personal Essay" (2001) 23(1) *Atlantis* 75–90, 79.
5. Virginia Woolf, *The Common Reader* (The Hogarth Press, 1948), 267–281.
6. *Ibid*, 184.
7. *Ibid*, 185.

ridden, ponderous, weaseling, overblown, pseudointellectual, hyperbolic, misleading, incivil, labored, bloodless, vacuous, evasive, pretentious, convoluted, rambling, incoherent, choked, archaic, orotund, and fuzzy.[8]

That is a remarkable array of criticisms, which rather suggests that Woolf's observations are as true of contemporary legal writing as they were of much modern fiction of her day. Although some of these criticisms have been touched on previously, it is worth briefly considering each of them.

Arcane writing

Writing that is arcane is understood by few. It is commonly referred to as 'legalese' and involves a form of writing that uses Latin and Law-French words and which ascribes unfamiliar meanings to familiar words. It has been suggested that members of the legal profession may use 'legalese' to enhance the importance of the legal profession (and their own competency at, and charges for, writing arcane text).[9] Former Chief Justice McLachlin of Canada once suggested that: "A lot of the wordiness that mars [modern] legal writing is related to the use of ... 'arcane phrases'."[10]

Archaic writing

Archaic writing is old-fashioned. Possibly because law continues to be gleaned in part from the writing of previous generations, legal writing has a tendency to be old fashioned, using antique/classic terminology, and drafted in an impersonal style far removed from the colloquial.[11] The Plain English movement in legal writing has seen various authors canvassing for a legal writing style that is more colloquial, by which is meant not writing that is written as one speaks ("That ... would appear unprofessional")[12] but writing that is clear, direct and simple and which "avoids pompous, turgid prose").[13]

---

8   Tom Goldstein and Jethro Lieberman, *The Lawyer's Guide to Writing Well*, 3rd edition (University of California Press, 2016), 3.
9   Matthew Arnold, "The Lack of Basic Writing Skills and Its Impact on the Legal Profession" (1995) 24(1) *Capital University Law Review* 227–256, 232.
10   Beverley McLachlin, "Legal Writing: Some Tools" (2001) 39(3) *Alberta Law Review* 695–702, 698.
11   Julius Getman, "Voices" (1988) 66(3) *Texas Law Review* 577–588, 578.
12   Wayne Schiess, "Writing for Your Client" (2008–2009) 12(1) *Scribes Journal of Legal Writing* 123–130, 128.
13   *Ibid.*

Bloodless writing

What is meant by 'bloodless' is writing that is wanting in colour (vivacity). Edmund Burke, in a review of the first edition of Blackstone's *Commentaries*, wrote how "[T]he law has long been looked on, as ... of so dry ... [and] heavy a nature, that students of vivacity ... were deterred from entering upon it".[14] Burke moves on to praise Blackstone for rescuing accounts of the law from the dreary mire into which they had fallen. Bringing vivacity to bear in the context of legal writing is not easily done: it involves mastering the basic building blocks of good writing and bringing a certain emotional (and self-) disinterest to bear, without which one runs the risk of producing text that is "heavy ... clotted and un-moving".[15] This may be why 'bloodlessness' remains a criticism of legal writing a quarter of a millennium later.

Boring/dull/grey/unimaginative writing

Writing that is boring, etc (the words boring, dull, grey and unimaginative seem to contemplate much the same deficiency) appears to be viewed as an especial wrong among writers. So, for example, Corkery writes that: "Lawyers are criticised for the[ir] complexity and prolixity. Worse, they are often said to be boring."[16] But there is a general consensus among writers on legal writing that it does not require to be dull and boring, albeit that some legal writers seem to think otherwise.[17] No one is contending for legal writing that moves at a breathless pace; however, there is a sense that legal writing which is not boring, etc succeeds in three respects: it grabs the attention of the busy reader, facilitates the reading-task, and provokes the reader into thinking (and hopefully agreeing with the writer).[18]

Choked writing

By 'choked' writing what appears to be meant is writing in which the writer's voice does not sound to the fullest. Voice is something of a

---

14   *The Annual Register (1767)* (J Dodsley, 1767), 287.
15   Irving Younger, "Let's Get Serious" (1987) 73(5) *ABA Journal* 110–111, 110.
16   Jim Corkery, *Study of Law* (The Adelaide Law Review Association, 1988), 129.
17   Arthur Miller, "Some Remarks on Legal Writing" (1955–1956) 18(3) *Georgia Bar Journal (Macon)* 253–269, 269.
18   Mark Osbeck, "What is 'Good Legal Writing' and Why Does It Matter?" (2012) 4(2) *Drexel Law Review* 417–466, 456.

literary oddity: many editors and writers think that it makes writing great, yet there seems to be no guaranteed way of acquiring a literary reputation.[19] Menand suggests that "The ... metaphor of voice in writing is not speaking. It is singing ... except that it comes out as writing".[20] And modern studies into the musicality of legal performance (including legal writing) suggest that an awareness of the musicality of that performance can inform the writing/reading processes.[21] One reason for 'choked' writing may be the desire to evince a professional voice which has the legitimate aim of trying to avoid prejudice,[22] yet which also tends to be "formal, erudite, and old fashioned".[23] Thus as a notion, it is well-intended in theory but can yield difficulties in practice. Perhaps the ideal to be aimed for in terms of voice as a writer is "your own voice with the hems and haws chipped out".[24]

Confused/foggy/fuzzy writing

Lord Bingham has observed (of judgment-writing, but his observations have a wider resonance) that nowadays the ideal judgment is seen to entail clarity (along with brevity and simplicity).[25] Such clarity will be impossible to attain if a legal writer's thinking or writing is confused, etc. And the primary problems with writing that is confused, etc are twofold: the reader will not understand the point being made and the writer may lose credibility.[26]

Convoluted/dense writing

Convoluted/dense text is complex and difficult to follow. Convoluted/dense writing can suggest that lawyers find it difficult to justify whatever they are stating,[27] or even that they do not understand what they are stating. Convoluted arguments have even been described by one United

---

19   Louis Menand, "Introduction" to Louis Menand (ed), *The Best American Essays 2004* (Houghton Mifflin, 2004), xiv.
20   *Ibid*, xvii.
21   Sean Mulcahy, "Singing the Law: The Musicality of Legal Performance" (2020) 24 *Law Text Culture* 480–514, 485.
22   Julius Getman, "Voices" (1988) 66(3) *Texas Law Review* 577–588, 578.
23   *Ibid*.
24   Sheridan Baker, *The Practical Stylist*, 4th edition (Harper & Row, 1977), 1.
25   Lord Bingham, "What Is the Law?" (2009) 40(3) *Victoria University of Wellington Law Review* 597–612, 609.
26   Kenneth Oettle, "Transition By Repetition: Take One Step Back to Go Two Steps Forward" (2008) 87(9) *Michigan Bar Journal* 44–45, 45.
27   Leah Sears, "From the Other Side of the Bench – A Brief is Called a Brief for a Reason" (2012) 18(4) *Georgia Bar Journal* 36–37, 36.

States Court of Appeals judge as "sleeping pills on paper".[28] Regardless of its cause, convoluted/dense writing can be remediated through simplicity.[29] That said, while the convoluted and dense seems best avoided, complexity in and of itself ought not invariably to be rejected if complexity of expression is necessary.[30] (Of course, as against this the legal writer needs to weigh the commercial reality that greater numbers of clients consider that one aspect of being professional is the ability to explain the complex plainly.)[31]

Disorganised/rambling writing

Legal texts require "overall organisation",[32] as well as an organised approach in terms of addressing each issue considered.[33] Apart from suggesting laziness on the part of the author, a disorganised or rambling legal text weakens one's force of logic, reduces credibility and makes the reader less trustful of the writer.[34] Legal readers understand organised text more than chaotic text.[35] They want to be taken firmly by the hand and led through each step of a writer's logical process,[36] not brought on a disorganised ramble which proceeds on the assumption that the reader somehow already knows what the writer is seeking to communicate.

Evasive/weaseling writing

Evasive/weaseling writing is writing in which the writer avoids committing him or herself to a particular point. A hallmark of such writing is the use of the passive voice[37] – what William Safire once referred to as the "passive-evasive".[38] Former Chief Justice McLachlin of Canada

---

28   Alex Kozinski, "The Wrong Stuff" (1992) 2 *Brigham Young University Law Review* 325–334, 326.
29   Adina Radulescu, "The Pitfalls of Simplifying Legal Writing" (2012) 4(2) *Contemporary Readings in Law and Social Justice* 367–372, 370.
30   Julie Baker, "And the Winner Is: How Principles of Cognitive Science Resolve the Plain Language Debate" (2011) 80(2) *UKMC Law Review* 287–306, 302.
31   Wayne Schiess, "What Plain English Really Is" (2003–2004) 9 *Scribes Journal of Legal Writing* 43–76, 53.
32   Nancy Wanderer, "The Secret to Legal Analysis" (2019) 34(1) *Maine Bar Journal* 34–38, 34.
33   *Ibid.*
34   Steven Katz, "The 33 Steps: Postgraduate Legal Writing" (2021) 44(9) *Los Angeles Lawyer* 18–23, 20.
35   Teresa Bruce, "The Architecture of Drama: How Lawyers Can Use Screenwriting Techniques to Tell More Compelling Stories" (2019) 47 *Legal Writing: The Journal of the Legal Writing Institute* 47–83, 56.
36   Susan Taylor, "Students as (Re)Visionaries: or Revision, Revision, Revision" (2005) 21(2) *Touro Law Review* 265–296, 269.
37   Michael Walsh, "Tips on Converting Legalese into Plain English (Part 2)" (2016) 62(5) *Practical Lawyer* 7–10, 8.
38   William Safire, *Safire's Political Dictionary* (Oxford University Press, 2008), 431.

has observed that the passive voice "saps text of its strength and hides too much",[39] while also wondering how it continues to be so popular with a profession that (ostensibly) aims for precision in language. The aim of legal language, after all, should be to communicate/persuade, not to "tantalise and pique the curiosity but ... leave ... questions unanswered".[40]

Flabby writing

What seems to be meant by 'flabby' writing is a certain want of tightness (or, conversely, a certain looseness) in wording – or, to put matters more formally, a want of concision in writing. 'Flabby' writing, it has been suggested, is prone to grammatical errors[41] (which seems to be but a reflection that the more one writes the more potential for error in one's writing). An interview done in the last decade with various judges of the United States Supreme Court indicates that they see concision (with clarity and simplicity) as a key virtue of good legal writing.[42] The fundamental attraction of concision is increased clarity of style. In *The Philosophy of Style*, the controversial English philosopher, Herbert Spencer, observes as follows in this regard:

> *Whatever the nature of the thought to be conveyed ... skilful selection of a few particulars which imply the rest, is the key to success. In the choice of component ideas, as in the choice of expressions, the aim must be to convey the greatest quantity of thoughts with the smallest quantity of words.*[43]

Heavy-handed writing

By 'heavy-handed' writing what appears to be connoted is writing that is clumsy, insensitive or overly forceful.

'Clumsy' structure has been referred to as one of three 'horses of the Apocalypse' in terms of judicial writing[44] – though much the same criticism might be brought to bear in the context of legal writing more generally. As Miller observes, "Words are clumsy tools ... [I]t is ... easy to

---

39 Beverley McLachlin, "Legal Writing: Some Tools" (2001) 39(3) *Alberta Law Review* 695–702, 698.
40 Arthur Miller, "Some Remarks on Legal Writing" (1955–1956) 18(3) *Georgia Bar Journal (Macon)* 253–269, 263.
41 Richard Hyland, "A Defense of Legal Writing" (1986) 134(3) *University of Pennsylvania Law Review* 599–626, 621.
42 Robert Anderson, "US Supreme Court Interviews on Effective Legal Writing – Part II" (2008) 37(7) *Colorado Lawyer* 103–106, 103.
43 Herbert Spencer, *Philosophy of Style*, 2nd edition (Allyn and Bacon, 1892), 29.
44 Leon Skomicki, "Simple Legal Writing Can Improve Business Outcomes in Latin America" (2019) 50(2) *University of Miami Inter-American Law Review* 122–143, 126.

cut one's fingers with them".[45] Footnotes have long been perceived as a resting place for clumsy text, Professor Rodell observing in the 1930s that footnotes breed "clumsy writing".[46] Clumsiness is also suggestive of a certain carelessness or haste on the part of the writer which diminishes the persuasiveness of the written word.

Insensitive writing shows no concern for the feelings of another. One of the valuable achievements of today's so-called 'woke' culture (with its general and desirable awakening to past and present racial and social injustice) is a heightened appreciation that there are words and terms in the legal vocabulary that have disturbing associations/origins[47] and also that legal writers must be careful in their word-choices as changes in society transpire.[48]

As to forceful text, legal writing often seeks legitimately to persuade the reader through forceful reasoning/writing.[49] However, to do so it must be accessible, attractive, constrained and generally function with the rules of legal discourse.[50] Overly forceful writing is writing that is unduly strong and assertive, that can leave the reader feeling "bludgeoned",[51] and which is likely to distract him or her from seeing the true merits of whatever argument is being advanced, indeed may even leave the reader feeling offended.[52] There is a difficult balance to be struck in this regard: personal voice (individual jaggedness) is what gives a person's writing its distinctive voice; so, when editing one needs to be careful as a legal writer to arrive at a finished piece of text that does all that is expected of it but is not refined into the "flat, placid ... [and] uninteresting".[53]

Hyperbolic/exaggerated writing

The essence of hyperbole is exaggeration for effect. The problems with hyperbole in legal writing are that it suggests that a legal writer considers his or her argument to be of dubious strength,[54] and has the tendency to

---

45 Arthur Miller, "Some Remarks on Legal Writing" (1955–1956) 18(3) *Georgia Bar Journal (Macon)* 253–269, 253.
46 Fred Rodell, "Goodbye to Law Reviews" (1936–1937) 23(1) *Virginia Law Review* 38–45, 41.
47 John Browning, "Should Legal Writing Be Woke?" (2022) 20 *Scribes Journal of Legal Writing* 25–50, 48.
48 *Ibid.*
49 Kathryn Stanchi, "Feminist Legal Writing" (2002) 39 *San Diego Law Review* 387–436, 389.
50 *Ibid.*
51 Pamela Samuelson, "Good Legal Writing: Of Orwell and Window-Panes" (1984) 46(1) *University of Pittsburgh Law Review* 149–170, 156.
52 *Ibid.*
53 Christopher Lutz, "Why Can't Lawyers Write?" (1989) 15(2) *Litigation* 26–57, 27.
54 Diane Kraft, "The Perils of Hyperbole" (2011) 75(3) *Bench & Bar* 31–49, 31.

distort the truth of what is being asserted[55] – and legal writing places an especial premium on truth. The opposite of hyperbole is understatement, "an effective tool of persuasion".[56] Chief Justice Rice of Colorado has even written of "the thrill of understatement",[57] observing how understatement can be so much more potent than overstatement. Walsh memorably describes hyperbole as "a noisy child's drum … we learn to tune out";[58] understatement, by contrast "is a flute … we strain to hear".[59]

Impersonal writing

Impersonal writing is writing that is not influenced by and does not evince or even purport to involve personal feelings. There is something of a paradox at play when it comes to impersonality in writing. Detachment is viewed as a virtue in the sense of a lawyer bringing perspective to bear;[60] professional legal writing is expected to be credible, formal, professional and structured;[61] yet personal voice (or at least an individualised professional voice) is part and parcel of being a legal writer.[62] Ultimately striking the right balance "is a personal choice"[63] with each legal writer being encouraged to settle on the voice "that sounds like you … [and] … means what you mean".[64]

Incoherent/indistinct/obscure/opaque writing

By incoherent, etc writing what is meant is writing that is unclear (to the point of incomprehensibility when it comes to incoherency). As Lord Bingham, a former 'law lord' has observed – of judgment writing, but his observations have a wider resonance – nowadays, the ideal judgment is seen to entail clarity (along with brevity and simplicity).[65] Sometimes

---

55   Wayne Schiess, "Ethical Legal Writing" (2002) 21(3) *Review of Litigation* 527–550, 530.
56   Patrick Hugg, "Professional Legal Writing Declaring Your Independence" (1991) 11(2) *Journal of the National Association of Administration Law Judges* 114–143, 139.
57   Nancy Rice, "Tips on Legal Writing" (2015) 44(5) *Colorado Lawyer* 61–62, 61.
58   Michael Walsh, "Using Literary Devices to Improve Your Legal Writing" (1998) 44(4) *Practical Lawyer* 9–11, 11.
59   *Ibid.*
60   Nancy Rice, "Tips on Legal Writing" (2015) 44(5) *Colorado Lawyer* 61–62, 61.
61   David Hricik and Karen Sneddon, "Voice and Tone in Legal Writing" (2019) 25(1) *Georgia Bar Journal* 84–85, 84.
62   J Christopher Rideout, "Voice, Self, and Persona in Legal Writing" (2009) 15(1) *Legal Writing: The Journal of the Legal Writing Institute* 67–108, 107.
63   Marcia Ziegler, "Legal Writing and Professional Identity: Finding Your Unique Voice" (2022) 86(1) *Bench & Bar* 30–31, 31.
64   *Ibid.*
65   Lord Bingham, "What Is the Law?" (2009) 40(3) *Victoria University of Wellington Law Review* 597–612, 609.

there can, of course, be a good reason for ambiguity; for example, the perception may present that it is simply impossible to be more precise.[66] In other instances (one often encounters this in statute) a text may be 'future proofed' by using suitably abstract language so as to try and ensure that future technological advances are caught by it).[67] When it comes to the clarity-ambiguity dichotomy, perhaps the wisest guidance is that clarity should be consciously aimed at, not some sort of reflexive process.[68] As the Supreme Court of Minnesota observed in *In re Petition of Disciplinary Action Against Hawkins*[69] – a case concerning an attorney who acted in breach of certain administrative rules and wrote incomprehensible documentation[70] – "Public confidence in the legal system is shaken when ... a lawyer's correspondence and legal documents are so filled with spelling, grammatical, and typographical errors that they are virtually incomprehensible".[71]

Infirm writing

Infirm writing is writing that is weak or irresolute, that is, showing hesitancy or uncertainty. To be avoided in legal writing is the "pusillanimous and irresolute".[72] Confident writing, it has been suggested, helps make the identified result seem inevitable and un-forced.[73] It is a pleasure to read because readers never have to pause to decipher meaning.[74] Weak writing, by contrast, seems to make "readers feel unintelligent ... just a little obtuse".[75] It has even been suggested that confidence is a manifestation of zeal and an aspect of *ethos* on the part of the writer.[76] That said, overconfidence can yield hubris, with some

---

66 Max Oppenheimer, "Clarity: Not So Clearly Good" (2007) 46(2) *Journal of the Legal Profession* 287–308, 295.
67 *Ibid*, 296.
68 *Ibid*, 308.
69 502 NW 2d 770 (1993).
70 *Ibid*, 771.
71 *Ibid*.
72 Judith Fischer, "A Contemporary Take on Strunk and White for Legal Writers" (2013) 15 *Scribes Journal of Legal Writing* 127–152, 136.
73 Timothy Terrell, "Organizing Clear Opinions: Beyond Logic to Coherence and Character" (1999) 38(2) *Judges' Journal* 4–41, 41. The observation is made of judicial writing; however, the point arguably applies with equal vigour to all legal writing.
74 Stephen Armstrong, "Writing with (Quiet) Power: What Makes the Difference?" (2005) *Utah Law Review* 127–168, 143.
75 *Ibid*.
76 Anne Mullins, "Source-Relational Ethos in Judicial Opinions" (2019) 54(4) *Wake Forest Law Review* 1089–1134, 1092. It will be recalled that Aristotle posited that there are three facets to being persuasive as an advocate: *ethos* (character), *logos* (reasoning) and *pathos* (emotional appeal) and that of the three, *ethos* is the most important (see Aristotle, *Treatise on Rhetoric*, T Buckley (trans) (Henry G Bohn, 1850), 12).

writers, it seems, considering that proofreading can either be ignored or left to others.[77]

Jargon-/cliché-ridden writing

Lawyers, it has been suggested, love or else just fall into professional jargon (law's "circumscribed vocabulary")[78] when they write, sometimes because the jargon enriches a legal text, but sometimes even when it adds nothing.[79] Deployment of professional jargon (technical legal terms) when it adds nothing to a legal text has been decried as "an ostentatious cloak to a complete vacuity of ideas".[80] So why do lawyers use it? It has been suggested that it may represent a desire for peer recognition, with lawyers "like modern teenagers"[81] using jargon "as much for peer acceptance as for communication of a substantive message".[82] And there is a sense that jargon is more tolerable in lawyer-to-lawyer legal writing than in other forms of legal writing.[83]

As to clichés (overused terms that betray a lack of original thought), Justice Cardozo has suggested that their usage may be beguiling because they are comfortingly familiar and seem to offer exactitude:

No one has been able to combat more effectively than [Holmes] … the tyranny of tags and tickets. Is it a question of the competence of a legislature to respond by novel legislation to the call of an emergent need? Fettered by the word, we are too often satisfied to say that competence exists if it can be brought within a cliché, 'the police power' of the state; and at home in the protective phrase, we settle back at peace … The familiar form beguiles into an assurance of security. Danger as well as deception may indeed be lurking ill-concealed, danger as well as deception in a false appearance of exactitude.[84]

Still another commentator has described clichés as "the archetypal use

---

77   Don Gibbons, "An Apostle's Screed" (1996) 42(4) *Crime and Delinquency* 610–622, 617.

78   Ken Vinson, "Law as a Foreign Language: Understanding Law School" (1996) 1(1) *New York City Law Review* 5–154, 66.

79   John Godbold, "Twenty Pages and Twenty Minutes – Effective Advocacy on Appeal" (1976) 30(5) *Southwestern Law Journal* 801–820, 814.

80   Jeremiah Buckley, "[Book Review] *Handbook of the Law of Evidence* by Charles T McCormick" (1955) 4 *DePaul Law Review* 340–346, 342–345, 345.

81   Donald Layh, "Plain English: Increasing the Power of Our Writing" (1992) 56(1) *Saskatchewan Law Review* 1–22, 6.

82   *Ibid.*

83   Mark Mathewson, "Law Students, Beware" (2001–2002) 8 *Scribes Journal of Legal Writing* 141–158, 149.

84   Benjamin Cardozo, *Selected Writings of Benjamin Nathan Cardozo*, M Hall (ed) (Fallon Publications, 1947), 83.

of outworn language".[85] Thus, whereas some level of professional jargon can sometimes be appropriate, clichés seem best avoided. Though it is perhaps difficult to excise altogether cliché from text, cliché-ridden documents, it has been suggested, tend not to read as good analysis.[86]

Laboured/ponderous writing

Laboured/ponderous writing is writing that is awkward and heavy. To the extent that it continues to manifest in legal writing, it is not clear why this is so. Lawyers are well-educated people and must know that "grimness is [not] ... a prerequisite to serious discourse".[87] Possible solutions to awkwardness/heaviness are to excise excess wording, substitute simpler (shorter) words in a text, and consolidate (streamline) one's thoughts.[88] A fundamental goal in writing is to attain a naturalness of style through being oneself, working on one's natural writing strengths, and remediating one's weaknesses as a writer,[89] such naturalness of style helping to maintain reader interest (just as speech variations in spoken language do).[90] The task of legal writing does not require that a writer avoid deploying any natural skill at elegance.[91] However, elegance (literary style) should not be confused with writing that is "ponderous, pompous ... [or] overburdened with irrelevant flourishes".[92]

Misleading writing

Legal texts are usually told from a particular perspective and to that extent they can be deceptive.[93] Stark suggests that one reason legal writing can be so bad is because lawyers grow disenchanted with language. The reason for this disenchantment, he posits, is because lawyers are paid to some extent to mislead, they recognise that they are participating in the task of misleading, they understand that language is

85   Yuri Kapgan, "Of Golf and Ghouls: The Prose Style of Justice Scalia" (2003) 9 *Legal Writing: The Journal of the Legal Writing Institute* 71–110, 75.
86   Ginette Chapman, "Apt Phrasing in Legal Writing" (2021) 50(9) *Colorado Lawyer* 10–11, 11.
87   Irving Younger, "Let's Get Serious" (1987) 73(5) *ABA Journal* 110–111, 110.
88   Jaro Mayda, "On Style and Form in Legal Writing" (1962) 31 *Revista Jurídica de la Universidad de Puerto Rico* 9–32, 17.
89   Pamela Samuelson, "Good Legal Writing: Of Orwell and Window-Panes" (1984) 46(1) *University of Pittsburgh Law Review* 149–170, 150.
90   Mark Osbeck, "What is 'Good Legal Writing' and Why Does It Matter?" (2012) 4(2) *Drexel Law Review* 417–466, 443.
91   *Ibid*, 464.
92   Edward Re, "Legal Writing as Good Literature" (1985) 59(2) *St John's Law Review* 211–227, 224.
93   Helena Whalen-Bridge, "The Lost Narrative: The Connection Between Legal Narrative and Legal Ethics" (2010) 7 *Journal of the Association of Legal Writing Directors* 229–246, 235.

the medium through which they mislead, and hence they grow disenchanted with language.[94] That said, there are ethical limits to the extent to which a narrative (with all its potential for deception) can be brought to bear,[95] in particular when it comes to court proceedings when deception could quickly amount to a breach of legal professional obligations as regards dealings with the court, or even perjury. There are also practical limits on the extent to which the legal writer can engage in deception as such deception can create a question mark as to the legitimacy of the facts, law and arguments contained in that text.[96]

Orotund writing

Orotund writing can be described as resonant, or even magisterial. Justice Cardozo has written in the following terms about the characteristics of magisterial writing (in the context of judicial writing but his observations arguably apply to legal writing more generally):

> [I]t is first in dignity and power ... It eschews ornament. It is meager in illustration and analogy. If it argues, it does so with the downward rush and overwhelming conviction of the syllogism, seldom with tentative gropings towards the inductive apprehension of a truth imperfectly discerned. We hear the voice of the law speaking ... with ... calmness and assurance ... born of a sense of mastery and power.[97]

The power of resonant text is remarkable. As the manifold citations in this book surely demonstrate, when it comes to published legal texts "resonant arguments written years ago are still read, discussed, and cited".[98] The rules of classical rhetoric suggest that an authoritative reading voice is resonant, that is, clear and impressive;[99] and an authoritative writing voice is the same. In terms of making text more persuasive, it has been suggested that when a fact is likely to resonate particularly with a reader it should be "lingered upon and luxuriated in".[100] And while any legal text should be drafted in a manner which is accessible, clear and

---

94   Steven Stark, "Why Lawyers Can't Write" (1984) 97(6) *Harvard Law Review* 1389–1393, 1392.

95   Helena Whalen-Bridge, "The Lost Narrative: The Connection Between Legal Narrative and Legal Ethics" (2010) 7 *Journal of the Association of Legal Writing Directors* 229–246, 235.

96   Michael Hyman, "Thoughts on Credibility: When Writing for the Court, Stick to the Facts, Write in Plain English, and Watch Your Tone" (2022) 110(8) *Illinois Bar Journal* 42–43, 42.

97   Benjamin Cardozo, *Selected Writings of Benjamin Nathan Cardozo*, M Hall (ed) (Fallon Publications, 1947), 342.

98   *Ibid.*

99   Susie Salmon, "Reconstructing the Voice of Authority" (2017) 51(1) *Akron Law Review* 143–188, 154.

100   Stephen Smith, "The Poetry of Persuasion: Early Literary Theory and Its Advice to Legal Writers" (2009) 6(1) *Journal of the Association of Legal Writing Directors* 55–74, 66.

precise, it has been suggested that it is especially important when law is used in pursuit of social justice that the language deployed be, amongst other matters, resonant.[101]

Pretentious writing

Pretentious writing is writing that seeks to impress through affectation. It has long been recognised as a bane of legal writing. Charles Beardsley, a past president of the American Bar Association, memorably cautioned in 1940 against "asinine affectation" by lawyers.[102] Pretentious writing exudes a gaudiness that is the opposite of robust, direct, plain English.[103] And nothing, it has been suggested, diminishes legal writing more than words such as "aforementioned, hereinabove, hereinafter ... and the like".[104] When it comes to legal writing the general view remains today as it was when David Hume wrote in the mid-18th century that: "Every voice is united in applauding elegance, propriety, simplicity, spirit in writing; and in blaming fustian [pomposity/pretence], affectation, coldness, and a false brilliancy."[105] In short, affectation/pretentiousness add nothing to the force of a writer's reasoning.[106] In the context of legal writing, pretension often comes clothed in the guise of unnecessary professional jargon ("talismanic phrases").[107] Possible remedies for pretentiousness in legal writing are (at the editing stage) to excise the "pompous ... pretentious or faddish"[108] and also to avoid "hanging on to something useless just because you think it's beautiful".[109]

Prolix/redundant writing

Prolixity is essentially undue wordiness (and wordiness involves the use of words that are unnecessary and hence redundant). Prolixity – and the

---

101   Andrea McArdle, "Teaching Writing in Clinical, Lawyering, and Legal Writing Courses: Negotiating Professional and Personal Voice" (2006) 12 *Clinical Law Review* 501–540, 523.
102   Bryan Garner *et al*, "The Legaldegook Awards: 1991–1992" (1992) 3 *Scribes Journal of Legal Writing* 107–122, 118.
103   Matthew Salzwedel, "Face It – Bad Legal Writing Wastes Money" (2013) 92(3) *Michigan Bar Journal* 52–53, 52.
104   Thomas Haggard, "Letters" (1998) 9(4) *South Carolina Lawyer* 6–14, 13.
105   David Hume, *Essays, Moral, Political, and Literary*, T Green and T Grose (eds) (Longmans, Green & Co, 1896), vol 1, 266.
106   Elliott Biskind, "Writing Right" (1972) 44(1) *New York State Bar Journal* 47–51, 47.
107   Thomas Spahn, "The Art of Legal Writing" (1989) 9(2) *Journal of the National Association of Administrative Law Judges* 137–152, 139.
108   Gerald Lebovits, "Take a Needed Pandemic Break! Thoughts on Legal Writing from William Zinsser" (2020) 56(5) *Tennessee Bar Journal* 32–35, 33.
109   *Ibid.*

use of redundant words – are the very opposite of concision – which is one of "the three C's of effective [legal] writing"[110] (the others are clarity and coherence).[111] Hatlen suggests that to keep sentences clear and comprehensible, one should excise the needless and redundant, as well as words implied by other words.[112] Wordiness diminishes writing by adding undue length and diminishing the degree of analysis.[113] Concision, by contrast, yields vigorous writing. Strunk observes in this regard that concision requires not that sentences be shortened or detail avoided but rather that the legal writer "make every word tell".[114]

Stilted writing

Writing that is stilted tends to be stiff and self-conscious, even unnatural. Perhaps its most common form is the type of writing which Justice Cardozo (in a consideration of judicial writing forms) has referred to as "the type refined or artificial, smelling of the lamp, verging at times upon preciosity or euphuism".[115] Of this type of writing, Cardozo later observes:

> With its merits it has its dangers, for unless well kept in hand, it verges at times upon preciosity and euphuism. Held in due restraint, it lends itself admirably to cases where there is need of delicate precision … Such a method has its charm and its attraction, though one feels at times the yearning for another more robust and virile.[116]

So Cardozo sees a use for refined – even particularly refined – language in matters which require especial precision. However, he suggests that such refinement needs to be kept in check if it is not to descend into 'preciosity' (excessive refinement) or 'euphuism' (artificiality or excessive elaboration). And while refined text has its merits (and seems often to feature in the judgments of Justice Cardozo himself) he rightly observes that, in the presence of such refinement, one sometimes feels the need for more vigorous language. Longinus, a classical commentator, writing of rhetoric observed that "[A]n exhibition of feeling has … most effect on an audience when it appears to flow naturally from the occasion, not to

---

110 Linda Furey, "To Write Well: A Primer on Concision, Clarity and Coherence in Legal Writing" (1992) 2 *New Jersey Lawyer* 18–26, 19.
111 *Ibid*.
112 Lisa Hatlen, "Conciseness in Legal Writing" (2009) 82(8) *Wisconsin Lawyer* 21–23, 21.
113 Ginette Chapman, "Apt Phrasing in Legal Writing" (2021) 50(9) *Colorado Lawyer* 10–11, 11.
114 William Strunk, *The Elements of Style* (New York: Harcourt, Brace & Co, 1920), 24.
115 Benjamin Cardozo, *Selected Writings of Benjamin Nathan Cardozo*, M Hall (ed) (Fallon Publications, 1947), 342.
116 *Ibid*, 349.

have been laboured by the art of the speaker".[117] His observations sound equally true when it comes to legal writing.

Uncivil writing

Uncivil writing is writing that is discourteous or impolite. In practice, civility may be required by professional or procedural rules and (when parties are uncivil in court) *may* wring criticism from the presiding judge/s. (This may not always happen and, of course, some judges may occasionally stray into uncivility in their own writing.)[118] Justice O'Connor, formerly of the United States Supreme Court, has suggested the advantages of civility among lawyers to be that it "enhance[s] the pleasure lawyers find in practice, increase[s] the effectiveness of our system of justice, and improve[s] the public's perception of lawyers".[119] There are other practical advantages to being civil: affronted victims may in the future be less facilitative of lawyers who are rude; lawyers with the reputation of being rude may find that their prospects of advancement diminish; and those who work for lawyers may prove less productive if they are treated with uncivility.[120] Being uncivil also does not tend to advance a client's interests;[121] and zealousness in the pursuit of a client's interests is not an acceptable reason for uncivility.[122] One suggested means of avoiding ever writing anything unacceptably uncivil is to write everything as if one's mother were going to read it.[123]

Ungrammatical writing

When it comes to clarity, a language requires agreed-upon rules (grammatical rules) if communications, such as legal texts, are to possess the clarity necessary to yield effective communication.[124] And when it comes to clarity in legal writing the same applies: the legal writer must

117 Longinus, *On the Sublime*, H Havell (trans) (Macmillan & Co, 1890), 42.
118 David Lee and Sarah Massarachia, "Kiss My Grits – And Other Eloquent Reports" (1999) 13(3) *CBA Record* 28–31, 29.
119 Sandra Day O'Connor, "Professionalism" (1998) 76(1) *Washington University Law Quarterly* 5–14, 8.
120 Sophie Sparrow, "Practicing Civility in the Legal Writing Course" (2007) 13 *Legal Writing: The Journal of the Legal Writing Institute* 113–158, 125–126.
121 Bryan Garner, "The Legal-Writing Skills Test" (1994–1995) 5 *Scribes Journal of Legal Writing* 107–140, 137.
122 Judith Fischer, "Incivility in Lawyers' Writing: Judicial Handling of Rambo Run Amok" (2011) 50(2) *Washburn Law Journal* 365–394, 370–371.
123 David Lee and Sarah Massarachia, "Kiss My Grits – And Other Eloquent Reports" (1999) 13(3) *CBA Record* 28–31, 30.
124 Mark Osbeck, "What is 'Good Legal Writing' and Why Does It Matter?" (2012) 4(2) *Drexel Law Review* 417–466, 428.

observe the rules of grammar.[125] Ungrammatical writing is possessed of three key disadvantages: it can cause ambiguity of meaning; it may irritate the reader who may therefore be less likely to be persuaded by the text in question; and it suggests a certain ignorance in a writer who is seeking to convey that he or she is knowledgeable. In this last regard, it has been observed that courts have emphasised how unprofessional prose raises questions as to lawyer competency (and courts cannot be alone in having such questions when they read text which proceeds in breach of grammar rules).[126]

Vacuous writing

Vacuous writing is writing that does not align with actuality,[127] or which evinces a lack of thought or intelligence. Leaving aside the Marxian notion that legal analysis is invariably vacuous (and but the means whereby rulers preserve power),[128] the following vacuities can usefully be avoided:

- Writing that makes superficial/vacuous comparisons between previous case law and the facts at hand without indicating why the comparison is significant.[129]
- Footnotes which make "worthless commentary"[130] and contain "material of doubtful relevance".[131]
- Qualifiers that add nothing much in themselves (save perhaps to suggest over-confidence or condescension on the part of the author).[132]

---

125   Timothy Blevins, "A Hallmark of Professional Writing Citation Form" (2003) 29(1) *Thurgood Marshall Law Review* 89–96, 96.
126   Heidi Brown, "Converting Benchslaps to Backslaps: Instilling Professional Accountability in New Legal Writers by Teaching and Reinforcing Context" (2014) 11 *Legal Communications and Rhetoric* 109–152, 123.
127   Marianne Constable, "Law as Claim to Justice: Legal History and Legal Speech Acts" (2011) 1(3) *UC Irvine Law Review* 631–640, 632.
128   Jeremy Miller, "Behind the Green Door, in Chambers: Is There a Limit to Judicial Discretion?" (1987) 12(1) *Oklahoma City University Law Review* 59–102, 88.
129   Maureen Arrigo-Ward, "How to Please Most of the People Most of the Time: Directing (or Teaching in) a First-Year Legal Writing Program" (1995) 29(2) *Valparaiso University Law Review* 557–610, 582.
130   Shane Tintle, "Citing the Elite: The Burden of Authorial Anxiety" (2007) 57(2) *Duke Law Journal* 487–516, 506.
131   *Ibid.*
132   In the United States, Supreme Court Justice Gorsuch's noted use of qualifiers in his judgments has been criticised for precisely this reason. See Nina Varsava, "Elements of Judicial Style: A Quantitative Guide to Neil Gorsuch's Opinion Writing" (2018) 93 *New York University Law Review Online* 75–107, 82.
133   Allan Hutchinson, "From Cultural Construction to Historical Deconstruction" (1984) 94 *Yale Law Journal* 209–238, 212.

- Writing that is too clever by half, with "glibness passed off as profundity and novelty as originality".[133]
- Grand, but largely empty, phraseology such as "It is important to remember that ...", "It is worth noting that ..." or "It is well established ...". (When it comes to the last-mentioned type of phrases the consensus view is that to achieve clarity and brevity in writing it is desirable that legal writers should "shun"[134] such "wordy ... expressions".)[135]

2.   Lifeless writing

Woolf disdains the type of writing that is solid but lifeless.[136] The problem of lifeless writing has already been considered above and is clearly an issue that addresses legal writing also. Justice Frankfurter of the United States Supreme Court in hypothesising (mistakenly, it is respectfully submitted) that "of the many mansions in the house of literature law is not one"[137] – an observation so eloquent it seems almost to defeat the proposition for which it stands – has written of "the inevitable lawyer's writing ... [with] lifeless tags and rags that preclude grace and stifle spontaneity".[138] The issue of whether legal writing is a form of literature has already been considered. However, the lifelessness to which Justice Frankfurter refers is not, it is respectfully submitted, quite the inevitability that he so clearly perceives it to be. There are proven means of making legal writing engaging and interesting, such as being clear, being concise and aiming for elegance.[139] Success in legal writing requires that one be correct but also readily readable, with readability being gauged by the degree to which readers understand a text, find it engaging and can read it at speed.[140]

3.   Forms of writing

Woolf is critical of the form of various modern novels, suggesting that the essential thing that ought to fill them (be it life, reality, spirit, or truth) can no longer be contained in such form as they are given.[141] Whenever

---

134   Brian Porto, "Past Tense: The Legal Prose of Justice Robert Larrow" (2020) 46(3) *Vermont Bar Journal* 24–27, 24.
135   *Ibid.*
136   Virginia Woolf, *The Common Reader* (The Hogarth Press, 1948), 186.
137   Felix Frankfurter, *Law and Politics: Occasional Papers of Felix Frankfurter*, A MacLeish and E Prichard (eds) (Harcourt, Brace & Co, 1939), 104.
138   *Ibid.*
139   Jillian Singer, "Four Principles to Help Guide Your Legal Writing" (2016) 8 *Solo & Small Firm* 4–6, 4.
140   Edgar Dale and Jeane Chall, "The Concept of Readability" (1949) 26(1) *Elementary English* 19–26, 23.
141   Virginia Woolf, *The Common Reader* (The Hogarth Press, 1948), 188.

one comes to the issue of form, it is difficult not to recall Saint Paul's observation in the Book of Corinthians that:

> *[I]f the trumpet give an uncertain sound, who shall prepare himself to the battle? So likewise ye, except ye utter by the tongue words easy to be understood, how shall it be known what is spoken? for ye shall speak into the air.*[142]

Mayda, having noted Saint Paul's renowned observation seeks to put what he says in terms more fitting for the legal writer:

> *Make it easy for your reader! ... [L]egal writers ... must above all – and second only to the content – care to communicate effectively ... To be effective is get across to your chosen audience your ideas with the maximum impact and understanding.*[143]

A question arises as to whether the traditional form of judgment is always the best means of achieving these ends. This issue is more closely examined in the Appendix to this book in the context of child and family law judgments. (And it is perhaps interesting to note in this regard that in the late-1960s the French courts began retreating from their traditional forms of judgment and writing decisions in a "much freer style".)[144] Although one finds enlightened judges such as Lord Bingham writing that the ideal judgment will be possessed of brevity, clarity and simplicity,[145] there has never been a systemic reappraisal of the adequacy of the traditional form of common-law judgment to determine whether it is 'fit for purpose' in a world that is radically different from that in which the present form of the typical common law judgment was originally conceived. (And that is to ignore for the moment the claim of the Legal Realist movement that judgments are but the *ex post facto* rationalisation of decisions arrived at for other reasons.[146] That is a proposition which is probably too strongly stated when put in the manner just stated but is not perhaps a theory entirely without substance.) With the post-COVID trend to greater use of online court hearings, the issue of judgment form seems even more pressing, not least as to consistency in the preparation and production of 'e-judgments' and the establishment of suitable quality control mechanisms.

---

142   Corinthians 14:8–9.
143   Jaro Mayda, "On Style and Form in Legal Writing" (1962) 31 *Revista Juridica de la Universidad de Puerto Rico* 9–32, 9.
144   Brigid McArthur, "French Judicial Decisions" (1984) 14(4) *Victoria University of Wellington Law Review* 463–475, 469.
145   Lord Bingham, "What Is the Law?" (2009) 40(3) *Victoria University of Wellington Law Review* 597–612, 609.
146   P Sim, "Jurisprudence and the Legal Process: Some Contemporary Trends" (1969) 2(1) *Otago Law Review* 1–14, 7.

4. Honesty and writing

Woolf considers that a book should mirror the author's mental conception if it is to be good.[147] She complains that modern writers not only depart from this ideal but positively work towards obfuscating the mental conception that yields a piece of prose.[148] In a similar vein, it has been suggested, for example, that just like literary writers "lawyers write to communicate ideas",[149] with the competency to communicate ideas being perhaps "the most important skill [that] a lawyer can master".[150]

When it comes to legal writing, it is only the thoughts in the writer's head that are real: the written text is 'merely' a means whereby those who read it intelligently "can reconstruct ... the imaginary tune that existed in the composer's [writer's] head".[151] The writer in this schema does not plant his or her thoughts in the reader's mind. Rather, what arises is a reproduction of the writer's thoughts in the reader's mind through the reader's own active thinking.[152] The test of a good legal writer is how accurately he or she manages to communicate to the reader what was in their mind as they wrote. This ability to communicate thoughts though perhaps the "most mundane feature"[153] of writing is also its most critical.[154]

The proposition that although a creation (such as a legal text) may sit physically before the reader the creative work presenting is in truth "something imagined"[155] is a proposition with a long intellectual history and was perhaps most famously propounded by Joseph Addison and William Hogarth in the 18th century. Addison, writing in *The Spectator* of 21 June 1712, posited that "pleasures of the imagination" can arise from our contemplation of physical objects (such as a legal text).[156] Four decades later, Hogarth treated even more fulsomely with this point in *The Analysis of Beauty*, observing:

> [L]et every object under our consideration, be imagined to have its inward contents scooped out so nicely, as to have nothing of it left but a thin shell ... and let us likewise suppose this thin shell to be made up of very fine

---

147   Virginia Woolf, *The Common Reader* (The Hogarth Press, 1948), 188.
148   *Ibid*.
149   Rebekah Hanley, "Want to Be a Better Writer? Read! Enjoying Other's Work Can Improve Your Own" (2020) 80(7) *Oregon State Bar Bulletin* 15–17, 16.
150   Thomas Collins and Ken Marlett, "New Tools Can Enhance Legal Writing" (2003) 75(5) *New York State Bar Association Journal* 10–18, 11.
151   R Collingwood, *The Principles of Art* (Clarendon Press, 1938), 139.
152   *Ibid*, 140.
153   Gertrude Block, "What Did You Say? What Did You Mean?" (1976–1977) 28(4) *Journal of Legal Education* 542–549, 549.
154   *Ibid*.
155   R Collingwood, *The Principles of Art* (Clarendon Press, 1938), 142.
156   J Addison *et al*, *The Spectator*, G Smith (ed) (Dutton, 1945), vol 3, 279.

> *threads, closely connected together, and equally perceptible, whether the eye is supposed to observe them from without, or within; and we shall find the ideas of the two surfaces of this shell will naturally coincide.*[157]

What both men are driving at is that evaluative judgment of a physical creation is more than a matter of sight, more even than the mind's eye,[158] in effect a learned form of perception that enables access to truth. Yet legal writers generally remain trapped today in a literary equivalent of the 19th-century theory of painting which held that the person who views a picture is merely seeing flat colour patterns.[159] Likewise, many legal writers look only to the 'flat text' of a legal text and derive nothing from it except what is contained in the particular combination of words presenting, even though the sensation of reading a legal text and treating with the thoughts reproduced in one's mind involve a much richer process than the mere reading of words. As the English philosopher, RG Collingwood has observed:

> *[I]n listening to music we not only hear ... sequences and combinations of audible sounds ... we also enjoy imaginary experiences which do not belong to the region of sound at all ... [P]oetry [too] has the power of bringing before us not only the sounds which constitute the audible fabric of the "poem", but other sounds, and sights, and tactile and motor experiences, and at times even scents ... in imagination.*[160]

The process of reading a creative legal text, it is submitted, is no different.

5.   Stream of consciousness

In what can be seen as praise of 'stream of consciousness' Woolf writes that to the writer life is not "a series of gig lamps symmetrically arranged".[161] Stream of consciousness is a writing method whereby the thoughts and emotions of a writer are in effect written out as they occur. Though not a commonly encountered style of legal writing it is not altogether unknown and is perhaps most obviously visible in the judgments of one of the greatest ever common law judges, Oliver Wendell Holmes, Jr (indeed it is a feature of his greatness). The free-wheeling style of Holmes's dissent in *Lochner v New York*[162] has already been considered previously above. His dissent in *Gitlow v*

---

157   William Hogarth, *The Analysis of Beauty* (The Silver Lotus Shop, 1909), 17.
158   R Collingwood, *The Principles of Art* (Clarendon Press, 1938), 144.
159   *Ibid*, 146.
160   *Ibid*, 147.
161   Virginia Woolf, *The Common Reader* (The Hogarth Press, 1948), 189.
162   198 US 45 (1905).

People,[163] a free speech case where a socialist was prosecuted for his authorship of a socialist tract, offers in its penultimate paragraph another example of where Holmes (in words that are not always altogether clear) spews forth a stream of writing that is so brilliant in form that it is almost blinding as to what it means in substance. Thus, Holmes writes:

> *It is said that this manifesto was more than a theory, that it was an incitement. Every idea is an incitement. It offers itself for belief, and, if believed, it is acted on unless some other belief outweighs it or some failure of energy stifles the movement at its birth. The only difference between the expression of an opinion and an incitement in the narrower sense is the speaker's enthusiasm for the result. Eloquence may set fire to reason. But whatever may be thought of the redundant discourse before us, it had no chance of starting a present conflagration. If, in the long run, the beliefs expressed in proletarian dictatorship are destined to be accepted by the dominant forces of the community, the only meaning of free speech is that they should be given their chance and have their way.*[164]

This prose is both stirring and euphoric (perhaps even a little frightening in the extent to which it would give sway to dangerous free speech that could up-end American democracy, the last great hope of the world), "[b]ut, when all is said and done, what exactly does this passage mean?".[165] Whatever about meaning, what Holmes's text involves is (for good or ill) law, learning, logic, and life experience fused into a single, piercing stream of consciousness in which the clearest flashes of brilliance can be discerned even if its meaning cannot perfectly be parsed.

In *United States v Schwimmer*,[166] in which the redoubtable Ms Schwimmer had been refused citizenship because she refused to swear to take up arms to defend the United States if that should be necessary (and rightly so, the Supreme Court held), Holmes offered yet another free-wheeling, stream of consciousness style dissent in which thought, emotion, judgment and sense all seem to fuse into a single effusive outpouring. Thus, Holmes writes in his closing passage:

> *She is an optimist, and states in strong and, I do not doubt, sincere words her belief that war will disappear, and that the impending destiny of mankind is to unite in peaceful leagues. I do not share that optimism, nor*

---

163   268 US 652 (1925).
164   *Ibid*, 673.
165   Gerard Hogan, "Holmes and Denning: Two 20th Century Legal Icons Compared" (2007) 42 *Irish Jurist* 119–135, 121–122.
166   279 US 644 (1929).

do I think that a philosophic view of the world would regard war as absurd. But most people who have known it regard it with horror, as a last resort, and even if not yet ready for cosmopolitan efforts, would welcome any practicable combinations that would increase the power on the side of peace. The notion that the applicant's optimistic anticipations would make her a worse citizen is sufficiently answered by her examination, which seems to me a better argument for her admission than any that I can offer. Some of her answers might excite popular prejudice, but, if there is any principle of the Constitution that more imperatively calls for attachment than any other, it is the principle of free thought – not free thought for those who agree with us, but freedom for the thought that we hate. I think that we should adhere to that principle with regard to admission into, as well as to life within, this country. And recurring to the opinion that bars this applicant's way, I would suggest that the Quakers have done their share to make the country what it is, that many citizens agree with the applicant's belief, and that I had not supposed hitherto that we regretted our inability to expel them because they believed more than some of us do in the teachings of the Sermon on the Mount.[167]

This is remarkable prose to find in a judgment. It moves from a description of what Ms Schwimmer believes of war, to what Holmes (a Civil War veteran) believes of war, to what most people make of war, to a consideration of Ms Schwimmer's views on her standing as a would-be citizen, to how those views sit in a constitutional architecture that places a premium on free thought, to a consideration of the essence of free thought, to a mention of the proud role played by the Quakers in American history, to a self-deprecatory suggestion that both the Quakers (and Ms Schwimmer) were adhering with especial rigour (and greater vigour than the majority of people) to the teachings of Jesus in his Sermon on the Mount, including Jesus's proposition that "Blessed are the peacemakers; for they shall be called the children of God".[168] All this in a mere 271 words – and all of those words comprising the most exquisite of prose. It is a remarkable achievement and all the more impressive because it combines facts, philosophy and faith so effortlessly and naturally in a single and incisive stream of words. In *Schwimmer*, as in *Gitlow*, as in *Lochner*, there is, to borrow from Woolf, no 'lining of the gig-lamps': what one gets is a spectacular amalgam of the head and the heart[169] – albeit following on deep thought and great mental labour. A

---

167   *Ibid*, 654–655.
168   Matthew 5:9.
169   Richard Posner, "Judges' Writing Styles (And Do They Matter?)" (1995) 62(4) *University of Chicago Law Review* 1421–1450, 1430.

word of caution is, however, required. Not every legal writer is a Holmes. So, for example, Judge Weltner of the Supreme Court of Georgia has cautioned against legal writing that contains a "flood of fuzzy stream-of-consciousness words".[170] A sequence of thoughts without due regard to logical argument or narrative sequence may work well when it comes to the extraordinary intellect of Holmes; it seems unlikely to work as well when it comes to a lesser legal writer.

6. Concision in writing

Writing in further praise of 'stream of consciousness' as a form of prose, Woolf points to how, as a prose form it emphasises that life may be found fully in the small.[171] Leaving aside her affection for the 'stream of consciousness' as a prose form, what Woolf points to is the importance to literary writing of focusing on the essential detail of a matter. In the legal writing context, this focus on essential detail takes the form of a recognition of the value (and efficiency) in concision. Concise text, it has been observed, is succinct, avoids superfluity, and presents "an appropriate level of detail".[172] For it is possible, of course, to 'go overboard' on detail. Thus, Justice Cardozo, commenting on the potential for "over-emphasis of details"[173] observes:

> [O]ne must permit oneself ... a certain margin of misstatement [ie, allow for some level of misstatement]. Of course, one must take heed that the margin is not exceeded ... On the other hand, the sentence may be so overloaded with all its possible qualifications that it will tumble down of its own weight ... The picture cannot be painted if the significant and ... insignificant are given equal prominence. One must know how to select. All these generalities are as easy as they are obvious, but, alas! the application is an ordeal to try the souls of men.[174]

Fundamentally (and this accords with what Justice Cardozo states in the above-quoted observations), regardless of the level of detail that one includes in a legal text, the constant aim and focus of the good legal writer must be clarity.[175]

---

170 Charles Weltner, "Effective Legal Writing: Views from the Bench" (1990) 26(4) *Georgia State Bar Journal* 154–163, 162.
171 Virginia Woolf, *The Common Reader* (The Hogarth Press, 1948), 190.
172 Mark Osbeck, "What is 'Good Legal Writing' and Why Does It Matter?" (2012) 4(2) *Drexel Law Review* 417–466, 437.
173 Benjamin Cardozo, *Selected Writings of Benjamin Nathan Cardozo*, M Hall (ed) (Fallon Publications, 1947), 341.
174 *Ibid.*
175 Catherine Fregosi, "The Importance of Finding Your Voice as a Writer" (2020–2021) 46(4) *Vermont Bar Journal* 36–39, 36.

7.   'Rules' of writing

Woolf sounds a useful note when it comes to 'rules' of writing, observing that any approach to writing is correct if the writer ends up expressing whatever he or she set out to express.[176] The fiction writer enjoys a greater freedom in this regard than the legal writer. The legal writer must organise information into "well-established formats",[177] observing "well-established patterns of analysis",[178] he or she must be methodical in terms of research,[179] grammatically correct,[180] and show consistent "creativity, insight, and judgment".[181] To cap all this the writer must seek to be concise and – as mentioned above – his or her constant aim and focus must be clarity.[182] Although the rules of good writing considered in this book are useful in terms of achieving these various (and not always consistent) goals, what Woolf points to is that it is the end result of one's writing rather than the rules of writing that ought to be the key focus of the legal writer.

8.   Long words and opening words

Woolf writes of the modern essay that of all forms of literature it is the one that least requires long words; it need merely yield pleasure.[183] Though a legal text sometimes calls for long words, they ought generally to be avoided: Floren, emphasising the need for a legal text to be readable, observes that "writing larded with big words is tough reading", even if a 'big' word is sometimes unavoidable.[184] To be remembered is that legal writing seeks to communicate/persuade and that there is no need to show off how clever one is by using long words unnecessarily.[185]

Opening words also count in a legal text. The beginning is where the legal writer creates the first impression with the legal reader. It may also be a point in a legal text where the potential for persuading the reader as to a certain view is optimal[186] or filtering what follows through whatever came first.[187]

---

176   Virginia Woolf, *The Common Reader* (The Hogarth Press, 1948), 192.
177   Laurel Oates *et al*, *The Legal Writing Handbook*, 3rd edition (Aspen Publishers, 2002), xxxiii.
178   *Ibid.*
179   *Ibid.*
180   *Ibid.*
181   *Ibid.*
182   Catherine Fregosi, "The Importance of Finding Your Voice as a Writer" (2020–2021) 46(4) *Vermont Bar Journal* 36–39, 36.
183   Virginia Woolf, *The Common Reader* (The Hogarth Press, 1948), 267.
184   M Floren, "Better Legal Writing" (1967) 13(4) *Student Lawyer Journal* 10–21, 11. See also Lisa Hatlen, "Conciseness in Legal Writing" (2009) 82(8) *Wisconsin Lawyer* 21–23, 23.
185   Arthur Miller, "Some Remarks on Legal Writing" (1955–1956) 18(3) *Georgia Bar Journal (Macon)* 253–269, 264.
186   Cathren Page, "Not So Very Bad Beginnings: What Fiction Can Teach Lawyers about Beginning a Persuasive Legal Narrative before a Court" (2017) 86(2) *Mississippi Law Journal* 315–364, 324.
187   *Ibid*, 325.

A good beginning, it has been suggested, should set the tone, identify the theme, pique the audience's interest and prime the audience to believe what is to follow.[188] The best introductions require introductions of their own by way of great opening lines.[189] Judge Wisdom of the United States Court of Appeals has observed that most judgments do not begin memorably[190] and suggests that a judgment writer should:

- attempt to state the key question in the first sentence;
- put the "sex appeal"[191] in the first and last sentences; and
- keep to one idea per sentence.[192]

Though Judge Wisdom is concerned with judgment writing his observations arguably have a wider resonance as regards legal writing more generally.

9. Writing engagingly

That essay-readers are not always enthralled by essays may be, Woolf suggests, as much due to the reader as to the essayist.[193] There are, of course, bad readers of legal texts also. As with literary texts, these include the "fearful reader … [the] reader in a hurry … [the reader who] reads the text his own way … [and the reader who] is … disrespectful of the text".[194] But perhaps of greater interest in a book about legal writing are Woolf's observations on what makes for more enthralling reading, as considered below:

A writer must have a knowledge of how to write[195]

For a person to succeed as a lawyer he or she must possess a variety of skills, including an ability to advocate, counsel and negotiate; however, these abilities are of limited use if he or she is not capable of effective writing.[196] As one commentator has observed, great lawyers are great writers, it being "commonly understood"[197] that the written word is a litmus test of good lawyering.

---

188   *Ibid.*
189   Charles Insler, "Opening Lines" (2016) 42(2) *Litigation* 8–13, 11.
190   Ellison Kahn, "A Trimestrial Potpourri" (1994) 111(1) *South African Law Journal* 198–207, 198.
191   John Wisdom, "Wisdom's Idiosyncrasies" (2000) 109 *Yale Law Journal* 1273–1278, 1273.
192   *Ibid.*
193   Virginia Woolf, *The Common Reader* (The Hogarth Press, 1948), 268.
194   Susanna Lindroos-Hovinheimo, "Retracing One's Steps: Searching for the Ethics of Legal Interpretation" (2009) 22(2) *International Journal for the Semiotics of Law* 163–178, 169.
195   Virginia Woolf, *The Common Reader* (The Hogarth Press, 1948), 268.
196   J Tim Willette, "Memo of Masochism (Reflections in Legal Writing)" (1993) 17(2) *Nova Law Review* 869–882, 869.
197   Edwin Torres, "Foreword" (2019) 73(4) *University of Miami Law Review* 1065–1070, 1066.

Learning should be fused in writing[198]

Woolf suggests that learning alone does not suffice to make prose potent and persuasive; that learning must fuse with the prose, rather than jutting out in some showy manner. In this regard, she, to some extent, echoes Justice Cardozo's earlier observation that when it comes to legal writing: "Form is not something added to substance as a mere protuberant adornment. The two are fused into a unity."[199] Strength and weakness in form are, he posits, "qualities of the substance ... tokens of the thing's identity. They make it what it is".[200]

A writer should not scold[201]

In the same way, a lawyer should avoid becoming (in his or her writing or otherwise) what one American commentator has colourfully referred to as a "junkyard dog ... unleashed",[202] that is, barking and growling and snapping at the unfortunate recipient of his or her prose. It has been suggested (and the suggestion chimes with common sense) that rudeness tends to be counterproductive, generating resentment, and reducing the prospects of success in the task at hand. To be avoided also is a moralising scolding (not least in judgments), a non-moralising, rule-bound legal system being the "most morally-defensible"[203] construct of law (and adjudication) in a liberal democracy.

A writer should not write carelessly[204]

Judge Weltner has contended that when it comes to legal writing, a carelessness of style is indicative of a careless mind, with the product of that mind being seen as poor work.[205] The reader of a legal text has enough to do in straining to comprehend whatever argument is being made without being put through the double trial of "careless style and

---

198   Virginia Woolf, *The Common Reader* (The Hogarth Press, 1948), 268.
199   Benjamin Cardozo, *Selected Writings of Benjamin Nathan Cardozo*, M Hall (ed) (Fallon Publications, 1947), 340.
200   *Ibid*.
201   Virginia Woolf, *The Common Reader* (The Hogarth Press, 1948), 269.
202   Douglas Abrams, "Incivility in Legal Writing Can Be Costly to Client and to Attorney" (2015–2016) 41(1) *Montana Lawyer* 14–23, 15.
203   Allan Hutchinson, "A Postmodern's Hart: Taking Rules Sceptically" (1995) 58(6) *Modern Law Review* 788–819, 796.
204   Virginia Woolf, *The Common Reader* (The Hogarth Press, 1948), 269.
205   Charles Weltner, "Effective Legal Writing: Views from the Bench" (1990) 26(4) *Georgia State Bar Journal* 154–163, 154.

cumbersome form".[206] Good legal writing is supposed to facilitate readers and the legal process;[207] to be avoided is the defensive abandonment of clarity and style in the face of a (typically hostile) reading audience.[208] As one commentator states of good legal writing, it can simultaneously "inspire, educate, entertain, explain, persuade, provoke, and seek a thirty-day continuance".[209] It will, I submit, fail to do so if drafted carelessly.

An essay should not be dull, dead or contain superfluities[210]

A legal text that is clear, concise, and readable is more likely to produce results than writing that is dull, wordy, pompous, and ponderous.[211] Again, as Lord Denning, "a towering figure of the common law",[212] has observed, legal reasoning presented "in a dull and turgid setting"[213] will be off-putting to readers; however, they will take notice if the same writing is presented "in a lively and attractive setting".[214] As to superfluities, these are consistent with wordiness and they are the enemy of that concision which should be the aim of the legal writer (and which has been touted, along with clarity and coherence as one of legal writing's "three Cs").[215]

Truth lends authority, shape and intensity to prose[216]

A legal text identifies the truth or at least the author's perception of the truth. However, it has been suggested that there is a closer relationship between non-fiction and fiction than is generally recognised because both are engaged in the manipulation of pen and audience to achieve a particular end.[217] So, for example, the legal writer has been described as a

---

206   Jaro Mayda, "On Style and Form in Legal Writing" (1962) 31 *Revista Juridica de la Universidad de Puerto Rico* 9–32, 9.
207   Adina Radulescu, "The Pitfalls of Simplifying Legal Writing" (2012) 4(2) *Contemporary Readings in Law and Social Justice* 367–372, 370.
208   Collyn Peddie, "Improving Legal Writing: The Triumph of Hope Over Experience" (1993) 13(1) *Review of Litigation* 83–104, 92.
209   *Ibid*, 85.
210   Virginia Woolf, *The Common Reader* (The Hogarth Press, 1948), 270.
211   Rebecca White Berch, "Legal Writing" (1988) 25(4) *Arizona Attorney* 51–52, 51.
212   Michael Kirby, "Lord Denning: An Antipodean Appreciation" (1986) 1 *Denning Law Journal* 103–116, 116.
213   Lord Denning, *The Family Story* (Butterworths, 1981), 216.
214   *Ibid*.
215   Linda Furey, "To Write Well: A Primer on Concision, Clarity and Coherence in Legal Writing" (1992) 2 *New Jersey Lawyer* 18–26, 19.
216   Virginia Woolf, *The Common Reader* (The Hogarth Press, 1948), 270.
217   Di Ricker, "Verbatim" (1994) 23(2) *Student Lawyer* 9–10, 9.

manipulator of prose for purposes that are less than noble.[218] But that might perhaps be contended to be unduly sceptical. Professional lawyers are subject to ethical obligations when it comes to truth-telling; and it seems, in any event, to be a truth of legal writing that it is facts that convince readers[219] and that what a legal writer does not want to be is a "street corner huckster"[220] (a salesperson) but rather should aim at being a trustworthy truth-teller.[221] Notably, Stark in his "Thirteen Rules of Professionalism in Legal Writing" devotes the first seven rules to the issue of truth-telling:

1. *Never lie ...*
2. *Don't ... disguise the truth.*
3. *[Unless] ... required, hedging [caveating] is ... dishonesty.*
4. *Avoid the use of hyperbole to distort ... truth ...*
5. *Ghost-writing [taking credit for another's work] is ... dishonesty.*
6. *An affidavit should be the assertions of the [signatory] ...*
7. *Always cite accurately.[222]*

A distinction falls to be made between truthfulness and candour: truthfulness involves explaining law and facts accurately and honestly; candour involves detailing all legally significant facts (even damaging ones) and also disclosing any adverse precedent.[223] Though the literary author may benefit from being truthful, the legal writer is often required to be candid. It has been suggested that candour is next only to integrity as a positive quality in the legal writer, and that a writer does an injustice to readers (and diminishes his or her own standing) if he or she does not strive constantly for candour (always allowing for error).[224]

A quality of good prose is "sobriety and hard-headedness"[225]

The word 'sobriety' when used in this context means 'solemnity', while the term 'hard-headness' refers to a certain detachment in one's writing. As to sobriety in legal writing, Justice Cardozo, following a review of the

---

218   Daniel Kornstein, "The Double Life of Wallace Stevens: Is Law Ever the 'Necessary Angel' of Creative Art?" (1997) 41(3/4) *New York Law School Law Review* 1187–1298, 1233.
219   James McElhaney, "Legal Writing that Works" (2007) 93 *ABA Journal* 30–31, 31.
220   *Ibid.*
221   *Ibid.*
222   Steven Stark, *Writing to Win* (Doubleday, 2000), 269.
223   J Christopher Rideout, "Ethos, Character, and Discoursal Self in Persuasive Writing" (2016) 21 *Legal Writing: The Journal of the Legal Writing Institute* 19–62, 56.
224   I Campbell, "Legal Writing" (1999) 30(2) *Victoria University of Wellington Law Review* 427–434, 429.
225   Virginia Woolf, *The Common Reader* (The Hogarth Press, 1948), 271.

various styles of judgment writing, suggests that his analysis might suggest that judgment writing is but a mix of the "solemn and the ponderous".[226] However, he is prepared to allow for a little lightness ("[f]lashes of humor")[227] in judgment writing – though he describes a judgment which seeks to be humorous from start to finish as "a perilous adventure"[228] that is best not embarked upon for a fear of suggesting that the law is an ass and the author a buffoon.[229] Cardozo's observations as to need for sobriety and the perils that humour poses have a resonance when it comes to legal writing more generally. Thus, even authors prepared to countenance the use of humour in general legal writing suggest that it should be used "sparingly".[230] At the very least, a legal writer must take care to ensure that the humour in a legal text "does not detract from its legal substance or humiliate ... parties".[231] However, any risk presenting in this regard is obviated if humour is simply avoided, so the better approach, it would seem, is to avoid using humour altogether.

As to hard-headedness (detachment) in legal writing, to some extent, all legal writing is less than objective. This is because lawyers typically manifest an ideological commitment to a legalism which sees ethics to be a matter of rule-following and moral relationships to involve rights and duties that rest on a construct of rules.[232] Nonetheless, detachment is seen by many as an attractive feature to bring to legal writing as commitment to a particular argument/cause may suggest a want of perspective on the part of a legal writer.[233]

Polished prose is not the same as ornamental prose[234]

Justice Cardozo, writing of ornament (fancy prose) in writing, praises the style of Matthew Arnold, the English poet, who deplored "ornament for the sake of ornament"[235] and always showed a sternness and severity in

---

226   Benjamin Cardozo, *Selected Writings of Benjamin Nathan Cardozo*, M Hall (ed) (Fallon Publications, 1947), 349.
227   *Ibid.*
228   *Ibid*, 350.
229   *Ibid.* See also Michael Bishop, "Why Must I Cry? Justification, Sacrifice, Loneliness, Madness and Laughter in Post-Apartheid Judicial Decision-Making" (2007) 1 *Pretoria Student Law Review* 33–56, 50.
230   Nancy Rice, "Tips on Legal Writing" (2015) 44(5) *Colorado Lawyer* 61–62, 61.
231   Lucas Hori, "Bons Mots, Buffoonery, and the Bench: The Role of Judicial Humor in Judicial Opinions" (2012) 60 *UCLA Law Review Discourse* 16–37, 35.
232   Arthur Miller, "The Myth of Objectivity in Legal Research and Writing" (1968) 18(3) *Catholic University Law Review* 290–307, 295.
233   Nancy Rice, "Tips on Legal Writing" (2015) 44(5) *Colorado Lawyer* 61–62, 61.
234   Virginia Woolf, *The Common Reader* (The Hogarth Press, 1948), 271,
235   Benjamin Cardozo, *Selected Writings of Benjamin Nathan Cardozo*, M Hall (ed) (Fallon Publications, 1947), 69.

his writing.[236] Much further back in time, ornament in oratory was also scorned by Demosthenes – perhaps the greatest of the ancient Greek orators – and its deployment in written texts seems also best avoided.[237] (There is, in truth, a danger that an excess of the ornamental may reduce serious writing to the comical.)[238] Hyman puts it simply and best when he observes that the legal writer should just "avoid grand and fancy words".[239]

Woolf suggests that a problem with ornamental prose is that it slows up the flow of the text,[240] causing the reader to pause to decipher the prose. And in legal writing, a form of writing which places a premium on clarity, concision, and coherence,[241] the writer should never leave a reader in a position where he or she is compelled to decipher meaning.[242]

Slightness of theme, Woolf suggests, may yield a temptation to add ornament to one's prose.[243] With legal writing, it perhaps results more often from a confusion of literary style with a style that is pompous, ponderous and unduly rich in needless flourishes:[244] the persuasiveness of a legal text "appears on the surface as discursive elegance".[245]

In his "Essay on Language", the 18th/19th-century English philosopher, Jeremy Bentham, makes various observations as regards ornament/decoration in language, among which are the following:

- the import of what one seeks to convey cannot be ornament;[246]
- ornament only arises in respect of ideas inessential to a text;[247]
- the addition of ideas which neither displease nor cause uneasiness, without increasing the number of words that would otherwise be used, comprises ornament; and[248]
- such ornament produces – or has a tendency to produce – pleasure.[249]

---

236   *Ibid.*
237   Robert Hanley, "Brush Up Your Aristotle" (2006) 3 *Journal of the Association of Legal Writing Directors* 145–153, 145.
238   *Ibid*, 150.
239   Michael Hyman, "Go Easy on the Legalese" (2018) 106(9) *Illinois Bar Journal* 48–49, 48.
240   Virginia Woolf, *The Common Reader* (The Hogarth Press, 1948), 271.
241   Linda Furey, "To Write Well: A Primer on Concision, Clarity and Coherence in Legal Writing" (1992) 2 *New Jersey Lawyer* 18–26, 19.
242   Jennifer Jolly-Ryan, "Who's on First?" (2019) 83(5) *Bench & Bar* 28–29, 29.
243   Virginia Woolf, *The Common Reader* (The Hogarth Press, 1948), 271.
244   Edward Re, "Legal Writing as Good Literature" (1985) 59(2) *St John's Law Review* 211–227, 224.
245   Richard Hyland, "A Defense of Legal Writing" (1986) 134(3) *University of Pennsylvania Law Review* 599–626, 620.
246   Jeremy Bentham, "Essay on Language" in Jeremy Bentham, *The Works of Jeremy Bentham*, John Bowring (ed) (William Tait, 1843), vol 8, 290–338, 306.
247   *Ibid.*
248   *Ibid*, 307.
249   *Ibid.*

Length

Victorian essayists wrote at length for a highly cultured public.[250] When it comes to the question of the overall length of legal texts, former Chief Justice McLachlin of Canada once suggested the simple rule that lawyers and judges should take care to "say what they need to say ... [and] [w]hen they have said it, they should stop".[251] Another commentator has suggested that if it takes too long to make a point, it might as well be a point un-made, as readers will simply give up on seeking to understand.[252]

As to lengthy quotations, a similar problem arises: they require readers to work too hard to understand[253] and they can be just too tiresome to read.[254] Judge Kozinski of the United States Court of Appeals has suggested that nobody reads block quotes and that if a block quote had something very useful to say, "the lawyer would have given ... a pithy paraphrase".[255] If quotations are to be used, there is a sense that cases are better summarised than quoted from,[256] and that quotes which require alteration through the use of ellipses and bracketing are just too long.[257]

When it comes to sentences it has been suggested that they should "lope along in strides no longer than those comfortable for the reader".[258] (In fact, there have been studies into what sentence length will suit an audience with a particular reading skill and in terms of gauging how long the 'lope' should be such studies can to some extent be brought to bear.)

A good essay should enfold the reader[259]

What Woolf appears to mean in this regard is that a text should be all-engrossing for the reader. Legal writing can be entertaining.[260] Every law library, it has been said, "contains an abundance of fascinating stories ...

---

250 Virginia Woolf, *The Common Reader* (The Hogarth Press, 1948), 273.
251 Beverley McLachlin, "Legal Writing: Some Tools" (2001) 39(3) *Alberta Law Review* 695–702, 700.
252 Bryan Garner, "Legal Writing: From Rough-Hewn to Refined" (2015) 86(5) *Oklahoma Bar Journal* 341–344, 341.
253 Sylvia Walbolt, "Young Lawyers: Keys to Successful Writing and Unlocking Your Talent" (2012) 31(3) *Appellate Practice* 22–27, 23.
254 Melvin White, "Writing Briefs for Overburdened Clerks and Busy Judges" (1997) 8 *Practical Litigator* 21–26, 25.
255 Alex Kozinski, "The Wrong Stuff" (1992) 2 *Brigham University Law Review* 325–334, 329.
256 Lawrence Grey, "Writing a Good Appellate Brief" (1985) 57(2) *New York State Bar Journal* 24–29, 28.
257 Tenielle Fordyce-Ruff and Jason Dykstra, "Legal Citation Part III: Using Citation to Convey Textual Meaning" (2018) 61(9) *Advocate (Idaho State Bar)* 52–55, 54.
258 Robert Littler, "Reader Rights in Legal Writing" (1950) 25(1) *Journal of the State Bar of California* 51–67, 60.
259 Virginia Woolf, *The Common Reader* (The Hogarth Press, 1948), 281.
260 Irving Younger, "Legal Writing All-Stars" (1986) 72(12) *ABA Journal* 94–95, 94.

that are ... engrossing and exciting".[261] In a similar vein, it has been suggested that when it comes to writing submissions (but the point has more general application) legal writers should seek to make "page-turners"[262] of elements of their legal texts, coupled with varied pacing.[263] By proceeding in an entertaining manner, the legal writer creates a situation in which the legal reader is encouraged to read on.[264]

Key propositions

- A legal text that is elegant in form but deficient in substance seems likely to disappoint.
- A question arises whether the typical form of judgment that courts now issue is fit for purpose or requires some variation of form if it is not to be seen as an ill-fitting means of conveying truth.
- Authors who wish to write better legal texts should seek always to convey the vision in their minds as to where the truth of a matter lies, avoiding details that blur/blemish/block the truth.
- A legal writer should seek to convey the uncertainty of life and law in his or her legal texts, not present "a series of gig lamps symmetrically arranged".[265]
- It is not a deficiency in a legal text if it focuses on the small rather than the big – legal writers are not required to raise their minds to great issues for their text to be great.
- The form of a legal text is perhaps more open to re-shaping and improvement than legal writers may instinctively imagine.
- Though a legal text sometimes calls for long words, they ought usually to be avoided.
- Opening words count – in them, a legal writer has a chance to draw the reader into the world of facts and law that is about to be depicted.
- People who come to read legal texts expect a particular form, expect (perhaps) to be mildly bored; and too often get what they

261   James Levy, "Escape to Alcatraz: What Self-Guided Museum Tours Can Show Us About Teaching Legal Research" (2001) 44(2) *New York Law Review* 387–428, 395.
262   Julie Oseid, "Liven Their Life Up Just a Little Bit" (2020) 24 *Journal of the Legal Writing Institute* 239–268, 240.
263   *Ibid.*
264   Patrick Hugg and Melanie McKay, "Classics Teach Legal Writing" (1985) 2(2) *Journal of Paralegal Education* 13–52, 39.
265   Virginia Woolf, *The Common Reader* (The Hogarth Press, 1948), 189.

come expecting. The following rules of better legal writing might usefully be observed:

- a legal writer must know how to write properly and well;
- learning alone does not suffice to make prose potent and persuasive;
- learning must fuse with the prose, rather than jutting out in some showy manner;
- a legal text should contain nothing inessential and speak to the now and have a wider resonance;
- a legal text that aims at the truth is necessarily a form of good;
- a moralising voice ought to be avoided in a legal text;
- prolixity/clarity are respectively to be avoided/pursued;
- a legal text should avoid dull/dead prose and prolixity;
- truth and a constant aiming for the truth give a legal text its shape and intensity;
- sobriety and hard-headedness (but not hard-heartedness) are desirable attributes of legal writing;
- ornamental/flowery prose slows up the flow of text and should be avoided;
- when a legal writer has the least to say he or she should not succumb to any temptation to say more;
- the best-written legal texts contain and conceal the legal writer; and
- a good legal writer should seek to enfold the reader in the thoughts and theme of his or her legal texts.

Afterword: Towards a code of good legal writing

Is it possible to discern some general propositions concerning good legal writing from the various observations made in the previous chapters? Numerous propositions are offered below – some of them could fit under multiple headings. To avoid needless repetition, such propositions are placed under the most relevant heading. Between them, they offer a rudimentary code of good legal writing.

1. Active/contemplative/reserved author

§1   A legal writer should have an active side (selecting facts and evidence and then writing up his or her text) and a contemplative side (thinking through what has been presented).

§2   To the extent that legal writers show reserve, it may be attributable to a sense that one is treating with a great subject (or that the writer is a great person).

§3   Writer reserve runs the risk of rendering a legal text colourless.

2. Brevity, clarity and simplicity

§4   Brevity of text may be a virtue. Undue brevity can be a barrier to profundity.

§5   Clarity is a paramount value in legal writing.

§6   The perfect legal text is arguably a text that is clear, brief, simple, passionate and possessed of transcendent idealism.

§7   A legal text involves the view of one or more legal writers on the sliver of life on which they are asked to opine or decide. However, their greatness has less to do with intensity of impression than with clarity of expression and analysis.

§8   No form of words should be selected or phrases employed that do not advance an argument and enlighten the reader.

§9   Meaningless/weak phraseology is to be avoided.

§10   It is by the brevity/charm/clarity/emphasis of argument that the aptness and fitness of prose falls to be judged.

§11 Sometimes reversing the natural order of phrases can be conducive to clarity.

§12 A legal text should contain nothing inessential, speak to the now and have a wider resonance.

§13 Professional lawyers are so busy that there can be a risk that they will end up producing 'skimmed' thought and avoid vesting each legal text with the best of themselves. This is a risk to be guarded against.

3. Carefulness/carelessness

§14 To be avoided in legal writing are carelessness, affected refinement and attention-seeking innovations.

§15 A legal text in which the legal writer has taken care to familiarise him or herself closely with the facts and law will be a superior form of legal text.

§16 A legal text is likely to be better appreciated the better it is written.

4. Central idea/theme

§17 A legal writer must bring a central idea to his or her legal text both as to outcome and as to what is meant to be said.

§18 A legal writer will be better equipped to write a legal text if he or she has a central theme.

5. Civility

§19 Being forcible/vigorous/strong in one's writing is not the same as being uncivil – civility counts.

6. Colloquialism/flippancy

§20 There is a necessary formality to legal texts – legal writers are engaged in serious business. However, there is a greater place for everyday language in legal prose than one typically encounters.

§21 That said, to be guarded against in legal writing is the inclusion of words that are too flippant/colloquial, thereby diminishing the quality of a legal text as professional prose.

7. Communication of thought

§22 A legal writer should take care that his or her prose is consistent with what he or she is thinking.

§23 The object of the legal writer is to make the reader realise the writer's conception of the 'tale' of fact and law recounted.

§24 A legal writer may commence with rough thoughts that then become refined thoughts – it is when he or she sits at the desk to write that the scale, spirit, particularity, style, etc of his or her intended text will be determined.

§25 The author who wishes to write better legal texts should seek always to convey the vision in his or her mind as to where the truth of a matter lies, avoiding details that blur/blemish/block the truth.

§26 Though the legal writer cannot sacrifice coherence/probability, he or she can seek to reveal the truth of his or her thoughts.

§27 In the best legal texts, the minds of the writer/reader are elevated: the writer writes what he or she sees; the reader is enabled to see that vision clearly.

§28 What remains after one finishes reading a notable legal text may not be a recollection of the detailed knowledge provided but a sense of the legal writer's vision.

8. Concision

§29 The legal writer's task is to select and compress in a bid at completeness, avoiding undue complexity and unwarranted error.

§30 In the best prose, the text shows a superior degree of organisation/concision/fluidity.

9. Condescension

§31 When writing a legal text, it is important to avoid condescension and to have a sense of what a non-lawyer would make of the text. This may not change the substance of one's legal texts and it may improve their style.

10. Detachment

§32 Detachment may not always best suit the subject at hand.

§33 A legal text should be honest and sincere, demonstrating the legal writer's legal knowledge but drawing also on personal experience. That cannot occur if the level of professional detachment brought to bear suggests the legal writer to be an unfeeling automaton.

§34 The legal writer may seek to be detached in his or her assessment of the law, but cannot be detached from the text that he or she writes.

11. Didacticism

§35 There may be didactic elements to a legal text but they are not the legal text.

12.   Digression

§36   A legal text such as a judgment or formal written advice has one purpose: to answer one or more issues presenting – a legal writer should not stray into addressing issues that are irrelevant.

§37   It is important not to get sidetracked into needless detail/ digression, placing undue importance on the unimportant.

§38   At the very least, the legal writer should not digress down logical sidetracks which merely display erudition rather than advancing an argument or informing the reader.

13.   Emotion/empathy/sympathy

§39   Although legal reasoning prefers the logical/objective/rational, there is a place for emotion in legal texts, provided it is couched appropriately.

§40   In terms of sustaining reader appreciation, sentiment (feeling) can heighten the value of a legal text, sentimentality (excessive feeling) lowers it.

§41   A legal text that evinces a degree of sympathy is likely to be more persuasive/powerful than a legal text possessing a surfeit of emotion.

§42   A legal writer with a sympathetic appreciation of life is more likely to draft a legal text that accurately delineates the human aspects of a case than one with less sympathy.

§43   Sobriety and hard-headedness (but not hard-heartedness) are desirable attributes of legal writing.

14.   Engaging writing

§44   A good legal writer should seek to enfold the reader in the thoughts and theme of his or her legal texts.

§45   Legal texts are stories of fact and law that can be written in an engaging manner which draws the reader in (making the text more interesting and memorable).

§46   There is no reason why legal texts cannot be written in an interesting style and every reason why they should be.

§47   Lord Denning's judgment style points to the legitimacy of the dramatic in legal writing.

§48   The potential for the dramatic must yield to the need for brevity.

§49   Suspense, to the extent it is thought desirable in legal writing, can be yielded through punctuation.

15. Ethics

§50 A legal text is meant to be ethical; as such it must appeal to the ideals of justice.

16. Exactness/precision

§51 In a legal text, the law should be stated exactly as it is (to aid clarity). That said, there can a temptation to indulge the 'cult of precision', that is, to write so exactly as to be incomprehensible.

§52 The legal writer must steer a course between "absolute accuracy"[1] and "slovenly inaccuracy".[2]

§53 It is not a weakness in a legal text if it focuses on the small – a legal writer need not raise his or her mind to great issues for a text to be great.

17. Experience

§54 Legal writers are expected to bring a knowledge of people and life to bear in their advice, opinions, etc – their knowledge of the law is assumed.

18. Footnotes

§55 Better-composed prose may eliminate the need for a footnote.

§56 Usage of a footnote may point to a want of completed development in the sentence to which it is attached.

§57 Restructuring of a sentence may obviate the need for the "excrescence"[3] of a footnote.

19. Form

§58 A question arises whether legal writing suffers from the deficiency that a certain constancy in form over time has generated a resistance to trying out alternative forms of legal text.

§59 A question arises whether the typical form of judgment that courts now issue is fit for purpose or requires some variation of form if it is not to be seen as an ill-fitting means of conveying truth.

§60 A legal writer should seek to convey the uncertainty of life and law in his or her legal texts, not present "a series of gig lamps symmetrically arranged".[4]

---

1   Anthony Trollope, *An Autobiography* (William Blackwood & Sons, 1883), vol II, 60.
2   *Ibid*.
3   Thomas de Quincey, *Essays on Style, Rhetoric and Language*, F Scott (ed) (Allyn & Bacon, 1893), 39.
4   Virginia Woolf, *The Common Reader* (The Hogarth Press, 1948), 189.

§61 The form of a legal text is perhaps more open to re-shaping and improvement than legal writers may instinctively imagine.

§62 People who come to read legal texts expect a particular form, expect (perhaps) to be mildly bored; and too often get what they come expecting.

§63 One cannot have form without ideas; ideas create form; when it comes to legal writing one needs to bring ideas and then form will follow.

20. Grammar

§64 A legal writer should ensure his or her prose is correct in terms of the grammar/words deployed.

§65 A legal writer should depart from good grammar where to proceed otherwise would diminish his or her thoughts.

§66 In a legal text, every sentence and word should be necessary and, if unnecessary, should be disregarded.

§67 Active verbs aid a text; the impersonal/inactive/transitive do not.

§68 To be avoided is the unduly long/cumbersome sentence. To be preferred are gracefully succeeding sentences, of varying length, one modifying the other and all well connected.

§69 The excessively conditional sentence is best avoided.

§70 Punctuation requires care: it can bring clarity and confusion.

§71 Each phrase of each sentence should comprise a mix of long/short, and the emphasised/understated, such as to gratify the inner ear.

§72 A question arises whether there is ever much desire for especially long legal texts – a legal text should certainly never be any longer than it needs to be.

21. Humour/amusement

§73 A legal text may aim to answer/instruct/interest – it should not seek to provoke laughter.

§74 A good legal text may amuse, not by yielding laughter but by being a balanced creation that is captivating, compelling or convincing.

§75 Legal texts should neither be frivolous nor excessively serious.

22. Hesitancy

§76 Writing in an unhesitating manner leaves less time for that storytelling to which lawyers may otherwise be prone.

23. Illusion

§77 A legal text is excellent to the extent it produces a coherent illusion of real life. Even so, real life, not the illusion, is its true focus (albeit that the illusion is necessary to success).

24. Language/vocabulary

§78 Language is the means whereby a legal writer creates as persuasive a legal text as he or she can, deploying the words necessary and bringing to bear his or her experiences.

§79 Law is a words-focused discipline, so a certain richness of vocabulary is necessary.

§80 A legal writer needs to deploy a vocabulary that is as simple as possible in all the circumstances but no simpler.

§81 Legal writers should take care when choosing and deploying words that they mean precisely what they state and state precisely what they mean.

§82 Though a legal text sometimes calls for long words, they ought usually to be avoided.

§83 Opening words count – in them, a legal writer has a chance to draw the reader in to the world of facts and law about to be depicted.

25. Foreign language/jargon

§84 The legal writer may use legal 'terms of art' and Latinisms. However, the legal writer who uses fewer terms of art and Latinisms can hope to produce more compelling texts.

§85 It may be that Latinisms give legal texts a lustre of learning. However, excess in this regard may come at the price of comprehensibility.

§86 Law is a technical discipline, so legal writers will sometimes need to use technical terms.

§87 Even when a lawyer comes spouting legalisms galore that is not necessarily bad (though it might need to be worked upon to improve comprehensibility).

26. Literary quality

§88 There is a general failure to recognise the literary quality of legal texts and the high literary quality to which many legal texts can stake a claim.

§89 If the inherent literary potential that legal texts entail is not duly recognised, legal writers seem less likely to attain that potential.

27. Moralising/morality

§90   Moral principle is a bedrock of legal writing, at least in liberal democracies.

§91   Moralising is to be avoided in a legal text – a legal writer is asked to decide issues of fact and law, not to opine or rule upon matters of morality.

§92   While a judgment may exhibit a worthy ideal, it is not a vehicle through which judges should pronounce on matters moral.

§93   The legal writer who engages in moralising will diminish his or her work by departing from the pursuit of legal truths.

§94   By chaining themselves to a particular perception of morality legal writers are chaining themselves to a star that is doomed to fade.

§95   To the extent that a legal writer engages in moralising, he or she is likely to be seen not to be presenting some objective morality but his or her own morality.

28. Observation

§96   The power of observation is a critical skill for legal writers.

29. Originality

§97   All writers compose works in accordance with their sense of originality. However, the potential for originality in legal writing seems under-appreciated.

§98   Originality in prose is the product of trial and error. Fear of error may hinder advancement in terms of evolving an ever-better system of legal writing.

§99   The near-complete absence of spontaneity in legal writing derives from self-censorship.

§100 It is typically the legal writer who shows an imaginative understanding of the law who ends up advancing legal knowledge.

30. Detachment

§101 The best-written legal texts contain and conceal the legal writer.

§102 It is undesirable that the persona/predilections/preferences of a legal writer should intrude unduly into a legal text – its abiding hallmark should be that the text predominates, not a sense of the author.

§103 Given that the skill of the author consists in not revealing him or herself to the reader, in the legal context this can (not un-controversially) be achieved through acquisition/maintenance of a professional voice.

§104 James observes of novels that they are as various as men's temperaments and successful in proportion to the extent that they reveal a particular mind.[5] The same observation might be made of legal writers and legal texts.

31. Quotes

§105 When quoting, a legal writer should take care to quote only that which is strictly necessary to advance the substance of the legal text.

32. Reading

§106 It is beneficial for the legal writer to read, for example, great past judgments and great literature.

§107 The truth of law is not to be found in fiction. However, in difficult cases, fiction may point to where real-life truth may lie.

33. Rhythm

§108 Prose should be rhythmical. It should not, however, be metrical – if it is metrical, it becomes verse.

§109 Poor cadence is a predicate for remoulding a clause, interpolating a phrase or striking out a superfluous word.

§110 When it comes to rhythm, one can distinguish between the famous opening 'da-da-da-dah' of Beethoven's Fifth Symphony as a rhythm that we all hear, and a second, separate rhythm that permeates the symphony as a whole. A legal writer may seek the first kind of rhythm but it is also possible for a separate rhythm to permeate a great legal text, yielding a feeling that everything within it fuses into a greater whole.

§111 Each phrase in a legal text must be apt, varied, satisfying to the ear and possessed of "ingenious neatness".[6]

34. Selection

§112 It is impossible for a legal writer to describe all the richness of the situation presenting in a case.

§113 What to include and omit from a legal text is a constantly presenting question; among the issues arising are whether inclusion of some fact is necessary or will weaken/obscure the general design of a particular legal text.

---

5   Henry James, *The Art of Fiction* (Cupples, Upham & Co, 1885), 60.
6   Robert Louis Stevenson, *Essays on the Art of Writing* (Chatto & Windus, 1919), 11.

§114 When it comes to selection, a legal text should exclude unnecessary detail.

§115 A legal text should be as close to reality as it can, though there will inevitably be selection of facts at play in terms of depicting reality.

§116 By blinding themselves to some material dimensions of what is at play before them, legal writers clear their minds for a consideration of more ethereal issues presenting.

§117 In a legal text, it may be necessary to include the tedious, but there seems no reason why the irrelevant cannot be omitted and the tedious kept to a minimum. To be avoided is unnecessary detail and carelessness in writing.

§118 In a legal text dedicated to the promotion/realisation of truth, legal writers should not succumb to selectivity in facts/law that aims solely at maximising a legal text's persuasiveness.

35. Sound

§119 The quality of prose rests on sound. A legal writer determined to write impactful legal text will be attentive to the sounds within/between words.

§120 Ordinary writers, in ordinary moments, content themselves with avoiding what is harsh (occasionally rising to alliteration or assonance) – in bad writing one finds "cacophony supreme".[7]

§121 With legal judgments, which continue to be crafted as though they are to be read out in court (and sometimes are), the need for harmony of expression presents. If a legal writer knows in advance how each sound in his or her sentences will affect the force of the text, he or she will engage readers.

36. Storytelling

§122 A legal writer should approach his or her task not out of a sense that he or she has to write but because there is a story of fact and law to tell.

§123 Legal writing involves a legal writer telling whatever 'story' he or she has resolved to tell in terms of facts, law, analysis and conclusion.

§124 The legal text as story has one merit (instilling reader desire to know what happens next) and one drawback (failing to instil that desire).

---

7   *Ibid*, 41.

§125 Just as a story is the repository of voice, so too are legal texts.

§126 Just as novels make the world seem more comprehensible, a legal text can make the world seem more comprehensible.

§127 A story may be told impartially from outside or omnisciently from within – in legal texts the external impartial tale predominates.

§128 A story involves a sequence of events arranged chronologically, whereas a plot involves a sequence of events but its emphasis is on causality. A legal text is akin to a plot.

§129 The concluding portion of a novel is often weakest because the plot requires to be wound up. By contrast, the concluding portion of a legal text is often its strongest point because it then that findings become manifest.

§130 A legal text should adhere to the ordinary and probable.

37. Style

§131 'Style' means the dexterous use of writing skill, having regard to the proportion of one part of a text to another and to the whole, the excision of useless words, emphasis of important words, and having a uniform form/style.

§132 The importance of style cannot be overestimated. In a legal text, as in a novel:

[T]here ought not to be ... a single sentence [that is] carelessly worded, [or] a single phrase which has not been considered ... There should be no unfinished places, no sign anywhere of weariness or haste ... The writer must so love his work as to dwell tenderly on every page and be literally unable to send forth a single page of it without the finishing touches.[8]

§133 Style in legal writing is important – language is the incarnation of thought and style is a part of that thought.

§134 Style is a quality of writing whereby a legal writer as author may improve him or herself.

§135 Less dedicated authors regularly adhere to a style that they settled upon early. Better authors (and those who seek to be better) view new texts as an opportunity to deploy fresh style.

§136 A legal text that is elegant (stylish) in form but deficient in substance seems likely to disappoint.

§137 Ornamental/flowery prose slows up the flow of text and should be avoided.

---

8   Walter Besant, *The Art of Fiction* (Cupples, Upham & Co, 1885), 30–31.

§138 Natural style ("disjointed babble")[9] is not the best style. To be preferred is a style which (unobtrusively) attains an elegance rich in meaning or (obtrusively) yields a richness and vigour of meaning.

§139 Whatever the intricacies/obscurities of a point, the polish of one's prose should not suffer.

38. Tone

§140 It is open to the legal writer as author to lighten/darken text and tone in such manner as he or she considers appropriate, though he or she should proceed with some moderation in this regard.

39. Transcendence

§141 Good legal texts have the power to touch the reader and to provide (or seek to provide) an answer to whatever questions arise.

§142 A legal text proceeds by reference to a loftier reality in which law reigns supreme.

40. Truth

§143 With legal texts, the criterion of worth is truth.

§144 A legal text that aims at the truth is necessarily a form of good.

§145 Behind the facts/law at play in a case is enlightening factual/legal truth.

§146 Substantive legal texts have much in common with Old Testament books – they are inspired by a desire for truth and, by way of purpose, they seek to reconcile identified facts and law into a unified truth.

§147 The writer, in his or her selection of law and facts and analysis and conclusions, should be a servant of truth.

§148 Honour and truth should be the guiding stars of the legal writer.

§149 Though legal texts come veiled in rationality, legal writers are to some extent involved in the task of making the reader feel/think/see a particular truth.

§150 When law and truth are combined in a legal text it can be a potent combination. (In the field of transitional justice, the notion of truth is especially significant as a means of individual healing.)

§151 The text which lingers is the text which most closely approaches the truth.

---

9   Robert Louis Stevenson, *Essays on the Art of Writing* (Chatto & Windus, 1919), 13.

§152 By serving truth lawyers can create "lasting unity from damaging conflict".[10]

§153 Each legal text is or ought to be engaged in the identification of the legal truth of whatever situation it engages with.

§154 Honest persuasive argument requires dedication to accuracy/truth.

§155 As a rule, truths need only be stated once – they do not become truer through being repeated.

§156 Wisdom in legal texts comes from the pondering and application to life of certain legal truths. Those truths are of great moment and not always complex.

§157 A legal text becomes mundane and of limited interest unless vivified by a sense of truth and an appetite for justice.

§158 Truth and a constant aiming for the truth give a legal text its shape and intensity.

41. Understatement

§159 It is preferable that a legal text proceed through understatement and action rather than moralising about truth.

42. Voice

§160 Voice in many guises (eg, professional, personal, social and discoursal) can creep into a legal text.

§161 In learning to craft 'legal writing' a lawyer acquires a professional voice, albeit one that belongs to the individual writer. (This concept of the professional voice is not without controversy.)

---

10   Paul Lannon, Jr, "A Lawyer in Pursuit of Truth and Unity: Mohandas Gandhi and the Private Practice of Law" (2011) 44(3) *Suffolk University Law Review* 665–682.

Appendix: Writing for the young and vulnerable

The need to write clearly but comprehensively for clients and litigants who are unfamiliar with the legal system has been touched upon in Chapters 9 and 14, and is a challenge that presents itself before lawyers and judges on a daily basis. In my own job as a judge, I find it is an issue that presents especially in asylum and immigration cases (in which applicants are in a vulnerable position and often do not speak English as their first language),[1] child law cases (where the litigants are young and often do not understand what is happening in court or what has been decided) and family law cases (in which the sheer emotion presenting and an unfamiliarity with the legal system often results in clients/litigants feeling overwhelmed by the process in which they are involved). As touched upon in the main text of this book, courtesy and respect demand that legal texts should be understandable and understood by those to whom they issue. The challenging but rewarding task of writing judgments in child and family law cases in terms that are respectful of litigants while also acknowledging their particular needs and demands was the subject of a paper that I prepared in July 2022 for a colloquium of judges. Extracts from that paper of relevance to the subject matter of this book are quoted below and seem also to be of relevance when it comes to legal writing more generally:

"**Creating a product that is needed and wanted**
1. *One pleasure of being a High Court judge in Ireland is that one does not spend an entire career hearing the same kinds of cases. In recent years, I have moved from the Commercial Court and tended to hear asylum/immigration cases and, recently, child/family cases.*

2. *Two things quickly became obvious to me when I started hearing child and family cases:*

---

1   English is the language in which I conduct court proceedings and write my judgments.

- *first, many people who come to court find the language of traditional-form judgments difficult to understand.*
- *second, in many such cases the parties presenting in court do not understand what is going on in court, sometimes even throwing desperate looks to the judge as if to ask her to advise what is happening. (I always respond to such looks by pausing to explain in plain language what is being said/done.)*

3. *With the above in mind, when writing child and family law judgments, I now generally add to my judgments a note in which I try to set out clearly what a particular judgment means for the affected child and/or family members. After all, 'the law does not belong to lawyers, judges or law professors – it belongs to the people who come before the courts to have their disputes resolved'.*[2]

4. *As new generations of people come before the courts, it is necessary for the courts to re-legitimate themselves as arbiters of disputes. Kane touches on this point when he writes of the International Criminal Court that to ensure its continuing legitimacy it must 'create and deliver a product ... needed and wanted by its consumer base'.*[3] *That is an observation which has a much wider resonance.*

Some innovations by various judges

5. *The English judge, Mr Justice Jackson, in* Re A: A Letter to a Young Person,[4] *an unsuccessful relocation application, wrote all of his judgment in the form of a note to the affected child. I quote a few sentences from that judgment to give a flavour of its style:*

'Dear Sam,

It was a pleasure to meet you on Monday and I hope your camp this week went well.

This case is about you and your future, so I am writing this letter as a way of giving my decision to you and to your parents.

---

2   See Robert Sharpe, "Brian Dickson, the Supreme Court of Canada, and the Charter of Rights: A Biographical Sketch" (2002) 21 *Windsor Yearbook of Access to Justice* 603–629, 611.

3   See Matthew Kane, "Accessible Judgments as a Practical Means to Re-engage African Interest and Salvage the International Criminal Court" (2015) 1 *African Journal of International Criminal Justice* 6–46, 8.

4   [2017] EWFC 48 (HC).

When a case like this comes before the court, the judge has to apply the law as found in the Children Act 1989, particularly in Section 1. You may have looked at this already, but if you Google it, you will see that when making my decision, your welfare is my paramount consideration – more important than anything else. If you look at s1(3), there is also a list of factors I have to consider, to make sure that everything is taken into account.

The information I have comes from a variety of sources. There are the papers from the old proceedings years ago. There are more papers from the proceedings this year, especially your own statements, your mum and Paul's statements, your dad's statements, and the report of Gemma, the Cafcass officer. Then there is the evidence each of you gave at court. I have taken all this into account ...'.

6. *My approach is slightly different. I write the judgment in a traditional form. I then attach a simple explanation of the judgment in the form of a note to the affected child and/or family members. That way the lawyers get the legal judgment they have come looking for and the child and/or family member gets a 'diet' version of the judgment. I quote a few sentences from one of my more recent judgments (in an adoption/surrogacy matter) to give a flavour of the approach that I adopt in the letter section:*

'Dear Mr A and Mr B
In the previous pages, I have written a quite long judgment about your case. The judgment is full of legal language and you may find it less than easy to understand. I am aware that family law judgments touch on important issues in people's personal lives. So I now typically add a 'plain English' note to the end of my family law judgments explaining briefly what I have decided. That is the least you deserve. Everyone else in this case will get to read this note but really it is for your benefit ...'.[5]

5   [2021] IEHC 785 (HC).

7. *Other approaches have been tried. Mr Justice Jackson also wrote a 'plain English' judgment in* Lancashire County Council v M and others *(an access/custody case).*[6] *However, he opted for a more conventional form than in* Re A. *I quote a few sentences from that judgment to give a flavour of its style:*

'1. This judgment is as short as possible so that the mother and the older children can follow it.

2. The case is about a white British family. There are four children – H [a boy aged 12], A [a girl aged 10], N [a boy aged 3] and R [a girl aged 10 months] ...

3. When H and A were born, the mother was living with their father, Mr B. They were together for about 8 years. After that, Mr B moved out, but he and the children still see each other and the children also see his parents. At times Mr B has been sent to prison for violence. He has also used drugs but says that he has not done that since the last time he went to prison in 2013. H and A see their father and grandparents at the weekends and everyone enjoys that ...'.

8. *Sheriff Anwar, a Scottish judge, also took a 'child-friendly' approach to the form of the judgment that she wrote and delivered in* Mr Patrick v Mrs Patrick.[7] *That was a parental contact case in which the Sheriff appears to have been advised that it was necessary that the children hear the decision as to contact from a neutral third person. Sheriff Anwar therefore took an approach like the approach that I use. Thus, she started with formal text and ended with a letter directly to the children. I quote a few sentences from her judgment to give a flavour of its style:*

'Dear Julie and Brian

My name is Sheriff Anwar.

Your mum and dad have asked me to make a decision on whether you should see your dad.

I think that as my decision is all about you, it is only fair that I should write to you.

---

6   [2016] EWFC 9 (HC).
7   [2017] Fam LR 128 (Sh. Ct).

I have not met you, but I have heard a lot about you. Your mum has told me all about how you are getting on at school and about your likes and dislikes. Your dad has told me about all the things you used to do together.

Your mum and dad have also told me about the problems they have had with each other after they split up. Sometimes, when parents split up it is very hard for them to stay friends. Your mum and dad have found it very hard to stay friends. Sometimes when people are no longer friends, they can say some nasty things about each other. They forget what is good about each other. That is not right and it is not nice. It shouldn't happen. You should not have to hear any of that. That is for the adults to sort out …'.

…

9. Writing at the turn of this century, Chief Justice McLachlin of Canada observed of the Canadian judiciary, though a similar trend is discernible more generally, that judges are becoming increasingly aware that getting the right answer to a legal question is not enough, and that 'we can maintain and enhance public confidence in the legal system not only by providing quality service, but also by doing so in a compassionate, respectful way'.[8]

10. My approach of appending to a judgment a 'plain language' note summarising the effect of a judgment (and indeed the approach of Sheriff Anwar), offers a practical answer to the question posed by Mr Justice Munby, then the President of the Family Division of the High Court of England and Wales when, in a public lecture on the involvement of children and vulnerable persons in the justice system, he asked:

'Should the judge be writing a letter for the child to read today, written in the kind of language appropriate for the child having regard to their present age or understanding? Or should the judge be writing a letter for the child to be read by the child at some – and if so what – point in the future?'[9]

---

8   See Beverley McLachlin, "Preserving Public Confidence in the Courts and the Legal Profession" (2002) 29 *Manitoba Law Journal* 277–288, 280.

9   See James Munby, *Unheard Voices: The Involvement of Children and Vulnerable People in the Family Justice System*, The Annual Lecture of the Wales Observatory on Human Rights of Children and Young People delivered by Sir James Munby, President of the Family Division at the College of Law, Swansea University on 25 June 2015, www.swansea.ac.uk/media/Sir-James-Munby-Annual-lecture-2015.pdf, 6.

11. *By providing a technical judgment that is clear, concise, and well-organised, followed by a 'plain language' note, one achieves, it seems to me, the two objectives identified by Mr Justice Munby. Thus one provides texts that can be understood now and in the future by the child (including when she becomes an adult) and also by the relevant legal audience.*

12. *Mr Justice Munby also highlights the risks of issuing the final judgment in child law cases in oral form. Doing so means that there will be children who will have no idea in the future as to why a judge made a particular decision, and 'Knowledge of who one is, who one's family is (or was) ... is fundamental to ... human beings ... [and] an aspect of ... private life which...the European Convention on Human Rights requires the State to respect'.*[10]

13. *Writing a simplified appendix to a judgment also neatly advances the therapeutic potential of judgments in the child and family law context, one Canadian commentator observing as follows:*

'Applying a similar approach to the child protection context has the potential to yield therapeutic benefits. A negative judgment in a child protection matter can, eg, acknowledge parents' strengths and positive motivations. Inclusion of this information has the potential of providing the parent with the comfort that their efforts, and usually their love for the child, were recognised, even though the frailties of their position have led to them ultimately being found unable to continue caring for their child.'[11]

What Twitter® users say

14. *In 2021, a photograph of one of my end-of-judgment notes was posted on Twitter® along with a kind remark. Within a couple of days almost 20,000 people indicated that they liked the note and hundreds of people made constructive comments. A few days later my judicial assistant drew my attention to what had happened. I read the online comments and found them interesting for a number of reasons:*
   - *First, they were overwhelmingly positive. So I knew that I was 'on to something' in terms of a helpful evolution of my judgment writing style.*

---

10   *Ibid.*
11   See Shelly Kierstead, "Therapeutic Jurisprudence and Child Protection" (2011) 17(1) *Barry Law Review* 31–44, 39.

- *Second, some of the observations gave a helpful sense of how I might improve further on what I had done, even pointing to some useful literature in this regard.*
- *Third, a number of commentators suggested that end-of-judgment notes need not be confined to children's cases. (They did not know that I have been doing something similar in asylum/immigration cases also; however, I agree with their suggestion that this approach could more widely be deployed.)*
- *Fourth, with so much brainpower brought to bear by so many well-intentioned people, I was given something of a 'road map' by which to navigate how I might improve what I was doing.*

15. *What the various tweets suggested was the following:*
    (1) There is an appetite for an explanatory note at the end of judgments.
    (2) When writing such a note a useful exercise is not to write as the judge but to write it through the mindset of the recipient/s.
    (3) Kindness and a lack of 'talking down' are necessary traits of any such note.
    (4) If the addressee is being addressed in anonymous terms, it is useful to explain why this is being done.
    (5) While some level of standardisation will inevitably creep in, it is important that each note should be personalised.
    (6) Each note should be down-to-earth, hopeful, respectful, empathetic, and informative.
    (7) Short sentences and the simplest vocabulary should be used.
    (8) Multi-syllable words are best avoided.
    (9) It is useful to include a line in judgments aimed at children requesting that a lawyer or guardian ad litem *take the time to read the note with/to the child and make sure that the child understands it.*

Children and the Council of Europe

16. *What might children think of child-friendly judgments? Research done under the auspices of the Council of Europe suggests that they welcome it:*

'[C]hildren … [are] critical of many officials … for not respecting them, for not appreciating their special needs as children and for not showing them empathy … [C]hildren want to be heard, they want to receive information in a form that they can understand.'[12]

---

12 Ursula Kilkelly, *Listening to Children About Justice: Report of the Council of Europe Consultation with Children on Child-Friendly Justice* 39 (Strasbourg, 5 October 2010. CJ-S-CH (2010) 14 rev).

17. *As a result of the UN Convention on the Rights of the Child (1989) judges have a duty to enhance the access and availability of child citizens to justice. As a result the Council of Europe, in 2010, adopted a series of 'Child Friendly Justice' Guidelines. A number of these Guidelines point to the need for a transformation of traditional judgment styles when it comes to children:*

'49. Judgments and court rulings affecting children should be duly reasoned and explained to them in language that children can understand, particularly those decisions in which the child's views and opinions have not been followed …

124. [C]hild-friendly justice … implies that children understand the nature and scope of the decision taken, and its effects. While the judgment and the motivation thereof cannot always be recorded and explained in child-friendly wording, due to legal requirements, children should have those decisions explained to them, either by their lawyer or another appropriate person (parent, social worker, etc).'

18. *My own experience suggests that Guideline 124 is not entirely correct. Sometimes the substantive issues in child proceedings are complex and the law needs to be reasoned through in detail. However, while reality can sometimes seem "resistant to explanation by simplification",[13] I have yet to encounter an issue/response that cannot be distilled into a child-friendly note that can be added to a judgment. And ultimately who better to explain to a child what she has decided than the deciding judge herself?*

Some possible concerns

19. *Stalford and Hollingsworth, in an engaging article, have pointed to a number of objections that might be and/or have been raised by judges about conveying the outcome of their decisions directly to parties, in particular children. These are considered below:*

(1) *There may be concern about exposing children to sensitive information that might impact on familial relationships.[14]*

---

13   *Ibid.*
14   See Helen Stalford and Kathryn Hollingsworth, "'This case is about you and your future': Towards Judgments for Children" (2020) 83(5) *Modern Law Review* 1030–1058, 1039.

I share such concerns. However, in terms of the notes that I append to judgments, I have not found this to be a real concern. This is because such notes largely reflect the conclusions reached and explain them in child-friendly language. Regardless of the form of judgment that issues, a child will obviously learn of the judge's conclusions. It cannot but help a child for an explanation of those conclusions to be furnished by the judge in language that is clear but not condescending.

(2) *Judges are often required to deal with complex factual and legal issues that may be too technical or nuanced to capture in a judgment addressed directly to a child.*

I am respectfully unconvinced that this is so.[15] *To the extent that it is true, this does not offer good reason why a comprehensive technical judgment cannot be followed by a child-friendly explanation.*

(3) *Demands for efficiency in the justice system may run contrary to the additional work involved in 'seemingly superfluous and time-consuming innovations in the form of child-friendly judgments'.*[16]

I am not sure that this is a convincing proposition when it comes to adding a child-friendly explanation to a technically complex judgment. Immediately after writing a complex judgment, when its every nuance is still fresh in my mind, I find it takes little time to reduce the substance of a judgment to a 'plain language' note.

(4) *The independence of the judiciary means that judges may legitimately resist incursions on their freedom to decide the form and tone of their judgments.*[17]

I respectfully do not agree with this line of possible resistance. The concept of judicial independence has never extended to writing judgments that are incomprehensible to their recipients.

(5) *Judges may consider that their neutrality and impartiality would be compromised by 'more involved', 'emotive' forms of judgment.*[18] *Detached language does not make one any less 'involved'. It is difficult,*

---

15   *Ibid,* 1040.
16   *Ibid.*
17   *Ibid.*
18   *Ibid,* 1041.

in particular, to see how a detached document followed by an explanatory note of that detached language renders a judge more 'involved' than she already is.

(6) *There may be a concern that simplified text is less precise. Questions arise, it might be suggested, 'as to whether a judge can alter the words and style of a judgment ... whilst still retaining the [precision] ... required for an 'appeal-proof' decision ... [T]hrough simplification ... the persuasive power of [a] ... judgment may be lost too'.*[19]

A number of observations might be made regarding this concern. There is no such thing as an 'appeal proof' decision. If an appellate court would have done things differently it will decide matters so. And the renowned judgments of Lord Denning are proof that simplification enhances comprehensibility and persuasiveness.

CS Lewis and writing for children

20. *Are there any wider rules when it comes to writing judgments for children? Perhaps the best advice in this regard has been given by CS Lewis, author of The Chronicles of Narnia and so one of the all-time 'greats' of children's literature. In his essay, 'On Three Ways of Writing for Children',*[20] *Lewis makes various observations that can be brought to bear in the context of judgment writing:*

(1) *Lewis is opposed to the notion of children as a special public, to whom one gives what they want, however unpleasant it may seem to the author. He considers that it is disrespectful 'to regale the child with things calculated to please but regarded by yourself with indifference or contempt'.*[21]

In the judgment writing context what Lewis effectively points to in this regard is the need to show empathy and avoid condescension.

(2) *Lewis observes how '[i]n any personal relation the two participants modify each other'.*[22]

---

19   *Ibid.*
20   See CS Lewis, "On Three Ways of Writing for Children" in *Of Other Worlds*, W Hooper (ed) (Harcourt Brace Jovanovich, 1975), 22–34.
21   *Ibid*, 23.
22   *Ibid.*

Hearing and deciding a case is an intensely personal process. For example, a trial-judge spends hours with people in a courtroom. She then goes home and spends hours in their imagined company as she constructs her judgment. She then issues to the parties a judgment written by her for the parties. So for all that the language of a judgment may be detached, it is actually a very personal (and inter-personal) task, with the judge affected by what the parties have said, and the parties affected by how the judge responds.

(3)   *Lewis subscribes to the theory that one should only write a children's story when that 'is the best art form for something you have to say'.*[23]

Bringing this to bear in the judgment writing context, what Lewis essentially points to is that one should write with children in mind when writing a child law judgment.

(4)   *Lewis observes how 'Sentimentality is so apt to creep in if we write at length about children as seen by their elders ... For we all remember that our childhood, as lived, was immeasurably different from what our elders saw'.*[24]

What Lewis is getting at in this regard is the need, when writing for children, to 'get into their shoes', to see the world as they see it and to write accordingly.

(5)   *Lewis posits that 'a children's story ... enjoyed only by children is a bad children's story'.*[25]

By this Lewis means that when a children's story is the right form in which to recount a story then it will be appreciated and read (and re-read) by children of all ages. This offers good reason for taking time to draft and add a 'plain English' appendix to a judgment. Unlike the judgment proper, it is likely to be read and re-read by the addressee and others, so it is important to pitch it right in terms of substance and tone. (And just as adults can enjoy the nostalgia of a children's book an adult who was once the child to whom a judgment was

---

23   *Ibid.*
24   *Ibid,* 24.
25   *Ibid.*

addressed may in later years enjoy and appreciate the kindness shown by the judge to the child that was.)

(6) *To judges who might shrink from writing child-friendly text, Lewis offers a useful word of caution when he observes that 'To be concerned about being grown up ... to blush at the suspicion of being childish; these things are the marks of childhood and adolescence'.*[26]

In a sense what Lewis suggests is that grown-ups should not be afraid to 'descend' to childish words if that is necessary to achieve empathy. While no one wants a judge who emotes from the bench, there is nothing wrong with a judge who writes in language that is empathetic.

(7) *Lewis suggests that writing for children 'imposes certain very fruitful necessities about length'.*[27]

In this, Lewis means that stories for children are typically shorter than other forms of story, though his use of the word 'fruitful' also carries the suggestion that such shortness is enriching. Two points arise from this. First, that when writing a judgment for a child the need for brevity should be to the fore. Second, that brevity aids clarity and enriches a judgment.

(8) *Lewis accepts that '[a] ... serious attack on the fairy tale as children's literature comes from those who do not wish children to be frightened'.*[28]

A like concern presents when it comes to writing judgments that will be read by children: one does not want, as a judge, to make a bad situation worse by writing something that may adversely affect a child. My own sense is that this is a very real concern. Certainly, it is one reason why I prefer writing a technical judgment in the traditional style that deals with the detail of a case (and which may be read by the child when older), whilst focusing in the child-friendly appendix on what the immediate implications of a judgment are for the child.

---

26   *Ibid*, 25.
27   *Ibid*, 28.
28   *Ibid*, 30.

(9)   *Lewis cautions against moralising, and the same point might be made of judgments. Moralising, Lewis suggests, is likely to lead a writer into platitudes and falsehoods. But he also considers it disrespectful, for 'in the moral sphere [children] ... are probably at least as wise as we'.*[29]

(10)   *Lewis cautions against patronising children but also against idolising them.*[30]

In terms of judgment writing, this again points to the need for empathetic text that is understanding, while at the same time bringing an adult understanding to the facts presenting. 'We must of course try to do them no harm: we may ... sometimes dare to hope that we may do them good. But only such good as involves treating them with respect.'[31]

An attempted summary

21. *What lessons might be taken from the foregoing? I would suggest the following:*

   - *Judges are often perceived as the human link between law/justice/litigants. It, therefore, behoves judges to show that the legal/justice system has feeling and is caring.*
   - *Getting the right answer to a tricky legal question is not enough; it is important to proceed compassionately/respectfully.*
   - *Many people who bring cases to court can find the language of traditional-form judgments difficult to understand. A useful innovation is to append, to a technical standard-form judgment, a 'plain language' note that sets out clearly but without condescension what a judgment means for the parties.*
   - *Writing a simplified addendum to a judgment advances the judgment's therapeutic potential.*
   - *For a court system to enjoy legitimacy it must create and deliver a product that is needed and wanted by its 'consumer base'.*
   - *The notion that demands for efficiency in the justice system may run contrary to the additional work involved in preparing 'time-consuming' litigant-friendly judgments is unconvincing. Immediately after writing a*

---

29   *Ibid,* 33.
30   *Ibid,* 34.
31   *Ibid.*

complex judgment, the time/work needed to reduce it to 'plain language' is not great.

- *As regards wider rules to writing for litigants in a manner that better meets their needs, the following might be posited:*

   (i) a judge must be conscious that what she writes will impact at several levels, so care and consideration are called for;

   (ii) while no one wants a judge who emotes from the bench, there is nothing wrong with a judge who writes empathetically;

   (iii) when writing a judgment for a person of limited language abilities the need for brevity which presents in all judgments is very much to the fore;

   (iv) a judge should avoid moralising: it will likely lead her into platitudes/falsehoods and assumes a moral wisdom that may not present;

   (v) one should neither patronise nor idealise litigants. Whilst a judge should lean towards empathy, she must bring critical understanding to a case.

   ...

Conclusion

36. The 'triple crown' of judgment writing is clarity, simplicity, and brevity. I hope that I have said things as clearly and simply as possible in the preceding pages. To achieve optimal brevity, perhaps now would be a good time to stop."

Table of cases

Index

Index

About the author

Max Barrett
Judge of the High Court of Ireland

Mr Justice Max Barrett is a judge of the High Court of Ireland. Having worked as a solicitor in private practice and also as an in-house lawyer in the financial services sector, he was appointed to the High Court in January 2014. As a judge, he worked initially on the Commercial Court. Over time he has worked in all major areas of the High Court's activity, including the Asylum, Chancery, Family, Immigration, Insolvency, Judicial Review, Jury and Non-Jury Lists. Judge Barrett has also headed the Competition List since his appointment to the bench.

During his time as a judge, Judge Barrett has delivered close to 600 reserved judgments. On the Asylum and Family Law Lists, he has taken a pioneering role in evolving a novel form of judgment – a traditional-form judgment to which a litigant-friendly letter in 'plain English' is appended – in a bid to maximise the comprehensibility of judgments for court users. Some of Judge Barrett's many judgments are now prominent/ leading judgments in their respective areas. In addition to his judicial experience, Judge Barrett holds a PhD in law, a first-class master's in English literature and first-class postgraduate diplomas in arbitration and financial services law. He is among the most widely published of the current Irish judiciary (books and articles). Judge Barrett is a member of the Law Society of Ireland and a bencher of King's Inns.

About Globe Law and Business

Globe Law and Business was established in 2005. From the very beginning, we set out to create law books that are sufficiently high level to be of real use to the experienced professional, yet still accessible and easy to navigate. Most of our authors are drawn from Magic Circle and other top commercial firms, both in the United Kingdom and internationally.

Our titles are carefully produced, with the utmost attention paid to editorial, design and production processes. We hope this results in high-quality publications that are easy to read and a pleasure to own. Our titles are also available as ebooks, which are compatible with most desktop, laptop and tablet devices. In 2018 we expanded our portfolio to include journals and Special Reports, available both digitally and in hard copy format, and produced to the same high standards as our books.

In 2021, we were very pleased to announce the start of a new chapter for Globe Law and Business following the acquisition of law books under the imprint Ark Publishing. Our law firm management list is now significantly expanded with many well known and loved Ark Publishing titles.

We are also pleased to announce the launch of our online content platform, Globe Law Online. This allows for easy search and networked access across firms. Key collections include the Law Firm Management Collection, Private Client and Energy and the Energy Transition. Email me at sian@globelawandbusiness.com for further details or to arrange a free trial for you or your firm.

Sian O'Neill
Managing director
Globe Law and Business
www.globelawandbusiness.com

By the same author

Globe Law
and Business

The Art and Craft of Judgment Writing

A Primer for Common Law Judges
Max Barrett

For full details, go to
www.globelawandbusiness.com/TACJW